The Best Humor from

PUNCH

THE BEST HUMOR FROM

PUNCH

EDITED BY WILLIAM COLE
AND ILLUSTRATED BY SPROD

THE WORLD PUBLISHING COMPANY
Cleveland and New York

Library of Congress Catalog Card Number: 53-6648

THIRD EDITION

CONTENTS

8

SPOOFS AND PARODIES

IN THE THROES OF LIVING

HOME AND FAMILY

SOME ARTS AND BELLES LETTRES

IN THE THROES OF LIVING

MAN AGAINST THE OTHER ANIMALS

ECCENTRICS AND INDIVIDUALISTS

❀

INTRODUCTION

Back in January of this year a noted literary pundit engaged in a column of speculation on the kinds of books that were badly needed. Among his desires for 1953 was "an anthology of humor that does not contain a preface arduously defining humor." Critics seldom get what they want, or so it would seem from their remarks on what they *do* get, but in this case, the prefacer and the critic find themselves hand in hand. A good laugh is a *rara avis*; to dissect it is ungentlemanly and ungracious.

Humor is one of those subjects like women, or the afterlife, or Who Put the Overalls in Mrs. Murphy's Chowder. People are always trying to figure it out. In most introductions to humorous books the author or editor starts with a fine resolve. He says right off that he doesn't know what humor is. But then, bowing obsequiously and walking out backward, he defines it for twelve pages. And other men write whole books about it. Long books. There was one a few years back by a much-lettered college professor. "Our risibilities," he said, "are provoked by what is inappropriate to the situation." If one goes by that definition, then a long and ponderous book dissecting humor is pretty funny.

This collection from *Punch* is unique in a number of ways. Its first claim to rarity has just been given. Another point is that, through one hundred and twelve years of oversight, there has never been an anthology of *Punch* prose and verse published in America. Why this should be, I don't know. I suppose nobody ever thought of it. Or perhaps it may have been that only in recent years have the peoples of the two countries paid much attention to one another. The English used to regard us as a nation of immensely wealthy men who ate in our undershirts. We on our part knew that England was inhabited solely by people who were forever dashing off to the hounds, by jove! (upper class), or dropping aitches and pulling their forelocks (lower class). A couple of wars have helped us progress in the direction of mutual understanding, if in no other direction. Until recently the English literary humor imported into this country was of a nature to arouse misconception. It was "Lord Cholmondeley (pronounced 'Chumley')" and towns named "Withering-on-the-Vine" or "Little Kumquat." The P. G. Wodehouse kind of thing; good, but limited. Bertie Wooster and his friends; vague youths with long front teeth and sandy moustaches. Now we know that there are people there, too.

"Englishmen don't think," somebody once remarked, "instead, they have traditions." *Punch* is one of the traditions. *Punch, or the London Charivari* was founded in 1841, inspired by a French humorous publication, *Paris Charivari*. There is still a good deal of haze enveloping the exact data on the founding; sufficient to say that there were three joint editors, one of whom, Mark Lemon, seems to have won out and is now acknowledged as "the first editor of *Punch*." An early prospectus for the new magazine indicates that the original intention was to title it "The Funny Dog—with Comic Tales." However, this tragedy was averted when one of the planners remarked that the publication should be "like a good mixture of punch, nothing without Lemon." Another man seized upon this happy witticism, and *Punch* it became.

The magazine was an immediate success, although it had a rocky time of it financially—the original investment was £25— until the printing and publishing were taken over by the firm of Bradbury & Evans in late 1842. (Bradbury & Evans became Bradbury & Agnew thirty years later, and the members of those two families still own all the stock.) The newspapers of the time expressed surprise at the lack of vulgarity in the new magazine of humor. One remarked editorially, "It will provoke many a hearty laugh, but never call a blush to the most delicate cheek." Such, indeed, is still the case.

England at the time of *Punch's* emergence was hot in the throes of the Industrial Revolution. In this era of crusades, the magazine

14

plunged into life with a bagful of its own. Cries for slum clearance, prison reform, and worker's rights were much in evidence on its pages. Thomas Hood's poem, "The Song of the Shirt," a plea for better wages for seamstresses, appeared in the Christmas issue of 1843, and the resulting uproar achieved international fame for *Punch* and trebled its circulation. Good circulation attracts good writers, and before long the best scriveners of the day were knocking hopefully on the door. Among those who were allowed across the threshold were William Makepeace Thackeray (he did drawings, too), W. S. Gilbert, Tennyson, Charles Lever, C. S. Calverley (the light-verse-poet's poet), Douglas Jerrold, and Coventry Patmore. Dickens's only contribution was rejected. More recently the stellar contributors have included A. A. Milne, E. V. Lucas, Alfred Noyes, Lord Dunsany, A. P. Herbert, and Stephen Potter, whose "Gamesmanship" first showed up in *Punch*.

Among the *Punch* artists have been Sir John Tenniel, of *Alice in Wonderland* fame, George du Maurier, and, still contributing, E. H. Shepard, illustrator of the *Winnie the Pooh* books.

After its first burst of radicalism *Punch* stood aside and became more the interested onlooker and commentator on the political happenings. Its tendencies through the years have been, like the upper and middle classes who are its largest public, conservative.

The editors of *Punch*—and there have been only eight in one hundred and twelve years—have all been writers themselves, with the exception of Kenneth Bird, who served from 1949 to 1953. Mr. Bird is one of *Punch's* best cartoonists, and signs his work under the pseudonym, "Fougasse." The editorial chair was taken over in January of 1953 by Malcolm Muggeridge, a political writer and former foreign correspondent for English newspapers.

Punch is edited from a comfortable, old-fashioned mansion on London's Bouverie Street, just off Fleet Street. People think of the "heart" of the building as the paneled dining room where, for the past century, the proprietors have gathered their top staff around them every Tuesday at the "*Punch* Table" to discuss, over and after a meal, the political cartoon for the following week's issue. To be "on the Table" is the highest distinction Messrs. Bradbury

& Agnew can bestow upon a staff member or a regular contributor. This elect group is usually made up of two members of the Firm, the Editor and Art Editor, a regular cartoonist, and perhaps five or six artists and writers of long standing. The only outsider who was ever allowed at one of these gatherings was Mark Twain. The political cartoon, which is the outcome of these meetings, has been one of the *Punch* traditions. It is the only drawing in *Punch* that the magazine refers to as a "cartoon." The rest—what we call cartoons here in America—are designated "Pictures and Sketches." The most famous cartoon (*Punch* style) appeared in 1890 and was titled "Dropping the Pilot." It showed a stoical Bismarck descending a ship's ladder, while the young Kaiser watched from the ship's rail above.

A wayfarer coming upon *Punch* on display at a magazine stand might think that it looked familiar. He could well be right, for the cover has been the same, with a few minor adjustments in color and typography, since 1844. This gives to *Punch* what is known in American advertising circles as "Identification Value." Once inside the magazine, however, any resemblance to the American advertising world of ads that shout and holler disappears. *Punch's* restrained advertisements are bunched together at the front and back of the magazine, making a kind of well-bred sandwich of the editorial content. This grouping-up gives the reader the opportunity to skip all the ads in one swoop, but if he does, he will miss out on some charming Anglicana. One reads, " 'Punchbowle tobacco stood me in good stead through the most harrowing examinations,' says this South African College-man." This statement is accompanied by a drawing of a clean-cut South African College-man, pipe in mouth. Or take the low-pressure charm of: "If your office is cold this winter, 'Fibreglass' insulation *might* help you" (italics mine.) The English are much addicted to kidding around with their language. "Did you MACLEAN your teeth today?" asks Maclean's Dentrifice, and the Scandinavian Airlines System advises Britishers to "Scandinaviate." Elsewhere we find "Wherever there's something afoot . . . you'll find Paton's shoe and boot laces."

16

The editorial meat of the magazine varies from week to week, but the flavor, and many of the departments, remains the same. For example the first page, the hors d'oeuvre, is entitled "Charivaria." "Charivari," according to my dictionary, is "a mock serenade of discordant noises made with pans, horns, etc. after a wedding." A selection of these discordant noises will be found on page 345 in this book. Among the other regular weekly departments is a lively "Impressions of Parliament" which some American magazine would do well to emulate for the Senate and Congress. There is also, usually, a political article by Malcolm Muggeridge, and sections of criticism on movies, plays, art, ballet, opera, television, and books —one long book review and a number of shorts. Once a month Charles W. Morton of the *Atlantic Monthly* contributes a witty American letter, and each issue contains one or two features on something of topical or general interest—census taking, Covent Garden, tea-tasting, lighthouse-keeping, etc. And then, of course, there is the real cream of *Punch*—articles and verse of the kind that make up this book, averaging five poems and seven humorous pieces per issue. The cartoons in *Punch* are on a par with the best produced in America—that would be the *New Yorker*—and there are fifteen or twenty per issue. The anthology of *Punch* cartoons published in America last year enabled the public over here to become happily acquainted with Emett, Fougasse, François, Langdon, Mahood, Searle, Sprod, and the few dozen other artists represented.

Malcolm Muggeridge, in a recent *New Yorker* interview, spoke of wanting to bring in some new writers to *Punch*, and to make it more topical. "Its role should be social history—to record the age," he said. Changes are made very slowly at 10 Bouverie Street, but one can, in the last few months, see that Mr. Muggeridge has been at work. Recent issues reveal some unfamiliar names (two of them almost unbelievable: Nesta Pain and Gideon Tode) and some others that, while familiar, are new to *Punch*: Angus Wilson, Cecil Beaton, John Betjeman, and William Sansom, to do some singling out.

Punch, of course, is written in English, not American. This is no particular handicap, but for us over here, reading *Punch* is not all beer and skittles. To work that analogy a little further, there is plenty of good strong beer, but what on earth are skittles? For that matter, who in the New World can immediately twig references to "elevenses" or "popsies"? And few of us can penetrate the occasional cricket articles in which a player will "steal cheeky singles" or "crack his ball through the covers for four"? I learned early in my *Punch* reading to pass quickly over pieces that began "Mummy! Mummy!"—the English are inclined to be treacly about small children, and pieces of this nature make A. A. Milne seem like a four-letter-word realist.

But every other prospect pleases; the flower of English humor transplants very well. Certainly the compilation of this book was as pleasant a task as a man could undertake. This anthology, selected for Americans by an American, is not designed to give a picture of contemporary life in England, or to reveal the English character, or to do anything solemn at all. These things may rub off on the reader *en route*, but there is really only one important thing—to laugh. That is the standard of admission.

And so—without further *Adieu*—America, meet *Punch*!

WILLIAM COLE

18

In the Throes of Living

DIVERSIONS AND DILEMMAS

SIMON CRABTREE

A Day in a Cream Bun Factory

THE TELEPHONE rang in the manager's office, and Miss Sibthorpe, the secretary, answered it.

"That the Garden Valley Cream Bun Factory?" asked an expressionless voice. "Good. This is Mr. Saville, of the East Hooting Victory Celebration Co-ordination Committee, speaking. I want forty thousand cream buns, standard type, not too much cream, delivered to the East Hooting Town Hall by noon to-morrow. Can you do it? Yes; it's for our Victory Tea-party. All right? I'll be there to take delivery. Right."

Miss Sibthorpe put down the receiver and looked at the manager, who nodded efficiently. In a few moments he was bawling down a speaking-tube.

"Exchange! Hello, exchange! Get me the works manager. That you, Hargreaves? Priority! Co-ordinate all work in A, B and D sheds. . . . Yes, priority. A big contract. Forty thousand cream buns ——"

"Standard type, not too much cream," prompted Miss Sibthorpe.

"—standard type, not too much cream, to be ready by eleven

o'clock to-morrow for immediate delivery. It's for the East Hooting Victory Tea-party. Yes, they'll be on night-shifts if necessary—yes. Of course. All right, Hargreaves, got that? Right, get busy."

And that was the beginning of the busiest day the Garden Valley Cream Bun Factory had ever known. To us cream-bun operatives, as we streamed into the factory at crack of dawn, it had seemed much like any other day. Wearily we tramped into the sheds, wearily we undid the string from the knees of our trousers, rinsed our mouths with antiseptic mouthwash, and began work. In Bay 26 of B shed I threw over the handle of my rotary bun-press and watched the mixture begin to feed into the pans, while a steady humming filled the air. This humming became louder and louder, until it was only possible to communicate with the man at the next machine by shouting loudly. Not that I had much to say to Sutcliffe anyhow.

"How's the missus?" I shouted.

"A bit poorly yet," answered Sutcliffe, peering at the flickering needle of the saccharometer, "she's——"

"Stop that talking!" shouted Pogson, our foreman, above the uproar, "and watch the pans. You'll have an accident in a minute."

I pulled over another lever and a jet of cream shot out with a squelching sound to where the buns, already baked and severed into halves, travelled slowly along the conveyor-belt.

The foreman paused to adjust a sprocket, checked the temperature-gauge of my machine, and passed on. He was a great flat-footed bully of a man, risen from the ranks as you might say, having been a cream-horn-filler in the old hand-filling days.

Gloomily I settled down to another day. I was minding my machine mechanically, dreaming my eternal dream that one day I might get into vanilla slices and have enough money to marry and settle down, when the alarm-bell rang, shrilly and insistently. Then the loud-speakers boomed out. Hargreaves, the works manager, speaking.

"Attention, A, B and D sheds—attention, everybody! A priority contract. Forty thousand cream buns to be ready by eleven o'clock to-morrow morning, for immediate delivery; standard type, not too

22

much cream. The buns are required for the East Hooting Victory Tea-party. The factory expects all operatives to give of their best. Right, get busy."

The loud-speakers were shut off. The humming rose to a scream as men dived for their machines and geared them up for a supreme effort. The sound of buns shooting out of the bun-slots into the metal containers was like machine-gun fire. Sweat poured off Sutcliffe's face as he wrestled with the knobs of his cream-pressure gauge, adjusting the quantity of cream which was to go into each bun with all the conscientiousness of the fine workman that he was. Young Gillespie, on the other side of me, had the light of battle in his eyes.

"We'll do it, yes, we'll do it," he muttered, looking round the great roaring clanging shed that shook with the incessant pounding of the machines.

All morning it went on. We had ten-minute shifts off for lunch. No one spoke in the canteen as we munched our sandwiches and gulped our tomato-sauce. Then back to work, back to the humming, pounding, clanging, stupefying rhythm of production. We looked up occasionally at the big screen where production figures were flashed up in coloured lights. A Shed, 4,296; B Shed, 4,057. Whipped into rivalry, we worked with redoubled vigour. The atmosphere grew tense.

But by the time the two-and-a-half-minute tea-interval came it was obvious that things were not going too well. The figures for B Shed stood at 9,470 only, with seventeen spoilt buns. The loud-speakers blared again. "Attention, all foremen, A, B and D sheds! Conference in works manager's office."

Our foreman hurried past with a grave face. Five minutes later he was back again, looking more self-important than ever.

"They're going to try music, mark my words," shouted Sutcliffe. Ours is a very progressive factory. Sutcliffe was right. Another minute and Sibelius' "Valse Triste," played by a brass band in march time, blared from the loud-speakers.

Bright-eyed, noise-drugged, we worked on through the pandemonium. The production figures on the screen shot up. Eleven thousand. Twelve thousand. Fifteen thousand. The five o'clock hooters sounded, and the operatives streamed out from C shed. C shed was the chocolate éclair shed. Nobody paid any attention. The loud-speakers, interrupting the "Toreador's Song" from *Carmen*, announced that work would continue throughout the night. Nobody even looked up from his task. We were working now like men possessed.

At seven-thirty my shift had five minutes off for soup and spoilt buns—that is, buns rejected for various defects, half-buns, or buns that had two layers of cream with bun in between. There are always a few of these, even in our factory. I looked round at the flushed, drugged faces. One or two seemed on the verge of collapse. Young Gillespie kept on muttering to himself, "Buns, buns, buns. We've got to do it. Buns, buns, buns." I tapped him on the shoulder. "Better take it easy for a bit, lad," I said. He looked up with a cry of fury. "Take it easy? My God, Clarkson, do you think ——"

The hooter sounded and we ran back to our machines. Looking out of the corner of my eye at Gillespie I saw him turn white. Next moment he collapsed on the conveyor-belt, while the machine methodically pelted him with buns and covered him with cream.

"Get that man out of here!" yelled the foreman. Jack Allgood, a small wiry Geordie, rushed forward to take his place.

"Fifty buns lost there," groaned Sutcliffe.

Night fell. Twenty thousand. Fourteen hours to go. We were working quite mechanically now, blind to everything but the buns leaping from the slots, deaf to everything but the rhythm of Mendelssohn's "Italian Symphony." On, on. Buns, buns, more buns. My brain seemed to contract in this mass frenzy. Buns, buns, buns, buns, buns. Every now and then someone fainted, and a reserve ran forward to take his place.

Dawn broke. Thirty-two thousand. Four hours to go. We were losing ground. "Conference!" boomed the loud-speakers. Anxiously our foreman hurried past. Vitamin tablets were issued to all operatives. Mountain air was pumped into the sheds. On, on. Buns, more buns.

And as the eleven o'clock hooter sounded we knew that we had won through. Forty thousand went up in purple letters on the indicators. The last bun sped on its way. We broke off work to join hands and sing incoherently before we sank back exhausted. We had won through. East Hooting would get its buns. And the honour of the factory was saved.

C. A. E. GREEN

Peanuts and Peaches

"This bit of Oxford Street has come down shocking," said the cornet-player sadly. "I'm fair sick of it."

"You mean the bomb damage?" I murmured.

"No, the hawkers. You can't give your best round here. Every time I do a top note a chestnut barrer catches me in the back." He lurched suddenly off the kerb and turned to scowl at a passing barrow. "That barrer was selling peaches not so long ago. You'd never believe the trouble I got into through peaches!" . . .

Then I remembered where I had seen him before. It was on the day I ate a peach while strolling along Oxford Street. Good society, I believe, recognizes that such a thing is nowadays as unavoidable as the barrows, but it lays down no rule for disposing of the stones. Even to-day I like to maintain a certain dignity, and I feel that one simply cannot in daylight fling peach-stones about regardless in Oxford Street. Yet few things are so searing to a sensitive soul as creeping about guiltily with a damp peachstone concealed in one's palm.

In desperation I had sidled into a saloon bar, thinking to deposit the stone surreptitiously under a seat. It seemed the only way. An astonishing sight met my eyes. A big, angry publican was leaning across the bar counter, glaring at his customers, who sat rigidly huddled near the door. They were well-dressed—typical men-

25

about-town, but their faces were grey and drawn with suspense, like those of trapped animals. The publican still watched them as he served me. The silence was uncanny. I joined them nervously.

"I can see through *you* all right," observed the publican.

"Psychic?" I asked affably.

"Peach-stones!" he hissed.

I blenched and stiffened in every limb, and a sort of shudder ran round the bar.

"I won't have it!" he went on. "I know 'em as soon as they come in, by their hands."

I glanced around me; every man's left hand, like my own, was clenched. There was another nerve-racking silence. You could have heard a pin drop. In fact there *was* a faint, mushy plop.

"Who dropped that stone?" cried the publican in an awful voice.

A young man, wearing the tie of a very good school, blushed scarlet. After a long pause he stooped and retrieved the stone.

"They all come in here, flicking peach-stones about," went on the publican. "Why don't they leave 'em in the fun-fairs? The back streets are full of 'em. This is a respectable pub."

There was another agonizing silence. We were all near breaking point. None of us could face Oxford Street again with our peach-stones. We had suffered enough out there. Only the hypnotic glare of the publican's eyes checked us from jettisoning our stones and rushing away. Then a cornet began wailing outside.

"We're closing in five minutes," announced the publican.

The tension became unbearable. Someone caught his breath in a sort of sob as the cornet-player entered. He held out a small velvet collecting bag. The relief was overwhelming. We relaxed and stretched our limbs and smiled. As the player passed among us we nodded kindly at him, dropped our stones into his little bag, and quietly left the premises. At the door I glanced back. The cornet-player was greeting the apoplectic publican.

"I must come in here more often," he was saying. "Very generous lot, I must say. I'll have a pint."

26

As I left he turned up the little bag and emptied its contents on the counter.

C. A. E. GREEN

A Moving Picture

I HAVE always thought well of Art. I even have a special stance for viewing pictures—with a soft collar I can hold it for minutes at a time, and people tip-toe round after me to see what pictures I deem worthy of notice.

Only the other day I met as ardent a lover of Art as you could wish. He was craning in rapt attention before a picture, peering minutely into the canvas as at a keyhole. Now you generally find that a man who wears a stringy tie, knotted to about the size of a pea, has a very tense nature, well suited to Art, and I thought it worth while spending a little time with him. I coughed and took up my stance beside him.

"Just look at them black currants," he said, pointing with an ecstatic middle finger. "I'll show you a beauty along here."

He sidled along the wall and pointed again.

"Just look at that," he said. "Apples!"

"Not a school I care for," I said, taking his arm. "Now here we have something rather better—a Pissarro."

"It's all little blobs of paint," he complained, thrusting his face within two inches of the canvas.

"Of course it is, at that distance," I said. "The way to look at a picture is to stand well back—about here."

"I can't see a bloomin' thing now!"

"Don't you find that the meaningless blobs take on a pattern now?" I asked. "Look at the picture as a whole."

"What picture?" he said, staring vaguely into space.

Then I divined his trouble—he was extremely short-sighted. His

27

eyes were round and shone with a slightly baffled melancholy, like those of a goldfish when you flip an ant's egg into the bowl. Yet it seemed a pity not to show him what he was missing. I suffer from the same trouble. I removed my glasses and fitted them on him.

It was obviously a revelation to him. He pivoted slowly on his heels, gazing round the gallery in wonder.

"Cherries!" he exclaimed.

I clicked my tongue in annoyance. He was looking at one of the poorest things in the place. As far as I could see without my glasses, it was a crude portrait of a woman in a Gainsborough hat with cherries on it—very badly done.

"A very poor thing," I said loftily, "but at least you can see it as a whole. Notice how badly that arm hangs, and the splayed feet too. The foreshortening of the face is all wrong."

"Like a horse," he said.

"Very like."

"Her face has gone very red," he observed.

"Strange you should notice that too," I said. "Some trick of the light perhaps. By jove, it seems to be moving now!"

Horrified, I snatched back my glasses and put them on just in time. The woman with the hat was rising majestically from her seat. She was brandishing an umbrella. I side-stepped smartly, but there was no time to warn my friend. Without a word she caught him a crack on the bare part of his neck at the back. He stared vacantly around.

"I'll have to get me eyes seen to," he remarked ruefully. "I've got a shocking headache coming on—a sort of shooting pain at the back of me head."

"Like a smart blow from an umbrella?" I asked, ducking again.

"Yes," he said, staring in the direction of my voice, although I was no longer there. "How did you guess?"

"I've just got one myself—above the ear," I said quickly. "I think we had better go at once."

"Yes," he said, reeling slightly as the umbrella came down again. "I think I'll go and have a lay down."

I hurried out of the gallery. Glancing back, I noticed that my

28

friend was already lying down—at the foot of a rather fine piece of modern sculpture. It made quite a striking group, although I thought his upturned boots gave it a slightly flamboyant note. There was no time however to adjust them, as the woman was bearing down on me, but it left a very pleasing memory in my mind as I lightly descended the marble staircase four steps at a time.

C. A. E. GREEN

My Pipe

"I SHAN'T be able to breathe in a minute!" cried Albert, thrashing wildly about him with his hat.

I admit that the smoke from my new pipe was rather depressing. It hung about like creeping swathes of purée, and it bothered him. It bothered me—in fact pipes repel me, especially my new one. It is fashioned somewhat on the lines of an over-blown saxophone, with a sort of glue-pot on the end. I carry it about quite easily in its velvet-lined case, but when smoking it the strain on my teeth is well-nigh intolerable, even with my head well back. If I relax for a moment the glue-pot raps me pretty sharply on the breast-bone.

"Has Mr. Wheel been round this evening?" I asked between desperately clenched teeth. It was in the Blue Duck Inn.

"No, he ain't," snorted Albert. "And don't start arguing with him again—you always get the worst of it. I've got enough to put up with with that there pipe of yours."

"We shall see," I replied loftily. The pipe somehow eluded my teeth and shot half an ounce of hot shag into my waistcoat.

"Here he comes now," said Albert, bridling.

I have suffered much from Mr. Emery Wheel. If you are a cigarette smoker you will know how futile it is to argue with a man who wields a pipe really well. You will recall sadly the forceful stab of the stem to emphasize a statement, the masterful gesture as he bites on it again, and the momentous silence as he fills it with tobacco to gain time to think up a crushing retort. A cigarette cannot cope with all this.

Emery Wheel joined us and puffed at his pipe for a while, considering his opening gambit. I smiled and casually placed a copy of the recent White Paper on the table. He rose to the bait at once. He cleared his throat and ran his pipe-stem ponderously down a column of figures. I immediately stabbed my own pipe at another column, and he drew back sharply. We smoked on, measuring each other in silence.

"The White Paper," I said challengingly.

"Precisely," said Emery, with a lordly flourish of his pipe. "Now this bears out what I was saying the other evening."

He brought down the pipe in a flash, but I was too quick for him. I aimed mine at the whites of his eyes.

"I think not," I replied loudly.

"What I say is—" he began, with a shrewd thrust.

"I couldn't disagree more," I cried, parrying like lightning.

Albert tried to make a point with his cigarette, but we waved him contemptuously aside. Emery sat back and rapped his pipe on his heel. I countered by churning about in the glue-pot and tipping more tobacco into it. It blazed up beautifully. Emery was badly shaken, but he pulled himself together.

"Let me tell you—" he shouted, with an authoritative lunge of his pipe. I checked him dead with a quiet stab.

"You would be quite wrong, Emery." My tone was icy cold.

Albert leaned across to speak. As I turned, teeth clenched again on my pipe, the glue-pot caught him a nasty crack on the chin, and he dropped out of the conversation. Emery and I smoked on fiercely. The air grew thick with fumes. I noted a few sparks floating about, and made a mental note to try a less pungent brand of tobacco on the morrow. Emery sprang to his feet.

"What I wanted to say is this—" he cried.

I silenced him with a resolute sweep of my pipe.

"Now *this* is the way I look at things," I said quietly.

30

He thrust his pipe into his pocket, completely baffled, and stamped out of the bar. I smiled triumphantly at Albert.

"That disposes of Mr. Emery Wheel, I think."

"What's the harm of letting him speak?" snapped Albert. "He talks very interesting, I think."

"Really, Albert," I said. "You amaze me."

I removed my pipe from my teeth—the heat was becoming oppressive.

"I know what he was trying to tell you," said Albert spitefully, "and he was right too."

"Indeed?"

"Yes. You've been and upset some ash on your tie. It's too late now—it's on fire."

A. B. HOLLOWOOD

An Organ of Public Opinion

"Excuse me, sir," said the man in the belted raincoat and beret, "would you mind telling me how you would vote if the General Election were being held to-day?" He licked the point of his pencil and looked up into the eyes of the Regular Customer.

The regular customer took a pull at his tankard and several shorter tugs at his right ear before replying. "Why," he said, "by puttin' a cross side of the name of the chap I . . . I was goin' to say like *best*, but there's such a thing as the ballot-box, isn't there? By putting a cross side of the name of *one* of the chaps. How's that?"

"Yes, yes, of course," said the investigator, smiling benignly. "I mean which political *party* would you vote for?"

"To-day, eh?" said the regular customer as he rubbed his left eye slowly with his knuckle.

"That's right—to-day," said the investigator.

"Bit late though, isn't it," said the regular customer, drawing his watch from a waistcoat pocket and studying it at arm's length. "Booths would be closed up by now, wouldn't they?"

"Well, suppose you'd voted this morning, bright and early," said the investigator.

"Ah, then you mean, 'ow 'ave I *voted*, not 'ow *shall* I vote," said the regular customer.

"All right—how should you have voted," said the investigator. He licked his pencil again.

"What kind of a choice did I 'ave?"

"Look, sir, I'm sorry I troubled you," said the investigator. "It isn't really fair to take up so much of your spare time. I'll be—"

"No trouble at *all*," said the regular customer. "In fact it's all very interestin'. Carry on."

"Well, let's say there are three candidates—Liberal, Socialist and Tory. Which would you vote for?"

"Which would you?"

"I'm asking *you*, sir."

"An' I'm asking you. Fair's fair."

"I'm independent, neutral."

" 'Aven't the courage of your confections, eh?"

"It's not that. Now, sir, *how would you vote?*"

"Well, I should 'ave to think, shouldn't I?"

"That's right—Liberal, Socialist, Tory?" said the investigator in a voice entirely devoid of enthusiasm.

"Who's the Socialist chap?"

"What chap?"

"The chap puttin' up, 'course!"

"Does that matter? Can't you give me a rough idea of your preference?"

"I can't very well vote for a chap I don't know nothin' about; now can I?"

"I mean which *party* would you support?"

"Not knowin' what they're proposin' to do, I can't say."

"But you know what they've *done*, their general principles—"

"I knows what they *'aven't* done," said the regular customer.

"Thank you, sir. I'll put you down as 'Don't know.' Thank you very much. Good night!"

"Hey, come back! Don't know what?"

"Which party to vote for," said the investigator wearily.

"Who don't?"

"Well, sir, you said yourself—"

"I said nothin' of the sort. I knows 'ow to use me 'ard-earned vote, me lad. You'll scratch that 'Don't know' out."

"With pleasure, sir, if you'll give me a definite answer."

"Ask me a def'nite question and you'll get a def'nite answer," said the regular customer, tapping the investigator on the chest with his pint.

"Would you vote for the Tories, the Conservatives?"

"Not much choice there, is there? But if I've got to take me pick I'll 'ave the Conservatives."

The investigator's eyes rolled in anguish. He flicked a tick at his pad. "Thank you, sir," he said. "I'm much obliged. Good night."

" 'Arf a sec.," said the regular customer, grabbing at the investigator's raincoat. "You 'aven't asked me yet about the Liberals."

"Some other time, sir. That's quite enough for the moment. I must be pushing." He broke free and walked rapidly out of the saloon.

"Sim'lar, Charlie," said the regular customer.

When the barman returned with the beer he found the regular

customer chuckling softly, shaking his head slowly to and fro an inch or two above the counter. "What's the big joke, Bert?" he said.

"That young chap in 'ere just now," said the regular customer. " 'E's gone away with me vote, an' 'e's forgotten to take me name. 'E won't 'arf be kickin' 'isself. I reckon 'e'll be back in a bit."

GERALDINE BUSSEY

The Silver Scream

FATHER is a kind man, who has never thrown a bucket of white-wash over anybody in his life; but he likes to see other people doing it. I nearly have to carry him home from the cinema after a really energetic comedy; he cries, and rotates in his seat, and his hilarity tends to burst out all over again in the middle of solemn flood-damage scenes on the news-reel.

If I am not able to accompany father to a film he will give me what he calls a rough idea of it when he comes home. Rough is the operative word; father thrashes about, slapping himself and utter-ing broken sentences like "The eggs—right through the paper bag —pin-stripe trousers!" Or, "Wallop! and the horse went right over him!"—while I just sit there feeling a bit precious.

Father is luckier than most people, for he can squeeze enjoy-ment out of a fifteenth-rate film as long as somebody falls over something. And last winter, when the early Charlie Chaplin com-edies were revived, I just don't know what the other passengers in the bus thought of father on our way home; but I know what the conductress thought. She told father to mind the step, and looked sorrowfully woman-to-woman at me.

"I go to be entertained" is father's dictum. On this principle he will scan the film advertisements in the newspaper, his com-mentary going something like this:

" 'You will thrill to their youthful—' so forth and so on. No, thank you. 'They Flew to the Moon.' Did they? How tiresome. Ah! here's a good one: 'Two Nuts on a Raft.' There's some ghastly stuff to sit through first, though. 'Life of Beethoven.'"

Mother hardly ever attends the silver screen with father now, because she would rather thrill to the youthful so forth and so on, or fly to the moon, or sit through Beethoven.

However, her conscience smites her about twice a year, and then she will endure the nuts on the raft for father's sake, although she pretends she cannot remember the names of the comedians afterwards. On these occasions father always has a wistful hope that mother will laugh at his choices, but so far I don't think she ever has.

One Saturday night three months ago father came home almost speechless with æsthetic appreciation of an offering called *Slap Me Down*. He broke the water jug in telling us about it.

"You girls simply must come," he kept saying. The film had finished its run locally, but father, hallooing, chased it into remote suburbs and saw it three more times, breaking an ash-tray and bending two forks in giving us further résumés.

For the sake of peace, mother and I finally gave in and agreed to see *Slap Me Down*, although it was by now twenty miles away. In the rain, we joined father, a train, a bus, and finally a wet queue outside the cinema. Father, eager as a child, kept saying "Wait till you see it. Just wait!"

"If only you'd let us, dear," sighed mother.

Mother did try hard to laugh, I will say that for her, but it was a dismal effort. Luckily, father, using his handkerchief constantly and overcome with delight at people sitting down suddenly in the pigs' dinner or having holes shot in their top hats, was in no state to notice. This time his mirth lasted right through the funeral of a foreign diplomat.

After it was over, poor mother looked wan and exhausted in the light of the foyer, but father was bursting with happiness.

"Wonderful, wonderful!" he said, and stepping gaily out into the rain with large gestures missed his footing on the kerb, rotated

35

desperately for a moment and finally sat down noisily in six inches of dirty water. When he got to his feet again he looked thoughtful. But mother laughed all the way home.

MARJORIE RIDDELL

Two's Company

I LIFTED the receiver and dialled.

There was a crackle . . . *burrr* . . . *click* . . . *pwsshk* . . . and a man's voice said: "Why do you want a monkey?"

"I beg your pardon?" I said.

"Who's that?" a woman asked.

"Is that Gerrard 49381?" I asked.

"What?" That was the man.

"What?" The woman's voice followed. "Are you there, Alfred?"

"Yes," he said. "Someone's on the line."

"Alfred," I said, "are you Gerrard 49381?"

"What?" he said.

I hung up.

Then I lit a cigarette and tried again.

This time the woman spoke first. "Of course I don't want a monkey," she said.

"Then why did you suggest it?" asked Alfred. "Really, Mabel, you are the limit."

"Mabel," I said, "are you Gerrard 49381?"

"It's that woman again," said Alfred. "Will you please get off the line?"

"We are holding," Mabel added haughtily, "a private conversation."

"You're not, you know," I pointed out, quite amiably. "And, anyway, why should *I* get off the line? Why don't *you* get off *my* line?"

"It's *our* line," said Alfred.

"Splendid," I said. "That's democracy for you. Now, is either of you Gerrard 49381?"

"What?" They spoke together.

"I am trying," I said, "to get Gerrard 49381."

"Then why on earth don't you dial properly," said Alfred irritably. "You women are all the same."

"What do you mean?" I asked coldly.

"I like that!" exclaimed Mabel.

Alfred had done for himself. Mabel and I were on the same side now.

"Asking for a monkey," muttered Alfred.

"It was a joke," said Mabel loudly. "It was supposed to be funny. You were supposed to laugh. Like this: Ha ha ha."

"All right. Ha ha ha," said Alfred.

"Funny, aren't you?" said Mabel.

"You're the funny one," said Alfred.

"I've got a sense of humour, anyway," said Mabel.

"That's what *you* think," said Alfred.

"Well, I go around with you, don't I?" said Mabel.

I cut in.

"Why," I asked, "do you want a monkey?"

"I don't!" cried Mabel. "I don't want a monkey. It's my birthday, see, and Alfred says to me what do you want for your birthday? You can have anything you like, honey ('honey,' he calls me —thinks he's Gary Cooper), anything at all. What, I says, anything? A pearl necklace or a motor boat or a monkey? It's a joke, see? It's funny."

"Ha ha ha," said Alfred.

"That's the trouble with men," I said. "No sense of humour. How long have you known him?"

"Three years," said Mabel. "Steady."

"What does he look like?"

"Well," said Mabel, "he's quite short, with freckles, and his eyes are a bit small."

"Hey!" said Alfred.

"Well, they are," said Mabel. "When Mum's on at me about you she always drags in your eyes."

"I can't help my eyes!"

"And his hair's going a bit thin," said Mabel.

"That's right," said Alfred bitterly. "Pull me to pieces. You're no Betty Grable, but it never made any difference to me. Here's your birthday and I'm giving you anything you want and you go on and on—"

"Oh, do you mean it, Alfred?" Mabel cried. "Can I really?"

" 'Course you can."

"Anything?"

"Anything."

"Oh, Alfred!"

"Honey!"

"He'll be quite bald," I said, "in a few years."

"You keep out of this," shrieked Mabel. "What's it got to do with you? Who are you anyway? Why don't you get off the line?"

"Yes," roared Alfred. "Get off the line."

I hung up.

C. R. W. FALWASSER

Wein Fest

THIS is the Wein Fest at Oberkirch, Schwarzwald, but I cannot speak any German.

The weather is Keats' Ode to Autumn; the town has been scrubbed and decorated; we have drunk the new wine. And now I stand on the balcony at the Gasthaus and watch the procession.

There are three bands and many wagons and much New Wine. We become very much excited. I listen to my fellow guests and learn shurn, sair shurn and voonderbar. Mein Host is very correct. He presents Herr Ludvig und Frau Ludvig. We bow. We shake hands. I tell them Ich spreche nicht Deutsch. They ask with many signs how I like Schwarzwald. I tell them it is shurn, sair shurn, and add voonderbar. They say Festzug is goot, nein? I say Vot is Festzug? They say Das ist Festzug and point to the strasse. This is a little confusing so Herr Ludvig calls for kirschwasser. By the time I have drunk this it is clear that Procession is in Kirche only, and three bands, etc. constitute Festzug. Das ist voonderbar. Kirschwasser ist sair goot. We bow. We shake hands. We return to the balcony.

Now come der kinder. We applaud ecstatically with much ach and many sairs. Frau Ludvig tells me she is a grosse-mutter and I simulate great surprise. We sit at little tables and Herr Ludvig shows me letters from his grandchildren. The kinder are so shurn that we drink more schnaps.

Here is Mein Host. He presents someone who has once been to America. We bow. We shake hands. Herr Once-to-America has also visited that lovely town Lewisham and the beautiful sea at Southport. So we shake hands again. We drink coffee and eat large slices of sair goot cake.

Also I meet a student. From lex, legis I understand that he studies law at Heidelberg. He teaches me the colours of the bandsmen's uniforms—vice, rode and schwarz—and I discover that Schwarzwald is Black Forest. Voonderbar. He puts coins on the table and teaches me about geld. I spit a little over pfennig. I learn to count up to five and laugh at fumf.

The Ludvigs are jealous. Herr Ludvig takes the chair of the student and says now ve vill sprechen English. He smokes a large and imaginary cigar and says Churchill. I say Ya. Goot. Frau Ludvig hems a fine seam and says Queen Mary? and I say Ya and das carpet is sair shurn. I also learn from them that Princess Elizabeth has zwei kinder and that Princess Margaret dancens goot and is sair shurn.

Herr Ludvig says that now ve vill sprechen politik. He tells me that the French are nicht goot but he has no word for the Russians. So we order more wein and fergessen them.

Dis wein ist vice wein and sair goot.

I assure Frau Ludvig that no one would take her for a grosse-mutter. I tell everyone that Schwarzwald is voonderbar. I recite the greater part of Keats' "Ode to Autumn."

Now we are dancing. I wear my hiking shoes and we dance on coconut matting, but it continues voonderbar. I jig up and down with Herr Ludvig who becomes sentimentalisch. I waltz politely with Mein Host. I tell him he waltzes goot. We bow. We shake hands.

We sit all together at one table and talk about me. They ask why come I to the Black Forest? Herr Ludvig says Ich binn rucksack girl. Herr Heidelberg says Ich binn botanik. Herr Ludvig says bloomen' forget-me-not and becomes sentimentalisch. His wife slaps him. Mein Host informs me that rosen Dorothy Perkins is sair goot. I tell him that I think highly of Frau Karl Druschki. We bow. We shake hands.

We drink more wein. They teach me Prost and I teach them Cheers and Herr America tries to teach everyone Mud in your Eye. I ask if crested tits are to be seen in this neighbourhood. Nobody understands. I remember vogel and draw one on the Essen Karte and give it a large crest. But Herr Ludvig makes it lay eggs and his wife slaps him. I give up Kulture and return to dancen.

Here is a Herr who remembers that he was a soldier. He demonstrates with bang bang much fighting and many wounds. So I demonstrate a direct hit on mein haus. This makes us freunds. He forces upon me his last and very unpleasant cigarette. We agree about the Russians. He tells me he has no mutter and no vater. This is good practice. I run through the whole family and inquire after his grosse-mutter and his grosse-vater. I learn that he has no little schwester but am not quite certain whether it is nein or nine bruders. It must be nein for he tells me he is now like myself—alone in the world and full of sorrows. I call him Werther and say he must cheer up and fergessen but perhaps I do not say it goot and he thinkens I mean something else. I say NEIN. He is be-drunken.

I talk Latin with Herr Heidelberg who explains Prosit.

Now we are dancen again. Now we are drinken champagne. I

say Prost and Herr Ludvig says Goo' Luck and Herr Heidelberg says Cheers and Mein Host says Mud in your Eye. Voonderbar. I tell them Ich binn fisch in wasser but cannot think how I knew that one. It is certainly voonderbar but I am tired and would schlafen. They say nein, dancen. So I dancen again but not sair goot. I tell Frau Ludvig that I think she does look like a grand-mother after all. She does not understand so we finish up the champagne. Now we all understand everything is sair goot. Herr Soldier is asleep. Herr Ludvig and Frau Ludvig hold hands and are sentimentalisch. Mein Host plays a violin that is not there. Herr Heidelberg and Herr America singen. I am all alone and continue to learn German. Ich binn in Schwarzwald und dis ist Weinfest. Ish bish nish tish. Ich sprechen Deutsch goot. Gooten arbend. Fee Fie Fo Fumf. In morgen, bitte, eins cup tea und zwei aspirin. Goot. Sair goot. Voonderbar. Ish bish . . . in Ober kirch. Goot Nacht.

BARRY CRAIG

The Fugitive Ticket

" 'Ere, this'll 'ardly do," said the ticket-collector moderately as he returned to me a card upon which was printed a choice of three correct weights with, on the reverse side, a statement to the effect that I had a determined disposition which would stop at nothing, but might be well advised, for some reason quite unfathomable, to avoid embarking upon new enterprises during the latter half of the week.

The ticket-collector snapped his clippers with an air of quiet boredom while I began turning out my pocket-book. There was a dry-cleaner's receipt on the reverse side of which was the admoni-tion that goods not reclaimed within a month would be returned to the depot, a warning of which I had evidently taken little heed as the receipt was six weeks old already. There followed a small folded paper containing lighter-flints sent to me by my wife when I had S.O.S.'d violently for them five years ago in Cairo—only to have my lighter stolen before their arrival. The ticket-collector's clippers snapped greedily on sight of an insurance agent's business-card and a bus-ticket from Belsize Park to Chalk Farm Stn Undg, districts which I have never visited, so that the presence of a bus ticket to and from such places seemed unexplainable unless someone had been borrowing my clothes. The insurance agent's business-card was more easily traceable, however, since I had one day seen a house of which the upstairs flat appeared to be empty, and on inquiry had encountered the occupier who promptly sold me an insurance policy by way of consolation. The ticket-collector had moved towards me as if the lighter-flints afforded him some manner of interest, only to step sadly away as the next train came in, its hurrying passengers dividing me from him for a few minutes. While he collected the tickets of these new arrivals I turned out an Algerian stamp I had been keeping for a nephew, a filled-in foot-ball-pool coupon, a farthing and the address torn off an envelope belonging to somebody called Tadpole. When the crowd had gone on its way, leaving me and my companion once more face to face, he suggested:

"Some people put them in the band of their hat. Some people put them under the silk band or the whatchumaycallit band on the outside, and there's blokes what stick 'em under the thingummy band on the inside wot goes to keep your hair oil from making the hat dirty." He paused, clipping the air thoughtfully. "Then there's blokes put them in matchboxes," he added.

Feeling for matches I encountered a bent packet of cigarettes, one of which I offered the collector who placed it between pencil and cap above his ear. I then asked if he had a match, but of course he had none either, a contingency which left me with an unused cigarette added to the pocket-book miscellanea in my free hand. Placing the cigarette between my lips I returned the pocket-book to my pocket and found there one non-safety match which the

42

collector struck knowingly against the railing. My overcoat pockets produced four handkerchiefs and, no doubt the sentimental souvenir of a forgotten day's outing, a sprig of white heather mixed with shreds of tobacco. This was followed by fourpence halfpenny, an ignition key, a calendar, a cloak-room ticket and an aspirin, with which items I was dealing when another trainload of passengers hastened through the barrier, marshalling their umbrellas, tickets and gloves with a nonchalance humiliating to me. At this point I found that fifty per cent. or more of the enjoyment in smoking a cigarette concerns itself with one's ability to leave off at intervals, and that I, having some of the contents of my pockets in each hand, could not take out of my mouth the cigarette which had been filming my face with a poisonous nimbus of smoke for some time so that big tears were descending over my cheeks.

"Don't take it so 'ard, mate," said a new voice when the crowd had passed on its way. "It'll turn up sooner or later. Some people try their trouser turn-ups."

I was confronted by a different ticket-collector, who countered my evident surprise with, "My mate's knocked off for breakfast."

With that air of wan desperation experienced when, having fruitlessly mobilized an entire family in a household pipe hunt, one begins a tour of such unlikely hiding places as picture-rails and the back of the gas stove, I turned down my trouser-ends to reveal a quantity of fluff, a button and some dried leaves.

"Then there's shoes," suggested the ticket-collector, as if determined to get the utmost value from my predicament. "Sometimes they falls into shoes."

Standing on one leg at a time I shook from alternate shoes a small piece of gravel and a scrap of material from a dress which my wife was trying to alter for the new look.

Plunging to the very bottom of possibility the ticket-collector said: "Let me see. You came in on the 8.11, didn't you? That'll be back again at 9.11, due in the one after next. Maybe you left it on the floor of the carriage." As we became suddenly enveloped in the crowd coming from the next train I experienced a barely controllable desire to squeeze through in the rush and have done with the business, a whim I might more easily have gratified but for the knowledge that ticket-collectors can see every passenger even though their eyes may be glued upon the tickets they are taking in. As it was I merely forced myself against the human tide to become once more a lonely castaway upon the platform.

"I once knew a bloke lost 'is ticket and found another one," pursued my companion. "'E was looking for a cheap-day single from Epsom Downs and found a return half monthly from Tattenham Corner. 'E was lucky, cos the fare was the same in them days, tho' it's now three-halfpence up."

By this time my overcoat and hat were hanging on the railing while, reflecting upon the curious adaptability of such garments to hanging up under almost any conditions, I went through my waistcoat-pockets—the coat and hat hanging beside me with a jaunty air of being on a spree after years of confinement to the same hooks in home and office. My waistcoat-pockets revealed a number of three-halfpenny stamps dating back to the days when letter post was that price.

"There's folks tear 'em up without knowing," advised the collector. "And folks that fold 'em cornerways to make little ashtrays. I mind when I was on the main line one time and tickets was all paper, people used to make them all sorts of queer shapes like paper boats and hats and gawky birds and kettles. Interesting, it was, some of the things they used to get up to."

When I turned my attention to my breast-pocket I found a stub of pencil jammed like a tent pole, while over it lay a collection of cards and tickets which it did my heart good to see.

Similarly encouraged was the ticket-collector who, with the air of one seeking bargains at a sale by auction, seized a portion of the booty.

"Ah! Now there's what I call a likely little lot," he said.

For a few minutes we sorted industriously until my helper said "'Ere, wot's all this?" in tones of injured suspicion as he handed me a scrap of paper upon which my own hand had once written:

44

> "And thus my life and this it is,
> that I who have embraced eternity
> and cupped my hands about the
>   sunlight's lip,
> and fondling revealed where the
>   palm trees softly lyeing laying
>   (lying)
> lieing of life that is dying (die-
>   ing?) . . ."

Deeply moved, my companion handed me back the whole miscellany he had been sorting.

"'Ave to carry on by yourself, mate," he said. "'Ere comes the twenty-seven."

And when some five minutes later we were alone again he offered one final suggestion:

"Some blokes 'as a special little pocket made for tickets," he almost soliloquized. "They make 'em in suits in different places and you put them in unsuspecting. There's the 'ackin' jacket style where they stick in a little extra outside pocket for carrying cartridges and golf-tees and cribbage-markers and the like, and then there's little pockets put in unexpected in the waist-band around your trousers, and then there's sometimes little pockets within pockets so to speak. Quite a lot of people overlook them and find 'em one day with all sorts of things in."

Fevered with last hope, my hands probed and explored every lining, seam and pocket in search of what I knew must exist somewhere on my clothing, one such pocket as the ticket-collector suggested. I explored my way back around pockets I had already visited, tossed on to the platform the rubbish accumulation of years of neglect, and, finally, Eureka! There in a place I had never previously suspected, just inside my overcoat, was a tiny pocket across the inside of which was strained a small piece of pasteboard. I pulled it out triumphantly and passed it to the ticket-collector, who gave a sigh audible even in a main railway terminus.

"'Ere," he said sadly, "this'll never do."

And he handed me back the piece of card with my weight on one side and my character on the other.

DACRE BALSDON

Junk

HE IS a foreigner and I am asked to entertain him, which I am happy to do, though I don't speak his language nor, I am warned, does he speak mine.

He comes and I say "How do you do?" To which he replies "Thank you, yes." And my wife says "How do you do?" And again he replies "Thank you, yes."

And then there is an ugly pause.

My wife rushes in impetuously, saying "What would you like to see? The Castle? The Cathedral? The Public Library? The River?"

"Please," he starts . . .

We are on tenterhooks.

"Please," he continues, "to see the junk."

Quick deciphering is evidently necessary. My wife, to give me time, offers him a cigarette.

He does not smoke.

"The junk," he says, warming up, for this is evidently his subject, "is a great problem, no?"

As a good housewife, my wife is sympathetic. "It *was* a great problem," she says; "one had dozens of things one did not want. But now one has got rid of them in the war."

She explains about salvage drives.

As I feared, salvage drive defeats him.

My wife explains patiently. "In the war," she says, "we were asked to give away our old junk. It has been made into bullets, tanks, cartridge-cases, you know."

46

"How," he asks, "is the junk bullets, please?"

Which of course is a difficult technical question.

My wife makes signs.

"Mr. Job," she says.

Mr. Job is where a few weeks ago we sold a bathroom stool which had lost a leg for twice the price that we originally paid for it.

I give supporting fire.

I say "Perhaps you would like to see Mr. Job. He has more junk than anybody that I know."

The stranger understands roughly. Very roughly.

"He has," he asks, "how many, this Mr. Job?"

"Hundreds of things," my wife tells him.

"*Hundreds?*" This evidently surprises him.

Not half as much as his next statement surprises me.

For he says, "I do not forget that I am once junk. And your wife," he adds, "she is junk, no?"

He says it, curiously, as if he was paying her a great compliment.

To save further embarrassment I fetch the car. Mr. Job's establishment is half a mile away and I have a feeling that our guest will not be happy till he gets there.

Introducing him to the car I say, "A fair piece of junk itself, this —but it still goes."

The remark defeats him.

We reach Mr. Job's shop, but it is shut. I remember sadly that the chief thing about Mr. Job's shop is that it is nearly always shut. There are one or two broken chairs in the window, some plates and a number of dusty and unreadable books.

I point. "Junk," I say.

But he replies, "No, not junk." And he looks at me curiously— almost as if I were insane. He looks no more flatteringly at my wife.

In the street outside the shop there are some children playing. They must have come from round the corner, for they were not here a moment ago.

Our guest looks at them, and his eyes light with interest. He looks at them, and then he looks at us. And then he sighs. There is much expression in his sigh. The stupidity of the English. The tragedy of the Universe. It is all there, somehow.

And then he says, with the air of a man pronouncing some tremendous, some world-shaking judgment: "The future of the world," he says, "it is with the junk."

Curious.

J . W . N I C H O L S O N

212° F. + +

"AT THAT moment," said Codd impressively, "at that phychological moment somebody—who it was we shall probably never know—*somebody*—"

"Switched off the lights?"

"No, no."

"Threw a fit?"

"No, NO!"

"Opened fire?"

"No!" shouted Codd. "For heaven's sake," he said plaintively, "who's telling this story? *Somebody*"—he again lowered his voice to get the full dramatic effect—"*turned on the steam.*"

"But how—?"

"Exactly," said Codd triumphantly. "You are asking yourselves how a head of steam ever came to be connected to the Downstairs Bar of my club. Most of the members who were lunching at the snack-counter that day are still asking themselves the same question. I don't suppose any of us will ever know the answer. Up to that moment there was nothing more to it than a spirited argument. Hard words, perhaps. No secretary of a respectable London club enjoys hearing it referred to as a Closed Shop or himself described as no better than a bureaucratic meat-porter. High feelings, certainly. The healthy cut-and-thrust of debate, yes. But

48

violence," said Codd. "No. And then," he said, "on comes the steam.

"My recollections of the next few minutes are confused. Men were milling about blindly in the dense white vapour. Members would loom up out of the mist, their faces disfigured with fury and the unconsumed portion of someone else's day's ration, and then disappear again in a dim welter of flailing limbs and broken furniture. Who amongst you can picture the full horror of the scene? Who—"

"I can," said Tench.

"You can?"

"Certainly I can," replied Tench. "I can not only picture it accurately, but I can, and will, describe a scene almost exactly similar to that of your own story, only differing from it in the greater intensity of its dramatic and emotional qualities."

Codd cleared his throat. "Sodden sandwiches—"

"I was standing outside in the hall of my club," went on Tench smoothly, "running my eye over the news on the tape and finishing my after-luncheon pipe, when my attention was caught by the door of the reading-room. This is a swing door, with a panel of clear glass framed in the woodwork. What caught my eye was that the glass at this moment wasn't clear. It was opaque."

Codd flopped back in his chair, beaten. Tench nodded gravely. "I didn't tumble to it at first," he said. "Even when one of the older members emerged, more in the manner of an ejected cartridge case than of one of the older members, his eyes red and streaming and his hard collar a limp rag round his neck, the obvious explanation never dawned on me. Two, and then three more men tumbled out with faces boiled crimson and hair hanging in dank fringes over their eyes. Their clothes—!" He checked a reminiscent smile. "The third man had evidently been unfortunate with the material of his demobilization suit. His jacket had separated completely down the back seam and the two halves, joined only by the collar, were hanging like pieces of sodden blotting-paper from either shoulder. The tell-tale cloud of vapour

49

which escaped from the room with each occupant should have told its story clearly enough; but I still stood dazed, listening uncomprehendingly to the hoarse cries and sounds of smashing furniture within. It was then that I overheard one of the porters say quietly to the hat-check man, 'I see they've got the steam on in there again.' "

" 'Again?' " asked Codd, incredulity and rage struggling for mastery in his voice.

"Again," repeated Tench. "I don't suppose any of you have ever—"

"I have," said Dace.

There was a pregnant pause. Codd and Tench were beyond words. I was beyond caring.

"You have what?" asked Tench in a choking voice.

"That and more," said Dace evasively. "You remember those specially shaped straw protectors they used to use for packing champagne bottles?"

Codd and Tench took advantage of the opening simultaneously.

"—great gobs of condensation dripping down into the *hors d'œuvre*—"

"—simply sitting round drinking their coffee when some sort of a wrangle started over a disputed right of possession to *The Times*—"

"Well, that's what this man's hat looked like," said Dace, raising his voice. "He was coming down the steps from my club, and it was only when I had walked up the pavement to the bottom of the steps that I realized it was the remains of a straw boater, almost reduced to its component parts. His companion, who at ten paces appeared to be wearing a sort of black hood, was revealed on closer inspection as the owner of a bowler, its crown shapeless and sagging and its once stiff brim hanging round his head like a vertical band of crêpe. He had what must have once been a bundle of documents in his hand, but these were stuck solidly together and resembled nothing more than an immense and sodden white sandwich. As they reached the bottom of the steps the man in the bowler made a vicious drive at his companion's stomach with a

50

rolled umbrella. He might as well have prodded him with a length of hosepipe."

Dace foolishly paused for effect and the other two came in neck and neck.

"—Superheated steam at four hundred and fifty pounds per square inch is no joke, let me tell—"

"—somehow or other got the front page over both their heads and before you could say knife, four or five of them—"

Dace made a despairing attempt to hold his audience. "As soon as I got inside I made inquiries," he said, speaking even more loudly and very much more rapidly, "though it was more like a swimming-pool than the entrance to a London club. The whole thing had apparently been touched off by some trifling incident in the billiards-room—"

"Who it was that found the cock," shouted Codd, "who turned the damned thing on we shall never—"

"At this moment," yelled Tench, "full belt, with a roar like the Niagara Falls, *on comes the*—"

All three men were on their feet now, their faces flushed with excitement and shouting, their eyes wild and bloodshot. For all the notice they took of me I might just as well not have been in the room. Better out of it, in fact. As I made for the door I could catch isolated phrases screamed out above the roar of contending voices.

"—cues bent and twisted by the heat"—(this was Dace again)— "Every colour of the rainbow running from the snooker-balls on to the sodden green cloth—"

"—eight and threepenceworth of loose change lying in a pool of water in my pocket—"

"—great wads of sopping newsprint—"

I closed the door softly behind me. This was clearly what Codd would have described as the psychological moment. In the ordinary way I would have estimated the odds against finding a steam-cock ready to hand in the hallway of Tench's flat at several millions to one. Fresh from listening to the three crazy raconteurs inside, however, the sight of a large wheel-valve fitted to a thick pipe running along the wainscoting seemed to me the most natural thing in the world.

I grasped the metal wheel and turned it firmly. . . .

It took three telephone calls and two plumbers, Mrs. Tench subsequently told me, to establish that some interfering idiot had turned off their water at the main. Who did it, she said, we shall probably never know.

ERIC KEOWN

La Perruque de Mme. Montargis

"IN NO CIRCUMSTANCES WILL MONKEYS OF WHATEVER SIZE OR COLOUR BE ADMITTED TO THIS HOTEL EITHER AS RESIDENTS OR CASUAL VISITORS."

"I've been wanting to ask you about that," I said to M. Tarragon, who came wandering in from the kitchen in his slippers, vaguely beating an egg.

"In that case I must tell you of a small, grief-ridden monkey whose eyes burned with primeval reproaches against the human race. It belonged to a somewhat bilious Mme. Boillot, and in my customary softness of heart I was prevailed on to allow it to accompany her to the restaurant, where it sat beside her soberly enough. Now, among his clients every hotelier has a few of whom he may not be especially fond but whom he is obliged to treat with respect owing to their agreeable habit of ordering for themselves the best of everything. One of these was Mme. Montargis, a shrivelled little woman with a vile temper but lots of money and admirably expensive tastes. You know what the restaurant is like on a Sunday, at lunch? Well, that was the time chosen by this infernal monkey to revenge its family's grudge against society. In one movement it bounded across the table, whipped the wig from the head of Mme. Montargis, and disappeared through the window. Often we had wondered if this really was a wig. Now we knew. Her skull was like an egg.

"*Figurez vous, mon ami*, the drama! Mme. Montargis screaming '*Assassin!*' Mme. Boillot screaming '*Lulu!*', all the restaurant laughing like madmen, while Hortense, the waitress, pelted the monkey with apples as he sat outside on the signboard wearing the wig and looking only a slightly more desiccated reflection of his victim. At last one of the apples got home, and after shouting some unforgivable things at Hortense the monkey streaked across the square and began climbing the church."

"Still wearing the wig?" I asked.

"A little askew. From gargoyle to gargoyle he went, shaking with rage. Speaking not as an hotelier anxious for the comfort of his guests but as a man of the world, I must admit it was magnificent entertainment. A large crowd left the monkey in no doubt of that. On reaching the top of the spire he briefly employed the weather-cock as a merry-go-round before planting the wig firmly on the central spike, and then he disappeared down the far side.

"In spite of its comedy the situation was grave far beyond the good name of my hotel, for our annual regatta was next day. The mayor and my brother councillors came to me in consternation, and we were heartily agreed that to have a wig on the top of the church at such a time would assuredly make us the laughing-stock of all Normandy. Just as we were considering what reasonable men should do, the monkey reappeared on the tower with a bottle of eau-de-vie he'd filched from a café on the other side. This he drank slowly and purposefully, with the air of one satisfying a long-cherished ambition, and as soon as he'd had enough he started to climb down the face of the church.

"In my time I've witnessed many prodigies of fuddled agility, but none in any way comparable. As you know, there is much fine old carving on our church. At one moment the monkey would be clinging by nothing but his tail to the halo of a saint, at the next he would be holding by a single finger to a devil's snout. All the time, however, his senses were fighting a losing battle, and halfway through this remarkable exhibition the eau-de-vie triumphed.

53

If it had not been for the outstretched arm of St. Peter which miraculously arrested his fall, the monkey would most certainly have been killed. I told them to take him to the kitchen and give him plenty of black coffee, and our council meeting was resumed. Steeplejacks? It was Sunday, and they would have to come from Rouen, with special ladders. *Pompiers?* M. Lasserre, our local commander, was frank about the limitations of his equipment. He couldn't guarantee his biggest jet to wet St. Peter's feet, much less dislodge the wig of Mme. Montargis. Rifle-fire? The sergeant of *gendarmerie*, brought hurriedly into consultation, declined to be responsible for filling the air with bullets on Sunday afternoon. 'The fact is, gentlemen,' said the mayor, 'only one person is capable of helping us—and he's tight!'

"We laughed, but our laughter stopped short as though some-one had cut it with a knife. For *the monkey was climbing the church again!* Very deliberately this time, with a puzzled frown on his face that suggested he was trying to remember something absolutely vital to his happiness. He'd sobered up a good deal, but I imagine he must have had a formidable headache, and every now and then he missed a hold and only just saved himself. This time there wasn't any cheering down in the square. Not a sound. Up went the monkey, up, up, up. When at long last he reached the weathercock he became tremendously excited at seeing the wig again, and he clapped it passionately on his head. 'Bravo, Mme. Montargis!' somebody cried. And then, having taken all that trouble to get it, in a moment the monkey grew tired of the wig. That seemed to me charmingly human of him, a beautiful justification of your M. Darwin. He grabbed it off and just flung it away, so that it floated down across the crowded square like a small auburn parachute. And it landed—where do you think?"

"In the Seine?" I suggested.

"On the very window-sill of Mme. Montargis's bedroom!"

"And the monkey?"

"You ask of the strangest thing of all. The creature made off across the roofs, a little unsteadily to be sure, like a farmer going

54

home on Saturday night, and never was he seen again. I suppose it seemed a heaven-sent chance to get away from Mme. Boillot. In case he ever thinks of returning from the *maquis* I hope I've stated my position politely but with sufficient frankness?"

"Indeed you have. And Mme. Montargis?"

"She didn't come near us for twelve years, until last week. Her curls are still in the very latest style."

J. B. BOOTHROYD

Ah! Youth

It is early evening and the trains are not full. At Goldhawk Road the pink-cheeked boy, dressed to kill in sports jacket and flannels, with a starched white collar a little large for him, has a wide choice of seats.

He selects the one opposite to me. I do not at this stage quite understand why he has such a bravado as he sits. He is so very young that I have an impulse to smile at him—a friendly smile with a wry little envious twist—but when he catches my eye he suddenly assumes an expression of great sophistication, throwing one knee over the other and tossing back his curly hair so that he hits his head on the back of the seat with a force which makes me wince in sympathy. My compassion is wasted; he does not deign to notice the mishap at all, but carelessly brings out a paper packet of cigarettes—so carelessly that he drops them on the floor. He fingers his yellow figured tie, which glistens from a recent ironing and sprouts out and down in a dashing jug-handle curve, before he stoops to pick up the packet, and the effort makes him surprisingly red in the face for one so young. His insouciance is almost offensive as he fumbles inexpertly with the wrapping; he would make better progress with it if he looked at what he was doing, but he is en-

55

gaged in reading every word of the advertisement over my head. The length of his sunburnt forearms fascinates me; they seem to be growing visibly out of their too short sleeves.

We are drawing into Wood Lane Station before he has got out his cigarette. The paper packet is almost in ribbons and the cigarette itself looks a little frayed at one end. He puts the packet away in his jacket pocket, although it came from his trousers, and taps the cigarette seven times on his thumb-nail; when he tries to put it in his mouth even he cannot conceal his surprise at finding that he no longer has it—that seventh tap has sent it flying under my seat. My heart goes out to him as he sits there in astonishment and dismay. It is my turn to read the advertisement over *his* head. As we rumble along towards Latimer Road he stealthily glances about the compartment with almost imperceptible movements of his head. I try to avoid his eye, but when, inevitably, our glances meet, he gives me a long defiant glare and then subjects the other scattered passengers to a similar inspection. Anybody who has noticed his little slip with the cigarette will never for a moment imagine that he is looking for it; he is just a self-composed young man.

As the doors open at Latimer Road I pretend a great interest in the only new passenger, following his every movement until he is seated at the compartment's far end; but out of my eye-corners I study my *vis-à-vis* nevertheless. Taking advantage of my preoccupation during those few valuable seconds he sweeps the whole floor with his gaze, opens and shakes his jacket, frenziedly digs his fingers down the sides of his cushions, but all in vain. When I turn my head to the front again he is sitting with his old composure, his lips pursed as if for whistling.

With interest I observe his search for the packet of cigarettes. As he tries first one trouser pocket, then the other, his mask of composure begins to crack. What game are the fates playing with him? First a cigarette that is snatched from his very fingers to disappear into thin air, now a whole packet of cigarettes vanished out of his pocket! He tries the side pockets of his jacket, his alarm increasingly ill-concealed; unable to believe that any man of the world would put cigarettes in his breast-pocket he then goes back

56

to his trousers again, even to the hip-pocket. When I meet his eye this time it registers frank bewilderment, but he is man enough to remember his code even at this crisis; under my gaze the bewilderment is ruthlessly suppressed and replaced by a glare which says, "I am looking for my handkerchief; what business is it of yours?"

It is none of course, but I have to bite my lower lip when he draws a spotted handkerchief from his breast-pocket and the bewitched cigarettes fall into his lap. He does not put the handkerchief to his nose but to his temples, dabbing delicately and carrying the thing off with an upward glance to see if the window is open.

His second cigarette is ready by the time we pull out of Westbourne Park, and the packet returned to his trousers-pocket this time. Thus we begin to learn those little routines of life which, when learned completely, make it such a dull, dull business. He puts the fresh cigarette in the extreme corner of his mouth. His search for matches causes him to lean over sideways in his seat and brings him quite accidentally, no doubt, into a position from which he can see his reflection in the draught-shield of plate-glass. He studies it with interest. I can almost see the idea come to him that the cigarette would look more becoming in a central position; he takes it between two fingers to move it but the wretched thing has stuck, his fingers slide vainly along it and leave it dangling absurdly from his upper lip; quick to cover up he seizes it between finger and thumb and tears it away—ooh! I can feel the ragged little pain. Perhaps I even exclaim, I don't know. At any rate he suddenly darts me a furious glance and rubs the plate-glass with his thumb to show me that he has been examining some mark or flaw all this time.

And now, at last, the moment has come. He has picked up somewhere the saloon-bar trick of striking, not the match on the box but the box on the match. He breaks the first two matches, the second falling flaming on to his trousers; he brushes it angrily aside; he does not look up. As he lights the third the compartment doors slide open and the incoming breeze blows it out. I can see the beads of perspiration on his fair young brow. With the fourth match—the doors having closed again—all is well. As soon as it flares he shoves the fiercely-gripped cigarette into the heart of the little flame, filling his lungs with sulphur and blackening the paper cylinder for more than half its length. He continues to draw furiously as if lighting a pipe, and it is only when he has burnt his fingers that he flings down the match and extinguishes it with a large and casual foot. Then with all the aplomb in the world he recrosses his legs and leans back in his seat.

The fun is over. I have enjoyed it, but without malice. I have kept a sober face, and I think I have earned a smoke on my own account. My case slides out of its accustomed pocket neatly; the cigarette is in my mouth, my lighter flicks, the first blue cloud puffs out, the case slides back—all in a matter of five seconds. I cannot help glancing across to see whether the pink-faced boy has been watching how it ought to be done. I think he has. His face, all pretence to sophistication suddenly gone, wears a delighted smile. I smile back. He leans forward and nods at my cigarette.

"Pooh," he says—"You've gorn and lit the cork end."

And so I have.

J. B. BOOTHROYD

You Have to be Born with It

"Not Thursday," I said. "I have to take a film man to dinner. Make it Wednesday." I spoke with a man-about-town's air, so much easier to carry off on the telephone. If I'd been talking to Westerbrook in the flesh I should have found myself explaining that the film man was nothing more than an acquaintance of my aunt's called Vasey, or very probably Riley, who was a chemist, or something, in a camera factory. But Westerbrook has a long-standing ascendancy over me. He is a genuine man-about-town, who can get a taxi on a pouring wet day in the rush hour without even looking out from under his umbrella. It's only on the telephone that I can stand up to him.

"Wednesday, then," he said. "I thought we might start at Emile's with a bottle of Chablis and a dozen oysters, then drop in to dine at—"

I let him get out the gilded name before I stopped him. I could see I was in for another evening of humiliation, with Westerbrook lining up managers, chefs and bandleaders at every stop, inquiring after their wives and families and leaving me nothing to contribute but a tired grin. Besides, I'm never quite sure about the etiquette with oysters.

"Oh, really," I said, my tones oozing boredom with high living of this kind—"Why not Crockett's?" The splendour even of Crockett's is something I would hesitate to aspire to alone, but I knew it was the least Westerbrook would consider.

"Crockett's," he said. It might have been some coffee-stall in the Old Kent Road. "All right, if you're not too finicky about your stomach-lining. Say six forty-five, in the lounge." He rang off.

I was early. I always am. I arrived at the run, and tried to give my coat to the doorman of the downstairs grill-room, who indicated, without speaking, the correct place for coats. The dining-room proper is upstairs at Crockett's, with the lounge adjoining. I felt, as I always feel when Westerbrook is imminent, that a drink's start would be an advantage, and said "A sherry" to a man in a white Eton jacket. He went away and came back with three gins for the party at the next table. I leaned round my pillar. My table is always behind a pillar. I leaned round and said "Did you get my sherry?" I won't say that he took no notice. He gave me a look but that was all, then or later.

Westerbrook was late. He always is. He arrived at the stroll, unbuttoning his coat, and a man was behind him, waiting to take it. Behind him was another man, with two sherries on a tray. "In the window, Arnold," said Westerbrook, not looking at him. I hadn't noticed the vacant table in the window. As a matter of fact, I don't think it was there before Westerbrook came in.

"To your health and prosperity," said Westerbrook, taking a sip. Before I could do the same he'd taken my glass and placed it with his own on Arnold's tray. He looked at the man with a sad expression. That was all. And the man—you will never have seen this—blushed. "Sorry, sir," he said. "I'll speak to the barman."

"Do that." Westerbrook's tone was affable. "And send someone with some menus."

When Arnold brought the replacement sherries the head-waiter, with two menus, was trotting behind. He seemed to comprehend perfectly that Westerbrook could scarcely be expected to subscribe to the degrading practice of ordering his dinner in the dining-room. Westerbrook, it seemed clear to the head-waiter, might very well decide to have the actual dinner in the lounge, even if it meant the trifling inconvenience for the management of running up a temporary kitchen nearby.

The menu began with the shameless item, "Lobster Cocktail, 6s. 6d. extra." Westerbrook said "Well, now. Suppose we start with two lobster cocktails, shall we . . .?"

Well, you know, you can't forbear to admire. In the dining-room the windows overlooked the bustling heart of London, and each one had two tables in it. Except ours. Ours had only one, discreetly distant from the band, near enough to the service-doors, yet far enough away. "You were lucky," I said (like a fool), "to be able to book this."

"Book?" said Westerbrook. His eyebrows went up very slightly. "My dear chap."

The meal was beyond reproach. Beyond mine, at least. Westerbrook sent back his napkin because it was worn a little thin round the monogram, and he had his Neapolitan ice brought for him to see, half-way through the roast duck, in case the colours should prove too garish. There was a little trouble (after Westerbrook had drunk his) over the quality of the brandy, but that was easily put right. As we left the dining-room a man met Westerbrook with his coat. At the street door I thanked him, and he drove off in a taxi which the commissionaire had had waiting for some minutes. As it was apparently the only disengaged taxi in London I walked, deep in thought, to Charing Cross.

The effect of Westerbrook's company takes three days to wear off. It was unfortunate that my engagement with the film man fell within this period of hypnosis. Otherwise I should never have said to him on the telephone, with a more pronounced man-about-town's air than ever, "I thought Crockett's—I mean, if you're not too finicky about your stomach-lining. Say six forty-five, in the lounge." I rang off.

I was late. I killed ten slow minutes fooling about looking in the lighted windows of closed haberdashers' shops. Then I arrived, at the stroll. I caught the cloakroom man's eye quite definitely as I ascended to the lounge unbuttoning my coat, but he didn't follow me, so I had to go back with it. It was not a promising start, but it did bring me face to face with Arnold, carrying two drinks on a tray, and I was able to give him a warm good evening. He side-stepped in silence and hurried on. There was no sign of the film man downstairs. I had hoped, rather, that I should find him trying to give his coat to the doorman of the grill-room, but returned upstairs without even this satisfaction. The swing-door of the upstairs dining-room was open, and I beckoned a waiter who seemed to be arranging condiments with all but unshakable concentration. "Send a menu over, will you?" I said, and strolled with iron composure into the lounge, a man whose wish is a waiter's command. He came quickly over and said, icily, "Seven o'clock, sir, we start serving." And he kicked the wooden wedge from under the door, so that it swung to with a faint, derisive puff. When I turned, hot words mounting, he was only a dwindling shadow behind the glass.

"It's all right," said a voice. "I've got one."

It was the film man—Travers, Spivey, whatever his damn name was—sitting at a table I hadn't noticed. He had two menus, and two men. One was the head-waiter, notebook poised, and the other was Arnold, bending low with two drinks on a tray.

"Barman's apologies," he was saying to my guest, "and he trusts these will be more to your satisfaction."

I took mine and drank it before I spoke. It tasted terrible.

D. H. BARBER

The Egg

IF MR. WILSON of Balham should by good fortune happen to read these lines I hope he will communicate with me so that I may send a personal apology. The whole business must, from his point of view, have looked extremely queer, and not so many people ask for my autograph that I can afford to offend any of them.

It began with the clock in the breakfast-room being ten minutes slow, so that when I went out to see if there were any eggs I thought I had plenty of time for my train. I walked to the end of the garden and entered the hen-run and looked into the boxes where Ermyntrude and the Queen of Sheba and Charity Pecksniff are supposed to lay their eggs. It was several days since they had obliged, and Edith had become quite bloodthirsty about them, talking of the joys of roast fowl and cold fowl in a way that would have made her proposed victims very uncomfortable if they had overheard. It was therefore with great delight that I found a fine brown egg in the box. From the coy look that Charity Pecksniff gave me I think it must have been hers, but as one can never be quite sure I felt that it would mean a reprieve for all three of them.

My intention was to knock on the breakfast-room window and hand the egg to Edith when she opened it. As by the breakfast-room clock it could now not be later than six minutes to nine I reckoned that I would have ample time to hand over the egg and also put in a strong plea for the lives of the birds. As I approached the window, however, with the egg clutched in my hand, I heard the church clock strike nine. My train goes at 9.3.

I reached the station as the train began to move, showing the egg to the astonished ticket-collector instead of my season-ticket. I then dashed through the barrier and clambered into a compartment in which there were twelve people sitting and seven people standing. To put the egg in my pocket in such a crowd I knew would be merely to invite its destruction, so I held it over my head.

A young lady in the corner whispered to her friend that I looked like the Statue of Liberty, and they both giggled. Why people should giggle at the sight of a man simply holding an egg aloft in a crowded railway carriage I cannot imagine. Eggs are widely known to be structures of peculiar fragility, and they are also known to be of great value. What more natural than that the happy possessor of an egg, obliged to carry it by train, should desire to preserve its integrity? Giggling, however, is infectious, and the other occupants of the compartment soon joined in, and several of them made facetious remarks which it is unnecessary to repeat.

At Victoria I changed to the Inner Circle, but Inner Circle passengers have an even more perverted sense of humour than passengers on the Southern, which is a rather high-class line, and I argued that if the Southerners had giggled, the Inner Circlers would roar, so I sat down on a seat on the platform and thought things over.

Before I went to collect the egg I had glanced through my morning mail and then stuffed it into my pocket. It consisted of a seed catalogue on nice thin paper, and a letter from a Mr. Wilson of Balham, saying that he had greatly enjoyed my recent book of verse, *Kugomba Kuplets*, and that he would like my autograph. He enclosed a large stamped and addressed envelope and a postal order for three-and-sixpence, and asked me to send him a copy of the book inscribed with my name. Atfer a moment's cogitation I carefully wrapped the egg in the seed-catalogue and then put the bundle inside the stamped addressed envelope and sealed it up.

I felt that with care the egg was now sufficiently armoured to travel safely in my overcoat pocket, and placed it therein. The Inner Circle happened to be having rather an off-day, and there was plenty of standing-room, and when I reached the office and extracted the package I could tell by its shape that its precious contents were still in one piece. I put the package carefully on my desk and then went to wash my hands.

A minute later the office-boy arrived. He is a new office-boy and full of zeal, and when I emerged from the toilet he informed me smugly that he had posted the package.

"What package?" I asked.

"The one to Mr. Wilson of Balham," he said.

As neither the office-boy nor I can remember the exact address we are unable to communicate directly with Mr. Wilson, but as I owe him three-and-six and he owes me an egg I should be glad to hear from him as soon as possible. The lives of Ermyntrude and the Queen of Sheba and Charity Pecksniff depend upon his early reply, as Edith is inclined to dismiss the whole episode as a figment of my imagination.

J. B. BOOTHROYD

Trained Minds

THE BALD man obviously had a lot to do before we got to Victoria, because his files and papers spread thickly over the compartment's only empty seat. I felt sorry for him, and if I hadn't wanted, as it happened, to write a short poem on the way to town I would have retired gracefully to the corridor. As it was, I stood over him with dumb menace while he scooped a clearing; as the train jerked into motion I sat down hurriedly on a sheet of figures headed "Time Series of Consumption Per Capita."

We settled ourselves, the bald man, the other two back-to-the-engines and myself engaging in a solemn bouncing bout, establishing frontiers and gathering coat tails; to the passengers opposite we must have looked like four boys jumping up to look over a fence. Then the bald man, quite unprovoked, began punching me in the ribs. He hadn't much room for this, but powerful blows travelling short distances are highly spoken of by boxing commentators, and with good reason.

I turned to protest, and was horrified to see his mouth open and his eyes starting from his head; fortunately he got out his handkerchief in time, and the sneeze crashed harmlessly into it. He was a man, as events proved, who tended to keep everything in his outside pockets.

When a moment later, owing to some subtle process of suggestion, a sneeze of my own began to give warning of approach, I was glad that I kept my handkerchief in an easily accessible pocket—except that it wasn't there to-day, and I was obliged to spring up like a jack-in-the-box to get the spare from my brief-case. But I wasn't quick enough, and had to smother my head in an old shirt of yellow and russet checks which I was taking to be re-collared.

No one took much notice. There were outbursts of throat clearing and leg crossing from those opposite, but these were just unconscious reactions to a dimly-sensed disturbance in the compartment. Even the bald man, now leaning sharply away from me to get out a leather notebook, seemed quite absorbed in a sheet of figures headed "Statistical Demand Function by Standard Barrels," and had to be banged on the shoulder before he would release the shirt-sleeve trapped behind him.

It was not until we had rebounced ourselves into an approximation of comfort that I realized what a chance I had missed of getting out my own work—a sheet of blank paper clipped to a piece of quarto three-ply. This, of course, was in the brief-case. It would not be fair to make another upward spring so soon. I closed my eyes and tried to polish an opening phrase . . . but my seat was suddenly torn from under me. The bald man, on whose coat tails I had evidently been sitting, had remembered something he wanted out of *his* brief-case, and, lacking my delicate consideration for others, had sprung up to get it. However, it was at least an opportunity for me to do the same, and for some moments we craned upwards together, our ears touching. Then he settled down with his *Journal of the Royal Statistical Society*, and I with my little piece of three-ply.

The next thing I knew, his head was on my chest, and for a second or two I could see right down inside the back of his neck. This was the result of his impulsive hunt for a red ball-point pen in his side pocket farthest away from me. I waited. I wanted my own pencil, but it was in my side pocket farthest away from *him*. When he transferred the search elsewhere, removing his head from my chest on to that of an old gentleman in a tweed hat, who grunted on impact but said nothing, I acted quickly; in the nick of time, in fact; because I'd barely fished up my pencil when the head came back; the bald man had got the pen all right, but was seized by a sudden desire to get at his cigarette-case. I waited again. Even when he'd got it, I still waited. I was curious to see where he went for his matches.

He went everywhere. After a few minutes it was clear that he hadn't got any matches. The only way out seemed to be to offer him mine, so I rose to my feet and dug into a trousers pocket. I was astonished to find, when I was up, that the bald man was up too, and we just stood there, like Tweedledum and Tweedledee, while I got my matches out of my trousers, and he got his out of his brief-case. We must have looked pretty silly to the passengers opposite, who crossed and recrossed their legs impatiently, while even the old gentleman in the tweed hat, who seemed to be sleeping, muttered something which sounded like "Montgolfier brothers, Montgolfier brothers," and brushed up his moustache with an irritable gesture.

Then, for a time, all was quiet. I twiddled my pencil and tried to polish an opening phrase; the bald man twiddled his ball-point and moved his lips in silent calculation. Inspiration reached us both simultaneously; the double mental snap of the fingers, the unspoken "Got it!" were almost audible; we flexed our writing instruments and looked down at our knees . . . then at the floor, then round the compartment, then at each other. Together we spoke: "Excuse me, but are you . . . ?" We were. He was sitting on my piece of three-ply: I was sitting on his *Journal of the Royal Statistical Society* and a spring-back file labelled "Estimation of Parameters from Time Series (Current Non-food Price Indices)."

It was while these articles were being exchanged that the train lurched into East Croydon. When it lurched out again our little company had been swollen by a young man with a small cabin trunk, two girls with knitting, two with hockey-sticks, and a sour-looking man of the retired police inspector type carrying a dismantled truckle-bed lashed together with rope.

Thus crushed, palisaded, literally put upon, the bald man and I exchanged our first glance of fellow-feeling. We did not speak; we could not move; but all the way to Victoria, by those tiny signs of understanding, the raised eyebrow, the restricted shrug, the semi-humorous wince through the wire mattress of the truckle-bed, we showed that adversity had drawn us close.

When we parted at the barrier we even exchanged polite, if wordless, salutes. And I, for my part, have been hoping ever since that I might see him again. Then I could return his sheet of figures headed "Short Comparison of Demand Analyses," and he my short poem, which must until then continue to consist of an in-spired opening phrase that I cannot for the life of me remember.

H. F. ELLIS

Mr. Strakus

M**ISS** F**OX** overtook me about a hundred yards short of the lodge
gates.

"I wonder," she began, "if you are going to the Fête, would
you be so kind—this gentleman is very anxious—and I simply
must get to the food office before it closes."

A small, very dapper man stood under her lee smiling affably.
He wore an unusually wide-brimmed very light-grey hat and a stiff
turn-down collar of quite surprising depth.

"Mr. Strakus," said Miss Fox, introducing us.

"How do you do, Mr. Strakus," I said.

He bowed, tapped himself three times on the chest and said
"Strakus" so loudly that I jumped.

"How do you do?" I said again.

"He is from abroad," whispered Miss Fox unnecessarily. "Rather
particular about his name. I think there's an 'h' in it."

"I see," I said. "Have you been over here long, Mr. Strachus?"

"Oos," he said, smiling more widely than ever.

"You have? Good."

"Na, na, na. Oos. Yes?"

I couldn't make head or tail of it.

"Oos," said Mr. Strakus again. "Stray-itch-oos."

"I could join you there," put in Miss Fox, "in about an hour." And she turned back towards the village before I could collect my scattered wits. From the appearance of her back she seemed, I am sorry to say, to be giggling. Mr. Strakus and I walked on together.

"We go?" he asked.

"Yes," I said. "To the Fête—the Fair. Miss Fox will join us, come later. You wish to see the Fair?"

It seemed that he did.

"Fair. Good. Very good," he said rapidly. It was like listening to a school report.

"Flower show," I went on. "Cokernuts. Vegetables." I outlined an enormous marrow in the air. "All that sort of thing. And round-abouts. You have roundabouts in your country?"

"Rounanroun?" he cried, and to my dismay began to spin rapidly on his toes, emitting shrill cries of enjoyment. I glanced anxiously up and down the road.

"So?" he inquired, panting. "The dance?"

"Well, no," I said. "Not that—At least, no." And I made rotatory movements with my hand. "Wooden horses," I ended feebly.

This threw him into transports of delight.

"Wooden 'orse," he cried. "I know him. You know Troy? Helen? Bad 'Ector, yes?"

I didn't know what to think. Was it possible that in whatever corner of Central Europe he came from they took their English Unseens from Lang, Leaf and Myers? And if so, what was the Homeric equivalent for cokernuts?

"Homer," I said, to gain time. "You like Homer?"

"Yes, yes, yes," he said, nodding his head in his excitement about eleven hundred times.

"Whoa-up!" I said nervously, for we were just turning into the drive of Lesley Manor (kind permission of Lady B—) and there were people about. "Even Homer didn't nod as often as that."

"How?" he asked. But I left it at that. For all I knew the joke might not go so well in Hungarian.

Mrs. Andrews was majestically in charge of the cokernuts as usual. "Good afternoon," I said. "Business good to-day?"

Mrs. Andrews thought it would be better after four, when the sixpennies came in.

"Of course," I agreed. "This is Mr. Strakus, who has come to see what an English Fête is like."

"Stray-itch-oos," said my companion.

"*Isn't* it a lovely day," said Mrs. Andrews brightly. "Wouldn't you care to have a try?"

Mr. Strakus, however, was deep in thought. He seemed to be searching his mind for something.

"Three for twopence," added Mrs. Andrews encouragingly.

"I'll have a go," I said. "Come on, Mr. Strakus."

He muttered something that sounded extraordinarily like "Rod, pole or perch," struck himself a violent blow on the chest, said "Na, na, na" several times over and relapsed into silence again.

I hurled my first missile—a near miss.

"Almost I have him," said Mr. Strakus to himself.

I hurled my second. Rotten.

Mr. Strakus gave a sudden shout of triumph. "Roly-poly bitchk," he cried (or thereabouts), turning a dazzling smile on Mrs. Andrews.

I threw my third with steam rising visibly from my head.

"I think he means 'Roll, bowl or pitch,' Mrs. Andrews," I said. "Miss Fox met me—"

"Yes, yes," cried Mr. Strakus, repeating his odious phrase over and over. "I have learned him since many days."

"Look," I said desperately, taking his arm. "Let's go and see the vegetables."

"But I have not rolled."

"Never mind that," I said. "You can do that later."

"Now," I said, when I had got him safely into a quiet corner of the vegetable tent. "What would you like to see? Tomatoes?"

He didn't seem to care about tomatoes.

"Runner beans," I said. "Big. Gross. Very good."

They seemed to depress him.

"Look," I cried, as one might with a child of five. "Potatoes. First prize. Very large."

But all the fire had gone out of the man. Only when we had got into the Fruit section and I pointed out some rather exceptional peaches did some spark of his old animation return to him.

"Good," he said.

"Very good," I said. "Delicious." And I made munching motions with my mouth to clinch the point.

"To eat?" he asked.

"Of course," I said nodding. "What else? Don't they have peaches in Bulgaria?"

He took one and ate it.

I suppose, if the judges had been at hand, I should have taken an easy First in the beetroot class.

"Not a half bad," he said, wiping his fingers with hideous ostentation on a silk handkerchief.

As we came out of the tent we ran, to my inexpressible relief, into Miss Fox.

"There you are," she said. "Been enjoying yourselves?"

"Well," I said. "Yes. Oh, yes."

Mr. Strakus, however, had a grievance and lost no time in airing it.

"I wish to roll," he said loudly.

And there I left them. From the appearance of my back I may have seemed, I am sorry to say, to be giggling.

LORD DUNSANY

Little Tim Brannehan

EITHER to deceive the Germans in case they should come, or some more local enemy, the people of Sheehanstown had twisted sideways the arms of the signpost that there is a mile from their village; and as some years later, when I came that way in a car, the arms had not yet been put straight, I asked the way of an old man who chanced to be walking by. And one thing leading to another, we got into conversation, and I asked him how things were in those parts. "Terrible. Terrible," said the old man. "Sure, they're terrible. And it's the same in the whole world, too. It's all going to ruin."

"As bad as that?" I said.

"Aye," he answered. "And worse."

"And what do you think is the cause of it?" I asked.

"It's all those inventions that they make," he replied. "Sure, I can remember when bicycles were new. But that wasn't enough for them, and they must go on till they invented aeroplanes and wireless and I don't know what all. And no good came of it, and the hearts of men has corrupted. Listen now, and I'll tell you. Did you ever hear of the house and family of Blackcastle? No. Well, I was thinking you came from a very long way away. And once there was no country in the world that hadn't heard of them; but they're all ruined now. And it happened like this: the estates fell into the hands of a young Lord Blackcastle, that had a hard, dry, withered heart. So that was the end of their greatness, for no man can be great with a hard heart. Aye, that was the end of them. God be with the old days."

"What did he do?" I asked.

"Do, is it?" he said. "Sure, he had a hard, withered heart. What could he do?"

"Did he commit a crime?" I asked.

"Begob, it was worse nor a crime," he said. "Sure, you wouldn't mind a bit of crime in a man. He grudged a sup of milk to a child."

"He shouldn't have done that," I said.

"It's what he did," said the old man.

"How did it happen?" I asked.

"Sure, the good Lady Blackcastle, that had been his mother, died," he said, "and there was nobody to look after him then. And he went abroad, and he went from bad to worse; and he

72

comes home, and that's what he did. Mustn't a man have a black heart in him indeed to grudge a glass of milk to an ailing child?"

"Are you sure he did it?" I asked. "And did he mean to?"

"Did it!" he said. "And mean to! Sure the whole thing's down in writing. Look now. It's in my pocket. I have it there night and day. Can you read that?"

And he pulled out an envelope holding a half-sheet of notepaper, with writing in faded ink; and, crumpled and thumbed though it was, I could still read the old writing. "Let a pint of milk a day," it said, "be given to little Tim Brannehan, since he is weakly. Moira Blackcastle."

He gave me time to read it and time for the import of the note to sink in, as he stood before me, a tall, white-bearded, reproachful figure, looking at the evidence which I held in my hand of the ruin that was coming to the world.

"He comes home from abroad," he said, "and goes into his dairy, and he stops that pint of milk being given out any more. And I shows him that very letter. And it has no more effect on him than a snowflake in the face of a charging bull or a wild lion. And you have seen the letter yourself, and a man must have a hard, black heart to go against a letter like that, written by such a lady as was Lady Blackcastle, now in heaven among the blessed saints. Sure, the world's going to ruin."

"But when did all this happen?" I asked. "And who is little Tim Brannehan?"

"Sure, it happened only the other day," he said. And the old man drew himself up to his full height, straightening for a moment the limbs that the years had bent. "And do you think I don't know what I'm talking about? Sure, I'm Tim Brannehan. And I was never refused that milk for seventy years."

ALEX ATKINSON

The Upturned Plate

"Excuse me," I said, dropping my olive-stone surreptitiously on the carpet, "but aren't you Evangeline Wellcome, of *Woman's Fun?*"

She smiled a smile full of comfort and hope, and we shook hands stickily.

"That's rather interesting," I said, "because I found myself in a bizarre situation the other day, and I've wondered ever since how I really should have reacted." As I spoke I edged her backwards out of the crowd, until she was forced to sit in a corner. "You don't mind, do you?" I said.

"I am only human, of course," said Evangeline Wellcome, "but if there is any advice I can give—any little gleam of sunshine I can direct into a dark, frustrated corner—"

"Yes, quite," I said. "Well, it was like this. I was dining in a crowded restaurant with an old school friend and his wife. We'd finished the soup, and the talk turned to omelettes."

"Before you go any further," said Evangeline, "I ought to warn you that I don't do the home-cookery page. That's Mrs. Codling."

"Yes," I said, "but this is more a question of etiquette. At least, I *think* it is."

"Ah!" said Evangeline, and sipped her sherry-and-water greedily.

"Now, I happen to be rather a dab at omelettes—"

"Many men are," she said roguishly, shaking her kiss-curl. "I remember a literary agent once—"

"Please don't interrupt," I said. "*You* should know better than that."

She giggled delightedly, and slapped my hand with her fan.

"My friend's wife," I said sternly, "confessed that she couldn't make an omelette for toffee. Stanley—that's my friend—recalled a wonderful savoury thing I'd concocted over an oil-stove in his attic in nineteen thirty-five, and begged me to give her the recipe."

"You did, I hope? That would be only proper."

"I did. Stanley found a piece of paper in his pocket, and I dictated. Now, the point is, Stanley wanted something to rest his paper on. What d'you think he did?"

"Called for the wine-list?"

"No. He turned his plate upside-down."

Evangeline began to look a little less sure of herself.

"After he'd written out the recipe," I went on, "we all forgot about the upturned plate, until the waiter came along in a hurry and served him with roast duck, gravy and green peas."

Evangeline opened her eyes wide, and put her sherry-and-water rather shakily on an occasional table.

"Well now," I said, "several questions arise. Should I, as host, ignore the fact that a portion of duck has slithered on to the floor and that my guest's lap is swimming in green peas? Should I, in fact, reminisce gaily about life in the Lower Sixth as though nothing has happened? Should I ask the lady if she'd care to dance? Or what?"

Evangeline groped nervously for her sherry-and-water, but somebody had drunk it. She blinked several times, and examined a crack in her colourless nail-varnish.

"Of course," she said at last, "such a situation is not likely to arise often."

"I'll grant you that," I said. "But what would *you* have done?"

She cleared her throat, and seemed to be looking for a friend across the room.

"I think," she said, "that first of all I should have helped Stanley to tip the peas out of his napkin into some—er—receptacle."

"He did that himself," I said. "He tipped them into his wineglass."

She licked her lips.

"In that case," she said, "I think I should have put the waiter at ease by explaining briefly how the plate came to be upside-down."

"The waiter," I said, "was *perfectly* at ease. He was fishing about under the table with a spoon and fork, and laughing like hell."

I thought for a moment that her eyes would brim with tears. but suddenly they were illumined as it were from within.

"Tell me," she said, "what did *you* do?"

"I began to talk about china," I said, "and while Stanley stood up to shake himself, his wife and I turned all the coffee-cups upside-down to see the markings on the bottom. Well of course after we'd finished the sweet—"

Evangeline gave a cry of terror and, leaping to her feet, pushed past me and was swallowed up in the crowd. I was sorry about that, because I always rather enjoy the end of the story.

H. F. ELLIS

From My Travel Book

THE SULTAN received me in the embroidered tent he uses as a
throne room. He is tall for a sultan and has the dignity and perfect manners of his race.

"Would you prefer the brailings up or down?" he asked me, as
soon as I had taken my seat on the low *pouffe* at his side. The sun
was striking down with tropical heat and the atmosphere inside
the little tent was stifling. Steam rose in fitful puffs from the bowl
of rose water by my side.

I asked that the brailings might be raised, but noticing that they
were already up, changed my mind and begged that they should
be lowered. The Sultan inclined his head and motioned to a
gigantic Nubian to leave them as they were. In his country, as I
should have remembered, politeness demands that the guest ask
always for the opposite of what he desires. Ignorance of this interesting custom has sometimes cost an unwary visitor dear.

"And your wives?" he inquired. "I trust they bloom like the lily
of the valley and wax fat as kine by the water-meadows of Yemen."

I said yes, that apart from a mild epidemic of measles in one
of the dormitories, they were all well at home. Though himself

77

monogamous, the Sultan naturally assumes that any guest of his has great possessions, and it would be discourteous to correct him.

"And the Sultana?" I asked boldly. "May I hope that no one has had the audacity to cut *her* currant off?"

The Sultan enjoys a joke, as I well knew, better than most men, but the reader must remember that we were conversing in Arabic and for a moment there was a baffled look in his fine, rather un-English eyes.

"In my country," I explained, "the power that flows along the pipes to bring heat and light to our houses is at times cut off—"

"How cut off?" he asked. "By the sword?"

I sought about in my mind for the Arabic for "switch."

"There is a handle," I said. "It is because there is a scarcity of the lumps of compressed vegetable-matter we dig up from the ground and burn to make the power that flows along the pipes."

"Here in this land," he said, "we do not dig vegetables from the ground to burn. That would be accounted a sin. My herd of four thousand camels—"

"These are very old vegetables," I said hastily, "buried many hundreds of cubits beneath the ground."

"The ways of Allah are strange," he said gravely. "But the ways of men pass all understanding. Let us eat." He clapped his hands and at once the customary whole boiled sheep, swimming in its cauldron of fat, was set before each of us. For some hours there was silence as we ate, but at last I threw the final bone back with a clatter into the empty cauldron and turned my streaming face to the Sultan.

"So," I said. "The jackals of hunger have been put to flight. Let us talk."

"Good!" said the Sultan. "But first—you will have another?"

"No, thank you," I replied—and could have bitten out my tongue when I realized my error and a second sheep was set before me. To have refused to eat it now would have been, in my host's eyes, a bitter insult, but it was, I confess, with some nausea that I fished up a forequarter and once more set my teeth in the scalding flesh. And when, just after sunset, I pushed the cauldron away and dipped my fingers in the rose bowl to signify repletion, the head and portions of the scrag-end still remained untasted.

"How then?" said the Sultan, frowning. "It is not to your liking?"

"It is excellent," I said, repressing a shudder. "But in my country there is a saying 'Enough is as good as a feast.'"

"It is true," he said. "But we have not feasted. To-night, if Allah wills, we shall feast—I and my brethren and my brethren-in-law and the husbands of my daughters and you, who are dearer to me than the father of my own sons. Be sure the feast will be as good as enough. Many sheep have been slaughtered in your honour."

"Your bountiful kindness," I replied desperately, "is sweeter to me than honey to the sweet-toothed Ethiopian. But in my country it is not the custom to eat the flesh of the sheep a second time before the sun has thrice completed the great circle of the heavens and returned again to his appointed place. The hindquarters of a single lamb is the portion that is set apart among my people for four persons to feast upon, here a little and there a little, until the space of seven days has passed by."

The Sultan expressed his astonishment. "The customs of one people are not those of another," he remarked courteously; and he gave immediate orders that two score goats and a hundred doves be broiled for the feast. "The flesh of the goat is not the flesh of the sheep," he pointed out.

But it was not until we strolled out together for a breather before the evening meal that I realized how boundless is the hospitality of the people of this forgotten corner of Arabia. Thick clouds of black smoke rolled across the velvety night sky and the air was heavy with the acrid smell of autumn bonfires. "They are burning old vegetables," explained my host, "to make hot the flesh of the goat. There is a saying among my people, 'The customs of the stranger are our customs.'"

I hardly knew how to thank him.

Verse

MARK HOLLIS

'Twixt Cup and Lip

THE introduction of a refrain
    (*With a Taisez-vous and a Vive le Roi*)
In a foreign language now and again
    Gives a poem a *je ne sais quoi*.

And a *je ne sais quoi* is what I need
    (*With an a, ab, absque, coram, de*)
To tell of Uncle John's good deed
    (*With a bene, melius, optime*).

For what do you think that Uncle did?
    (*With Sitzen Sie and a Komm herein*)
He gave me a cheque for fifty quid
    (*With a Kraft durch Freude and Wacht am Rhein*).

I flung my arms round Uncle's neck
    (*With a Far niente and Nada hoy*)
But the bank have just dishonoured the cheque
    (*With a Mene Tekel and ὀτοτοτοῖ*).

EVOE (E. V. KNOX)

My Own Simplified Spelling

(*I cannot be bothered with other people's systems, new or old. I have chosen what I liked from any source that suited me. I have tried to clarify not only pronunciation but sense. And to make things easier I have omitted punctuation, always a nuisance to children and often, no doubt, to foreigners.)*

AWLTHO I no how 2 and fro
Sum peepul go with spade and ho
    And doutless have gud reason

I doo not so
I plahnt no ro
I neether dig nor proon nor mo
    Throo awl the singing season

If ruff winds sow
Across the slow
They cannot cow my glad hart now
    To werk wer well ni treason

Come with me Flo
Thine ainshent bo
Wair hi and lo we yoost 2 go
    Wair virelets bloom in every coom

Wair leeps from lair
The startuld hair
Wair springs from brake the trembling do
    Wile yet the yung yere fleas on

Wot ho dust thow
Or I need now
Amungst the ferze beneeth the bow
Wen brites the sun weel cair for nun
    But wonder wudlands throo

No racking coff shall keep us off
    Nor trace of winters floo

Wot not shall not
  Our troo luv twine
In cops or grot
  Thi hand in mine
By sum trees bole weel make our gole
Sole speek to sole time onwud role
  And hevvn luk down benine

Wile mounts the lark
In that hi ark
Weel from the bark
Cut out the names
Of Flo and James
  With tangled harts for sine

Is life not o and 2 sho
Wen browze b lined with ankshus tho
  And cairs 2 closely clinging

Wot ho wot ho
Need we to no
Wen wites the blossum on the slo
  And meeds with joy r springing

Wot sox 2 nit
Wen skize r lit
And down on floury banx we sit
  With larx awl round us singing

RENÉE HAYNES

Ingenious Raconteur

LAST autumn's chestnuts, rather *passées*,
He now presents as *marrons glacées*.

PHILIP A. STALKER

Talk

OFTEN I talk to men, on this or that,
Through the long night, and chiefly through my hat;
And they, in turn, through hats of different size,
Build confident assertion on surmise.

So it continues, hour succeeding hour
As each small bud of thought bursts into flower,
While, listening in limbo, sit the sages,
The Great Ones of the contemplative ages,
And all the sons of knowledgeable Man
Who ever talked since Time itself began—
Listening now, eager to catch one glow
Of thought not born five thousand years ago,
One little curtain raised, one tiny pelmet,
One word not said through some old Roman helmet.

A. P. HERBERT

Hattage

Iт's kind of you to let me have my hat:
  And I will give you sixpence for it now.
No, no, I think you should have more than that:
  Name your own ransom, sir, and I shall bow.

It was so kind of you to guard my hat,
  While I was lunching in this costly hole.
You did not jump on it, or squash it flat:
  You did not sell it to a single soul.

You did not lend it to a minstrel-troupe;
  You did not give it to the dog to dine;
You did not plunge it in to-morrow's soup
  (I think there was a hat or two in mine).

The *mousse de veau* reminded me of cats;
  The room is draughty, and the bills astound:
But when it comes to the control of hats
  The management is absolutely sound.

Let highway robbers gather in the street;
  Let burglars prowl, and fellow-lunchers stare:
My heart is light (whatever I must eat).
  My hat's impregnable. For you are there.

This hat is dear to me. We've had such fun.
  I was betrothed in this beloved lid.
I should not like to use another one:
  I should not have the coupons if I did.

This hat is dear to me. My hat, it is!
  I know of nothing that has cost me half.

I should not care to count the sixpences
I have invested in the cloak-room staff.

Yachts—first editions—caviare—and gin—
    Champagne and diamonds, and things like that—
Silk stockings—motor-cars—and even sin
    Are less expensive than the common hat.

Capital value! Search the Island ground
    From London City to the hills of Minch:
A piece of property will not be found
    That carries so much money to the inch.

Men must pay "corkage" for the wine they bring,
    Which always struck me as a puzzling plan:
I do not get the logic of the thing.
    But I will pay my hattage like a man.

Maybe, one morning, when the credit cracks,
    I'll give this dear old monument away
To my dear Chancellor, in lieu of tax.
    Meanwhile, I'll buy it back again. Good day.

VIRGINIA GRAHAM

Mr. Mackenzie

WE learnt about Mr. Mackenzie in the flat above,
because when he moved in
he started almost at once to play
his violin.
    He began, at seven, by playing some Bach,
so we knew he was serious,
and then he stopped, for dinner I suppose,
which wasn't so very mysterious;
but you see at eight,

he foxed us a bit
by playing the "Caprice Viennoise."
We didn't know *what* to make of it.
　At 8.30 we knew he was industrious
because he practised his scales,
and then suddenly he played
Wales! Wa—les!
So odd! We decided, erroneously, he was Welsh.
　At nine we knew he was in love.
The Chopin nocturne sounded quite different;
rather as though he were wearing a woolly glove—
all muffled and tender, a little mawkish really,
but when he began to play
Debussy, we realized
that tho' he might be in love, he was also gay.
And intelligent—yes, he sounded very intelligent.
　But it wasn't until ten
or thereabouts,
when
Mr. Mackenzie hit a piercing high note,
and having hung
on to it for hours hurled himself like a cataract into
　boogie woogie,
that we knew, for certain, Mr. Mackenzie was young.

MARK HOLLIS

Careless Talk

Bill
Was ill.

In his delirium
He talked about Miriam.

This was an error
As his wife was a terror

Known
As Joan.

H. J. HANN

!

CONFOUND that man
I asked to dine;
He neither   turned up
Nor

dropped a line.

DONALD MATTAM

In a Town Garden

LOVELIEST of trees, the cherry now
Is hung with bloom along the bough,

As every urchin by my fence
Notes for future reference.

THOMAS EVAN RYVES

Amoeba

THE very first Amœba
  Once said to his inside:
"I can't get on together, George;
  I really must divide.

"There is a surge, a wild surmise,
  That troubles my—er—breast.
You shall have half the chromosomes
  And I will take the rest."

'Tis done! 'Tis done! Bisectitude!
  O Rhapsody in two!
Amœba is beside himself
  And both of him is true.

"Hail and farewell," Amœba said,
  "This is the day of days.
We must put out our pseudopods
  And take our parting ways.

"The centuries that lie ahead;
  Those flying years of grace!
Who knows what we may yet become?
  We'll set a pounding pace."

Amœba's road is hard and long
  To Nineveh and Rome,
But still Amœba's on the grade;
  On, on, to kingdom come!

The very first Amœba
    Is getting old and grey,
But still his dreams are far ahead;
    His future far away.

Oh, not for him is history
    And human joy and pain.
In twenty minutes he'll divide
    And then set out again.

VIRGINIA GRAHAM

Disillusionment

SHYNESS and modesty, they said,
    Will bring love to your side,
Seek not to gild the gingerbread;
    Dear heavens, how they lied!

The ointment pots are full of flies,
    And bitter is the cup
For those of us who drop our eyes
    And no one picks them up.

JUSTIN RICHARDSON

La Carte

It takes much art
To choose à la carte
For less than they quote
For the table d'hôte.

The Human Races

THE human races
All live where time and space is;
Their nature uniformly base is.

The Nordic races
Hop round in continual metastasis
Leaving hideous industrial traces.

The Mongol races
Have flat faces
And live in most extensive places.

The Hamitic races
Play in jazz bands with wild grimaces
And wear purple shoe-laces.

The Mediterranean races
Have many graces
And like to fill their lives with embraces.

The Semitic races
Divide their time between the oasis
And the widest of wide open spaces.

The Celtic races
Drink whisky by the dozen cases;
Each man can hold as much as his own weight displaces.

The Alpine races
Live on top or half-way up or at the bases
Of mountains where the air is vilely cold but braces.

The Coptic races
Walk in processions at unseemly paces
Carrying enormous maces.

The Carib races
Inhabit upturned carapaces,
Eating seaweed, mussel shell, and uncooked daces.

The Balkan races
Live roughly north-west of the place where Thrace is.
Their conduct a perpetual disgrace is.

The human races
All live where time and space is;
Their nature uniformly base is.

D. H. A. ALEXANDER

Rencontre

Mrs. Canticle's coming up Waverley Street,
  Aggressive and ample as Venus.
She knows that I've seen her, she's seen me I know,
But there's still the best part of a furlong to go
Before I salute her, and each must ignore
The other's existence until there's no more
  Than a couple of paces between us.
    So look to the left, brother, look to the right,
    Pretend Mrs. Canticle isn't in sight;
    Look down at the pavement, look up at the sky,
    It's too early to catch Mrs. Canticle's eye.

Mrs. Canticle's coming, I cannot retreat,
  She's a stickler for social convention.
I'll be charged with a quite unforgivable sin
If my features relax in a premature grin;

And how can I banish an impulse to run?
Shall I do up my shoe-lace? It isn't undone.
  Is there nothing to rivet attention?
    Look nonchalant, brother, and don't think it weak
    To pretend it's the wind that is flushing your cheek;
    There is justification for acting a lie
    In the strain of avoiding La Canticle's eye.

Mrs. Canticle's coming, her mind is effete,
  Her talk superficial and hollow.
I'm reputed a wit, but what is there to say?
"Good morning," to start with; "A beautiful day,
I hope you are well, what an odd place to meet,
Whatever brings you in to Waverley Street?"
  I suppose that's the line I should follow.
    Well, brother, she's gone. You can look where you please
    And expand in regaining your natural ease . . .
    But there's something that irks me, I cannot deny,
    In failing to catch Mrs. Canticle's eye.

G. C. POLSON

!Nightmare Setter's Type

WE're told to read—to rest our eyes—
.Contrarywise lines alternate
For prose the scheme is worth one's praise,
Raise dilemmas unforeseen but
My doubts where poetry is concerned,
,Turned are lines when rhyme should what for
The last word or the first? And can
?Scan its reverse line backwards each
I've tried one way—it's only fair
.Compare and other the try to

You will, although you backwards read,
,this scan to forwards look to need
And forwards only will it rhyme.
.Preferred are ways which tell will time
We'd rather these than always see
.Before used always method the

So let's make writing poems brighter—
:Typewriter "ways-both-work" a invent
We'll be the first to try the stunt
.Front to back poetry writing of

R. P. LISTER

The Gem-Like Flame

THERE was a chap— I forget his name—
Who burned with a hard and gem-like flame,
His spirit was pure, his spirit was white,
And it shone like a candle in the night.

This singular state that chap achieved
By living up to the things he believed;
He spurned the Better, pursued the Best,
He wedded the Form to the Thing Expressed,

He strove for beauty with all his heart,
And worshipped Life as a form of Art;
And everything Vulgar he flung aside
Till his soul was perfectly purified.

And that explains how the poor chap came
To burn with a hard and gem-like flame;
And that explains why my old friend Mike
Laid him out with a marlinespike.

✺

JUSTIN RICHARDSON

Back-Room Joys

Mending Fuses

WHEN the lights go on after we've mended a fuse
Don't we feel a sort of magnification of the thews!
We are an expert who has been consulted,
Who has prescribed and something has resulted.
We have exercised our excellent mystery
And as we have said it should be, so we have made it be.
We have been brave, dealing with occult forces.
We have been scientific, tracing things to their sources.
We are rewarded also with admiring eyes,
Showing, as do our own, no small surprise.

Being Brave

IT's very great fun being brave,
Making light of some personal disaster—
A toothache, a thumb set in plaster—
With an airy, insouciant wave
And a marked shift in the conversation.
This not only limits consolation
To the point where we're fed but not choked,
But attracts admiration—which isn't normally evoked.
The resignation of our opening tone
Precludes the thought that the fault is probably our own,
As our subsequent lucky attempt to be gay and convivial
Completely disguises the fact that it's really quite trivial.
All this is incense, a sweetly inebriate savour

That makes us get braver and braver
Until, often, long after we're well.

A warning. There *are* cases—it *has* occurred—
Of people taking brave sufferers at their word;
That *isn't* so swell.

Knowing Better, Keeping Quiet

KNOWING better, keeping quiet—
This is an ambrosial diet.
Contradicting is bad form,
Knowledge kept inside keeps warm.
"Botticelli's 'Mona Lisa' . . ."
"Avignon was built by Cæsar . . ."
". . . Panthéon . . . Napoleon's coffin. . . ."
Listen to the crass old boffin—
Every single fact mixed up!
This is nectar in your cup;
Do not spill it; sniff its savour—
Once it's gone where is the flavour?
Now it's the Croisette at *Nice!*
Now it's "gendarmes" for *police!*
Do not stop him—let him utter;
Speech is bread but silence butter.
All day long you'll hug it tight—
How you could have put him right!
But you didn't—that's the fun.

Sometimes there's another one,
Someone keeping quiet too.
Then the merest wink will do,
Showing that you knew, but more,
Like an epicure, forbore.
Then the joy finds full fruition—
Modesty *plus* recognition.

ERIC WALMSLEY

The Tuba

TUBA, tuba, shining bright
At the Danceodrome last night,
Oh, what mortal hand or eye
Hath framed thy fearful symmetry?

In what overheated cell
Did that proud musician dwell?
Daring what fantastic jape
Conceived he thy most monstrous shape?

Say, by what outlandish art
Could he even make a start?
And, once started, how could he
Invent an instrument like thee?

Why those knobs? And to what ends
Created he those fearsome bends?
Those pipes? That horn? Those pistons? And
That funny little music stand?

Why, too, when the time had come
For thee to be no longer dumb,
Did thy maker's fancy stoop
To perpetrate that boop-a-doop?

Tuba, tuba, shining bright
At the Danceodrome last night,
Oh, what mortal hand or eye
Could frame thy fearful symmetry?

EVOE (E. V. KNOX)

The Mental Cure

Tom, Tom the piper's son
Stole a pig and away he run,
The pig was missed, and Tom was hissed
And sent to a psychiatrist.

This gentleman, whose name was Squeers
Allayed the young delinquent's fears,
And penned a note of even date
To the police court magistrate,
Which ran "The little mind is split
But we must make the best of it;
Subliminal desire for pork
Is often much too hard to balk,
And in some cases may extrude
The sense of moral turpitude;
Complete dispersal of the former
Should metagrobolize the Trauma."

The beak, at once impressed by this
Superbly phrased analysis,
Dispatched to a Remedial Home
The adolescent gastronome.
And here were pigs of various size
And various breeds in painted sties,
And every day from earliest dawn
The boy was given bits of brawn
And chitterlings and sausage meat
And rather more than he could eat—
However hard he tried to cram—
Of roasted pork and Wiltshire ham;

Till he forgot that ancient sin
For which the cops had pulled him in,
And nothing in his mind was left
Associating "pigs" with "theft."

The moral of this tale is plain:
He never stole a pig again;
And if he had not found some lead
And coshed a bank clerk on the head
When he returned refreshed and gay
From his delightful time of play,
He would not be in jug to-day.

J. B. BOOTHROYD

"And Now . . ."

IT's a *rum—*
Ba band another *rum-*
Ba band a never *slum-*
Ba band there's any *num-*
Ba of *rum-*
Ba bands
     Shicker-shicker-shicker.
Turn on the radio,
Mammoth set or midget,
All you'll ever get
Is the everlasting fidget
Of a *rum-*
Ba band another *rum-*
Ba band a pluck and *strum-*
Ba band with a
Shicker-shicker-shicker-shicker
Shee shicker-shick and a

Ticker-ticker-ticker-ticker
Tee ticker-tick and a
Boom and a nobble and a clang
And a bang
And a chatter and a natter
Let it clatter
Let it shatter
Let it spatter
Doesn't matter
Getting flatter
It's a *rum-*
Ba band another *rum-*
Ba band another *rum·*
Ba band another *rum-*
Ba band another Rum!
      Shicker-shicker-shicker.
Turn on the radio,
Mammoth set or midget,
All you seem to get
Is the orchestrated fidget
Of a *rum-*
Ba band another *rum-*
Ba band another *rum-*
Ba band, there's any *num-*BA . . .
To play the *rum-*BA . . .
Can't someone have the rumba banned?
      (*Shicker-shick*)

VIRGINIA GRAHAM

Delius in the Evening

THEY shouldn't play Delius in the evening,
   it is too sad to be borne;

those lonely notes on the clarinet,
    those sultry hums on the horn,
the sweet rush up of the violins
    as they leave the bass bassoon
twiddle me round like a baby
    in a treacle molasses cocoon.

I seem to be drowning in butter,
    with caramel sauce in my hair,
and the sad soft harps pull me under
    whenever I rise for air.
I know I'm not forced to listen,
    I could easily twiddle the knobs,
but I want to have some sort of reason
    for racking the room with my sobs.

E. V. MILNER

Tree into Poem

I think that I shall never see
A poem lovely as a tree . . .
Yet, oddly, I have heard it hinted
That trees are pulped and poems printed.

M. KEEL JONES

Election Reflection

EACH day into the upper air
Ascends the politician's prayer—
"Grant me the gift of swift retort
And keep the public memory short."

E. V. BOOTH

The Alliterative Dodo

WHAT can I do, the Dodo asked,
　Before I quit the scene—
Where worldly triumphs were so few—
　To keep my memory green?
Whereto the gods replied: Good Bird!
　The roads to Fame are many,
And dying—with a name like yours—
　As good a one as any!

DACRE BALSDON

Endurance Test

I'VE heard it said that Sir Barnabas Beer
spent most of his long and distinguished career
in moving great masses of paper about,
from a tray marked *In* to another marked *Out*.

JUSTIN RICHARDSON

All Awry

I WANT to know, am I the only stooge
Who has this trouble between "gauge" and "gouge"?
Or is it "gowge"? Am I a problem child
Because, to me, "misled" is always "misled"?
Does one pronounce the "Mall" as I do "Mall,"
Or does it rhyme with "shall"; or not at all?
I have—I think I have—my "orgy" taped
But "prosecute" is still not firmly shaped
And gets mixed up with "persecute" at times.
I can't divorce "executor" from crimes,
And have internal struggles when I say
"Quayside"—I want to call it "quay"—
Do there exist some types who, without fail,
Can spot the winner between "goal" and "gaol,"
Unerring supermen who know their stuff
And call it "slough"? (or, dammit, is it "slough"?)
I hope there are, to prove it *can* be done;
Meanwhile, I ask again, am I the one—
The *only* one in our rough island story—
Who always gets such words as these all awry?

R. C. SCRIVEN

One-Man Farm

I WORK a one-man farm in Slaithwaite:
my farm has but one field. I plaithwaite

in Saxon linchets (to allaithwaite
proper crop-rotation). Naithwaite
bears beet, peas, wheat, grass, and one caithwaite
won't support two—and a saithwaite
has nine piglings. Ee, by gaithwaite
is by the sweat of my own braithwaite
shows a profit. Aye, and haithwaite
does, caps all t'farming chaps
   i' Slaithwaite!

R. J. P. HEWISON

Genius

A SCIENTIST living at Staines
Is searching with infinite pains
   For a new type of sound
   Which he hopes, when it's found,
Will travel much faster than planes.

J. B. BOOTHROYD

Please Excuse Typing

IF YOU have ever, like me,
Missed the "r" and hit the "t,"
Addressing some fat blister
As "Mt." instead of "Mr.,"
I trust you left it unamended?

Splendid.

J . R . POPE

A Word of Encouragement

O WHAT a tangled web we weave
When first we practise to deceive!
But when we've practised quite a while
How vastly we improve our style!

G . N . SPROD

Request Number

TELL me a story, Father, please do;
 I've kissed Mama and I've said my prayers,
And I bade good night to the soft pussy-cat
 And the little grey mouse that lives under the stairs.

Tell me a story, Father, please do,
 Of power-crazed vampires of monstrous size,
Of hordes of malevolent man-eating crabs
 And pea-green zombies with X-ray eyes.

In the Throes of Living

IN THE SHOPS

❀

PATRICIA HELBRICH

A Bottle of Ink

"I WANT a bottle of ink," I said firmly.

"Certainly, miss. Black, blue, or blue-black?" he asked.

"Black," I said definitely. I wavered. "No, blue," I said. My eyes fell before his gaze. "Blue-black," I said meekly.

He brought it. It was covered with a thick layer of dust.

"Seven-and-a-half without dust, eight-and-a-half with," he said, jocularly.

I looked at it. I rather liked the dust. It made the bottle look more aristocratic—like old brandy.

"With the dust," I said.

His mouth widened. "Ha! ha! ha! ha-ha-ha-ha-ha! he! he! he . . ." he caught the eye of the manager and coughed. He wiped the bottle with his coat-sleeve.

"Is the top firm?" I asked.

He held the bottle upside down. A thin blue-black trickle slid down the label.

"No," he said briefly.

He screwed tighter. He held the bottle upside down. Another trickle emerged and joined the first.

"No," he said, still more briefly.

He screwed tighter. There was a sharp crack. A river joined the two trickles and together they rushed to form a sea on the counter. "No."

He brought out another bottle. He wiped it. He held it upside down. A thin trickle . . . He put it hastily back in the farthest corner he could find. Likewise a second, and a third. The farthest corner began to protest and pushed its collection into the open again.

*　　*　　*　　*　　*

Wearily he held the fifty-sixth bottle upside down. And nothing happened. He shook it. And nothing happened. He banged it on the counter, grabbed my money and dived into the recesses behind the shop.

I tucked the bottle in my handbag. At the door I paused. I looked at my handbag. It must have been that final bang on the counter. I turned back.

"I want," I said firmly, "a bottle of ink eradicator . . ."

ERIC ROBERTS

Buying a Tennis Racket

"I want a tennis racket," I said, hooking my umbrella on the counter and wiping my spectacles with my handkerchief the better to examine the selection of instruments that would be put before me.

"Very good, sir," said the assistant. "Had you any particular make in mind?"

I was not really acquainted with any make at all, but this was something I preferred the man not to know.

"I'm not fussy," I answered, "except that I do rather prefer to have the strings that run vertically a contrasting colour to those that run horizontally, if you know what I mean."

"Yes, I follow you, sir," the man said, focusing his eyes on me in a peculiar sort of way. "Only I'm afraid we have nothing in stock like that. It was a fashion that found favour rather earlier in the century, I believe."

"Indeed?" I said. "Oh, well, never mind. Show me what you have."

While the man was away I picked a cricket ball off a small

ebony stand and tossed it into the air with a twist of my fingers that in my younger days produced an off-break that turned a full ten inches.

"It's a sad thing when *Anno Domini* curbs our sporting activities," I said, when the man returned. "The racket is actually for my nephew."

I placed the cricket ball on the counter, whereupon it rolled to the edge, fell on the floor, and disappeared under a pile of bicycle mudguards. The five rackets that the man was hugging to his bosom made it impossible for him to spare a hand to stop it.

As soon as he had unburdened himself I selected one and held it at arm's length, squinting at it in the way I had seen people do.

"You will be able to detect any bow in the frame more easily by holding it edge on," advised the man as he lowered himself to his knees and grovelled amongst the mudguards.

By the time he had recovered the cricket ball, replaced it on the ebony stand, and tucked his tie back inside his waistcoat, I had completed my preliminary inspection.

"Good," I said. "None of them seems to be bent in any way. Now, if you don't mind, I should like to test the amount of go there is in the gut."

"These rackets are all strung to a tension of seventy pounds," said the man.

"That means precisely nothing to me," I remarked. "Have you a ball with which I may try for myself?"

The man took one out of a box, and apprehensively biting his finger ends passed it to me across the counter. I noticed that his hand shook slightly, and he seemed paler than when I first saw him.

I selected a racket at random, threw the ball a foot in the air, and as it dropped on to the strings I gave a fierce upward flick with my wrist. It was, to the best of my recollection, precisely the same movement that I used to impart to my old "Wizphast" that had served me so faithfully between the years 1921–29, and it should have resulted in the ball rising to a convenient height of approximately eighteen inches.

I can only conclude, however, that the tension on my "Wiz-phast" must have been a good deal less than 70 lb., for I was both surprised and alarmed to see the ball rise to within six inches of the ceiling, strike the corner of a suspended folding canoe, and be deflected in its downward path towards a pyramid of golf-balls mounted on a small mahogany table.

With commendable presence of mind the assistant leapt into action like a panther, and with outstretched hand strove frantically to avert the destruction of a morning's work. No doubt, too, he would have succeeded had not the turn-up of his trousers caught in the bottom bicycle mudguard . . .

As he dusted himself down I explained that I thought a tension of 70 lb. would be too much of a liability in the hands of my young nephew, but that, as I disliked putting people about to no purpose, I would gladly purchase one of his mudguards for my wife's bicycle.

D. A. DYER

Shopping

WHILE we drank coffee under the disinterested eyes of a group of waitresses she made a shopping list on the back of a menu card. I did not like the look of "A present for Timothy."

The pavements were deep with people. The sky was drab, and from it grey rain was falling.

We drifted into a shop which sold, among other things, photographical equipment. She wanted for Timothy an exposure meter; not an electrical one, as that was too dear. The assistant was delighted. He produced a thing through which he invited us to look. Did we not see a row of five figures? Good. The number which we could see the least plain of the five was the important one. It formed the basis on which mathematical calculations, that were made plain in a booklet provided, were to be set in motion. He suggested that, for example, the number might be four . . . He thumbed through the booklet and scratched his head. If the number were four it was easy to deduce that . . . Well, say the number was six . . . We wandered around the shop. The assistant had by now become thoroughly absorbed in the booklet; he was jotting down figures on a piece of paper. She asked him several times whether he had in stock any other kind of meter. After a while he looked up in a bemused kind of fashion and suggested desperately that she was to suppose that the number was eight.

Leaving him to calculate whatever was to be calculated from that figure we moved into another shop. The fellow there was much more encouraging; he had in stock a very superior kind of meter. He padded about the room, shooting his eyes hither and thither and prodding out an occasional hand. His manner became harassed. He ought to have in stock a very superior meter . . . Would we in the meantime like to look at one of this type? The figure which one was able to see the least plain of the five formed the basis on which mathematical . . . No, we did not want to look at that kind. He was sure that somewhere he had . . . Ah!

She had, he explained, only to look through this thing and she would see dots; she would see the dots more plainly if she were to take her hand away from the end. Now, those dots were not all . . . She unscrewed her eye and declared that she could see nothing at all. He snatched it away from her and glared through it. He walked up and down, the thing clamped to one eye, pointing it up to the ceiling, down to the floor. It was evident that a certain amount of practice was required in the use of it. He declared after some giddy perambulations that he was now beginning to see spots. Hundreds of them.

We slipped away to look for a music stand. She wanted one which would fold up; the one Timothy had now, if old and rusty, would fold up to a size no bigger than this . . . well, that, anyway. The girl said she was sorry, all she had was a chromium-plated one in two parts. Perhaps we would like to see how it worked? She undid various screws. She shook it. Then she held it up to the light in a reflective manner, and a leg suddenly shot out like a sword from a scabbard. She looked pleased. She gave a tug here and a pull there, and the thing stood quiveringly upright. The bit to hold the music, which was separate, would now fit quite simply into the stand, thus . . . She twiddled some more screws, tried gentle persuasion, brute force . . . it was just the knack, she explained. We said it was obviously a very good stand, but we were not all that keen on chromium. Was there another music shop? There was, but it was the other end of the town.

As we approached this building the roar of a wireless set almost blasted us from the pavement. We plucked up courage to enter, and a rush of furious sound slammed back the door upon its hinges. The man beamed at us. She took a deep breath and in a violent screech asked whether he had any music stands. Just then someone switched off the wireless. The man recoiled with a very pained expression. Later, he said No.

ALEX ATKINSON

Hep

"Get *Hep*," a notice on the door of The Music Mart advised me in alternate black and red letters: *"Use a Boppa Tonal Colour Stone Lined Bla-Bla Mute."* I took a deep breath and entered the shop. It smelt of drums, and as I eased myself between a 3 oct., c.c. elec. Vibraphone and a dazzling pyramid of Santa Anna piano-accordions (41 treble, 3 voices, 120 bass, aluminum pallette boards, 4 registers on treble grille) two young men with long hair turned from the counter to inspect me. Dancing girls had been painted on their neckties, and they seemed to be wearing other people's jackets. A solemn old lady assistant with a bun was riffling expertly through a catalogue entitled "New Orleans Style."

I stood politely at the far end of the counter, and taking up a six-months-old issue of *Down Beat*, pretended to read about a gentleman called Jelly Roll Morton.

"Here, friend!" said one of the young men suddenly, "settle an argument. Who took alto in the N' Yorleans Wanderers nineteen twenty-six disc of 'Gatemouth'?"

I started nervously, and the brim of my hat brushed against a Giant Nyfty Cymbal, which hissed like a panther.

"Alto what?" I said.

Their eyes narrowed, and the old lady stuck her pencil through her bun and blinked at me. I selected two or three super, deep cup, cushion rimmed mouthpieces from a cardboard box, and began to examine them, pursing my lips critically.

"Here," said the second young man, "weren't you with Biff Maul at Aldo Holiday Camp year before last—trumpet doubling piano?"

"No," I said casually. I picked up a shop-soiled copy of *Sixty Hot Licks for Clar.*, and read the advertisements on the back.

"Why, man! I know," said the first young man delightedly. "You did vocals and guit. with Buzzer Loftus at the old Melodion."

I shook my head mysteriously. "Tar and Feather Me Blues," I read musingly. "Royal Tournament Dixieland Shout. Beef Steak Stomp. Coffin Lid Drag, arr. pno. Hm."

The old lady looked along the counter with her finger in the catalogue. "Can I show you anything?" she said.

"Yes, please," I said. "I want a 'Swanee' Plastic Toot-Floot."

In the silence that followed, the two young men pushed back

their hats and stopped chewing, and I picked up a hand-made Cuban Wonder maraca and balanced it on the palm of my hand until it fell into a box of nylon drumheads.

"A what?" asked the old lady frigidly.

"A 'Swanee' Plastic Toot-Floot," I said. "For my nephew. You have them in the window."

"*We* have?"

"Yes," I said. "On a card. Just to the left of the reconditioned single tension tom-toms."

"You're kidding," she said sternly.

"Oh no," I said, and added with a brave smile, "I'm right in the groove."

Nobody else smiled. The old lady made her way incredulously to the window. I la-la'ed the hottest number I could remember ("Betty Co-ed") and the youths, swallowing nervously, moved closer together for protection.

"These?" said the old lady, reappearing with the card of dusty Floots.

"Yes," I said. "I think I'll have a yellow one."

She slid a yellow one from its slot and looked at it suspiciously. "They seem to be three shillings," she said.

"Well, man alive!" said one young man, wide-eyed. "I call that real cute. Ernie, you could use that in 'Whistle Stop Rag,' for a laugh!"

He slid out a green one and blew down it heartily, making a sound of rushing air.

"Nah, nah," said his friend. "It fingers like a sax."

They experimented for a while, talking excitedly about control of stomach muscles, slap-tonguing, and over-blowing for upper-register, without producing a single note.

I smiled paternally at them as the old lady gave me my change. "If you'll allow me," I said. "You're blowing down the wrong end."

They passed it over, rather awed, and I played the first two lines of "Three Blind Mice," accurately *ma non troppo*.

"You young people," I said, as I handed it back, "ought to become hep." And pausing only to pop a clear gum into my mouth, I jived out of the shop, clicking my fingers and chewing vigorously.

H. F. ELLIS

Letter to a Man Called Hobling

Sir,—I write in more annoyance than can be communicated without the aid of gestures to inquire whether you think it right that a little newspaper and tobacconist's shop like yours should be shut at three o'clock on a Sunday afternoon. It must be perfectly well known to you that the only hope of getting tobacco after midday on Sunday is to find one of those little newspaper and tobacconist's shops (like yours) that also sell sweets and have doors that go *ping* when opened. I need hardly add that shops of this kind have a step down immediately inside the door, so that the customer enters with enough noise to render the bell as unnecessary as it is unmusical.

Whether your door actually goes *ping* I cannot say, since I was unable to open it. But that is a detail which in no way invalidates my argument that you have a responsibility to the public, as the proprietor of the sort of shop that stays open on Sundays, *to* stay open on Sundays. If you want definite proof that the public expects you to be open let me tell you that I only came round to your place because a man I asked in the street told me he didn't know anyone nearer than you who would be likely to be open. "Try Hobling's," he said. So I tried Hobling's—with what results you know.

It was a long way out of my way, Hobling. In the days of unfettered motoring I might not have said anything about it, but on a bicycle it is a long pull out to your place from the High Street —particularly for a man without clips, as I was. You have never had the experience, I dare say, of riding nearly two miles with your

feet on the very extremity of the pedals and your knees sticking
out at right angles to keep the turn-ups of your trousers clear of
the chain, but you can take it from me that when you try the
door of a newspaper and tobacconist's shop at the end of it and
find it shut, the view you form of the owner of the shop, Hobling,
is gloomy indeed. Of course *you* are all right if you run out of
tobacco on a Sunday afternoon. All you have to do is to step into
your own shop from that dark little room at the back and give
yourself a packet of whatever decent stuff you keep hidden away
under the counter. No turning of the knees out at right angles for
you, Hobling. No hopeless pushing and straining against a locked
door with your nose glued to the glass panel and a whole shelf full
of two-ounce tins to drive you pretty well crazy with frustrated desire. Oh, no. People can have nervous breakdowns right and left for
all you care. It gives an added flavour to your pipe, I shouldn't
wonder, to hear the faint sounds of people like me scrabbling
frantically at your shop door.

My bicycle blew over while I was spread-eagled against your
barricades. You shrug your shoulders, perhaps, disclaiming any
responsibility for what happens to my front mudguard outside your
shop on a Sunday afternoon. All right. Shrug away. You are
probably right in your smug assumption that the law cannot touch
you, away there in your noisome cubbyhole at the back, in a case
like this. But there is such a thing as good-will, Hobling. And I
can tell you that any lingering traces of good-will I might have had
towards your name and business were wiped out for good and all
when my bicycle blew over. The mudguard gave out a resonant
clang with every revolution of the wheel as I rode away, and because of this, and because of the humiliating angle of my knees,
people came out of their houses and laughed openly. I don't blame
them. They had finished their Sunday papers, very likely, and
needed a change. But I blame you. I also hold you responsible
for my fall at the corner of Blenheim Avenue. If I had been smoking a full pipe instead of sucking away at an empty one I should
not have drawn a shred of old tobacco into the back of my throat.
I believe that to be incontrovertible. I had a fit of coughing, ac-

companied by watering at the eyes, that lasted until well after the time I found myself at the feet of a man in a blue serge suit, at the point where Blenheim Avenue joins Albemarle Crescent. It was a nasty fall. I have the evidence of the man in the blue suit for this (his actual words were "You had a nasty fall"), and he advised me to lie quiet in case anything was broken. He also advocated a cup of sweet strong tea—despite the early hour. I had landed, as it turned out, with my knees still in the riding position, and this misled him, naturally enough, into conjecturing a possible limb injury. I explained the cause of my mishap and he thereupon very civilly offered me a fill of Workman's Ecstasy. What a contrast with the attitude of some others I forbear to name!

I had to refuse his offer on the grounds that the bowl of my pipe was now missing. Nor could we find it anywhere, though I turned over the contents of the gutter very thoroughly for several yards both in the Avenue and up the Crescent. It was only when I attempted to ride away that I discovered that the bowl had become lodged in the spokes of my rear wheel—an unusual reason for a spill.

The man in the blue serge suit said he reckoned the pipe was now beyond repair. I blame you entirely for this.

But I want to make it absolutely clear to you, Hobling, that wherever else I go for my new pipe it will not be to your dingy little place.

P. M. HUBBARD

Plenty of Clementi

THE woman pushed open the door with vigour and made straight for the counter. She swept past the gleaming splendour of the Blüthner grand, past the rows of smiling, romantic faces on the song-hits, even past the percussion band incongruously painted with rabbits and toadstools. She poured a wave of matronly charm over the counter at the assistant and said "Good afternoon. I wonder if you've got a piece of music my little gel is very fond of. By Clementi. It was in a book her cousin had." She smiled powerfully to fill up the gaps in her description and stood with her head slightly on one side awaiting results.

Her husband neatly side-stepped the vicious back-swing of the door and whipped through without touching it as it swung open the second time. Pleased with this dexterity, which he did not often bring off, he turned and ran an expert eye over the door. He tested the spring with his finger, prodding the plate-glass like a farmer sounding the flanks of fat stock. Then he nodded, pulled out a small pocket-book and made a note. This done, he wandered across to the song-hits and, feet apart and hands clasped behind his back, began to examine the faces minutely.

The assistant was a plump girl with a fresh complexion and untidy reddish hair. The woman's inquiry had in any case left her slightly at a loss, and the sudden and acrobatic entrance of her husband, coming immediately on top of it, had disastrously distracted her attention. With an effort she brought her eyes back to the tilted, smiling, formidable face in front of her and said "Clementi, madam? Oh yes. What was the piece called, now?"

The woman, sensing obstruction, bridled slightly. "Well, really," she said, "I don't think it had a name. It was in a book with several other pieces. My gel is fourteen," she added, as a further concession.

A sharp ping from the other side of the shop brought her round as though she had been shot at from behind. "John!" she said. Her husband, one pale-blue drumstick poised for a blow at the dangling triangle of the percussion band, looked at her over his shoulder. "John," she said, "what was that piece called?"

He raised the drumstick an inch or two higher without looking at it. "Which piece?" he said. "You know," she said, "the piece Betty played—" Her voice rose with a note of increasing urgency and then stopped suddenly. The triangle went *crsssh* as the stick caught it smartly on the open side. He nodded appreciatively.

Then he put the stick down with the others and sauntered pleasantly over towards the counter. He said "I know, the Clementi." He fixed the assistant with a wild and quizzical eye but spoke to his wife. "You should ask her," he said, "if she has Moments with the Masters."

"Has what?" she said, but the assistant blossomed instantly into smiling relief. "Moments with the Masters?" she said. "Oh yes, madam. Which series would it be, now?" She dived suddenly under the counter and produced a pile of different-coloured volumes of music, which she slapped down on the glass.

The woman said "Well, really—I didn't know there was more than one. Let me see, I wonder if it was the blue one?" Her husband said "Can't we see which has got the Clementi?" and the assistant flicked open the blue cover and ran her eye down the index. She said "There's two Clementis here—no, three." She tried the pink volume. "Oh dear," she said, "there's plenty of Clementi."

The husband said "Ha! Plenty of Clementi, eh?" and made for the percussion band as though to develop the theme. Half-way across the shop he stopped and turned round. "I know," he said, "it was this one. Dah, dah, dee-dee, dah—Dah, *dah*, dah—Do you know it?"

The assistant frowned. "Not Clementi," she said, "no. Was it La, la, la *lah*, la—La, la, la, *lah*, la—that one?" She fumbled with the pink volume, but the wife, frowning with unaccustomed concentration, fingered stiffly on the glass the opening bars of a sonatina in the blue book. "Was this it?" she said. She cleared her throat, stared fiercely at the music, said "Dee" in a high squeak, tried an octave lower and went ahead. "Dee-dae, *dah*, da—Da, *dah*—"

A glass door opened at the back of the shop, and a little man with a bald head and glasses put his head out and looked at the assistant. "All right, Miss James?" he said. The assistant nodded wildly, but the little man hesitated as the woman, flicking over pages and fingering as she hummed, opened up again. "Deedle-deedle, dum-di, dum-di—Deedle-deedle, dum-di, dum-di," she sang, and her husband, whipping away from the percussion band, shouted "That's it!" "Deedle-deedle, dum-di, dum-di—Deedle-deedle, dum-di, dum-di," he carolled triumphantly under his wife's soprano, and the assistant, gripping the counter with both hands, came in in a rich contralto. "Deedle-deedle, dum-di, dum-di—Deedle-deedle, dum-di, dum-di."

Heads collected outside on the pavement, and a nervous woman, entering the shop silently with a string bag full of onions, turned and went quickly out. The manager, now right out of his office, produced an unexpectedly resonant bass, and the four voices soared to a triumphant climax. "Deedle-deedle, dum-di, dum-di —Deedle-deedle, *dum!*"

In the sudden silence the Blüthner grand moaned faintly in response to the last tremendous unison. Then the manager gave a high, neighing laugh and said "Yes, well—" and dived into his office.

"Five shillings," said the assistant weakly, wiping her eyes.

The woman found two half-crowns in the depths of her enormous bag. She put them on the counter, took up the blue book and, still dazed, followed her husband into the street.

"Moments with the Masters," said the assistant, "I'll say." She collected the coloured books and arranged them under the counter. She said "Deedle-deedle, dum-di—" and shut her teeth with a snap. From behind the glass door a rumbling bass said "Dum-di," and then, just as suddenly, stopped.

Spoofs and Parodies

ALEX ATKINSON

Chapter the Last

Merriman Explains

IT MUST have been a full twelve and a half seconds before anybody broke the stunned silence that followed Merriman's calm announcement. As I look back, I can still see the half-humorous smile playing about his satyr's face in the flickering firelight. I can hear again the hearty cracks he made as he pulled his fingers one by one. I couldn't help feeling that the old fox was holding something back. What lay behind the quizzical look he fired at Eleanor? Did I detect a flutter of fear on her pasty (but somehow curiously attractive) face? What was the significance of the third onion? *Was there a third onion at all?* If so, *who had it?* These and eight other questions chased themselves around in my brain as I watched Merriman pick up his Chartreuse and look round at us with quiet amusement.

It was Humphrey who spoke first, his voice echoing strangely through the quiet room, with its crossed swords, Rembrandts, and jade. "But—great Scott!—if Alastair Tripp *wasn't there* . . . !"

"Alastair Tripp," said Merriman, breathing on his monocle (the only time I ever saw him do such a thing in all the years I knew him), "wasn't, as you say, there. *And yet, in a way, he was.*"

Humphrey gave a snort of disgust, and drained his crème-de-menthe noisily. Even Chief Inspector Rodd gave vent to a half-stifled groan of bewilderment.

Merriman frowned. "You really are the dumbest crew I ever struck," he snarled. His gay wit was so infectious that the tension eased at once. He pointed at Humphrey with an olive on the end of an ebony-handled poniard. "Take your mind back," he said,

127

"to a week last Wednesday, at sixteen minutes past seven p.m., in the hall of Mossburn Manor. Haven't you realized yet that the Mrs. Ogilvie who flung the grand-father clock over the banisters was in reality her own step-mother—Eleanor's sister's aunt by marriage? Even by the light of a single candle you should have noticed the blonde wig, the false hands, or the papier-mâché mask—*the very mask which was found later up the chimney in Simon's bedroom!* Don't you see?"

Eleanor gasped. I could see Humphrey's knuckles whiten as his bony hands tightened their grip on the handle of the lawn-mower. I felt that the pieces were beginning to drop into place like bits of an enormous, sinister jig-saw puzzle. The trouble was, they didn't seem to fit.

"A left shoe, my half-wits," rumbled Merriman. "A left shoe with the lace missing. One onion where there should have been three. A half-chewed sweet in an otherwise deserted goldfish-bowl. By thunder, surely you *see?*" He rose to his feet and began to pace the room, with his head bent to avoid the oak beams. Sometimes as he walked he trod on the Chief Inspector, and once as he stood upright to emphasize a point, he brought down the chandelier with a crash. "It was a chance remark from Lady Powder that tipped me off," he bellowed, pounding a huge fist on the top of Eleanor's head. Eleanor's eyes widened, and on her face there was a look I hadn't seen before. "We were on the roof, you remember, trying to find a croquet ball, and all of a sudden she said 'It hasn't rained since Monday.'" He stood in the middle of the room, with one hand on the picture-rail and the other in his trousers pocket, and surveyed us. "From that moment," he said quietly, "I knew I was on the wrong track." He started to walk about again, and some of the floor-boards didn't seem any too safe down at my end of the room.

"But—great Scott!—if Alastair Tripp *wasn't there* . . . " Humphrey began again.

"I'm coming to that." Merriman fixed me with his eccentric glare. "I believe I have told you more than once, my foolish ape," he said, "that there are a hundred and four ways of getting into a

128

room with no doors on the inside and no windows on the outside. But that's beside the point. Consider, if you will, the night of the murder. Here we have John Smith taking a nap in the pantry. The door is locked. The window is locked. The cupboard is bare. The carpet—and mark this—the carpet is *rolled up in a corner,* tied round with ordinary common or garden string. Now then, in the first place, as you will have guessed, the lightly-sleeping figure on the camp bed was not John Smith at all." Merriman fixed Eleanor with a penetrating stare. "*You* know who it was, don't you, *Mrs. Anstruther?*"

"Mrs. *what!*" The question left my lips before I could stop it. Eleanor turned deathly pale, and tore her cambric handkerchief in two with a convulsive movement. Chief Inspector Rodd stirred slightly in his sleep. A frown of impatience played fitfully over the chiselled features of Humphrey Beeton. Outside the rain whispered eerily against the panes.

"Good Kensington Gore!" swore Merriman, wrenching a handful of stops from his treasured organ and hurling them at the Chief Inspector: "it was so *easy!*" He sat suddenly in the wicker armchair, and all but flattened Professor Meak, whom we had somehow forgotten. "Let me take you through it step by step. A bootlace is fastened to one end of the blow-pipe, which has previously been filled with sugar. This whole deadly contraption is lowered down the chimney—oh, there was plenty of time, I assure you: remember that Mercia Foxglove had been concealed in the shrubbery since dawn, and in any case at that time nobody knew that Paul's father was really Janet's uncle from Belfast."

"But if Alastair Tripp *wasn't there* . . . " Humphrey's voice was desperate with curiosity. The lawn-mower trembled in his hands.

"I'm coming to that," said Merriman, filling his pipe with herbs. "Three onions," he went on steadily, "have already been placed midway between the door and the golf-club—which, you will observe, is leaning unnoticed against the wall. Very well, then. Recall, if you will, the evidence of the so-called Alfred Harp— actually, of course, as I will show you, he is none other than our friend the mysterious 'milkman': but more of that anon. Where did he find the decanter after—I repeat, *after*—the gardener's cottage had been burnt to the ground? He found it, my pretty dumbbells, in the pocket of Sir Herbert's dressing-gown—*which was nowhere to be found.*" He beamed expansively. "*Now* do you understand?"

Humphrey rose unsteadily. His face was working, and I thought I detected a fleck of foam on his tie. I reached unobtrusively for my hat. "But if Alastair Tripp—*wasn't there*—" Humphrey almost shouted.

"I'm coming to that."

It was too much. With a mighty roar of rage and impatience, Humphrey swung the lawn-mower over his head in a flashing arc.

As I groped my way down the back stairs I reflected sadly that this would probably go down in history as Merriman's Last Case.

D. BROCK

Science: Is It Instinct or Reason?

I SEE that Science once more (O ye scientific laurels, and once more, ye old jokes never sere) has proved that dogs are not intelligent. This time it was done by locking dogs in boxes with trick

130

latches, strings, springs, and the rest, and the dogs proved less adept than apes at setting themselves free. There were other tests of course . . . dogs refused to recognize photographs (in common with savages and sitters for portraits), and they failed to remember which of three identical light-bulbs had last been lit, and they got cross and stubborn when people kept locking and unlocking the four doors of a specially-built room.

It seems to me that Science, as usual, has failed to take a lot of things into account. To begin with, some dogs are brighter than others (and you cannot have different degrees of Nothing). And then there are different *kinds* of brightness. And then, while some dogs may lack the aplomb of an ape in a box, their very hysteria may be slightly more reasonable than the sang-froid of an ape who doesn't even realize himself to be in a very queer situation. And for that matter, some of the dogs probably spotted the tests for what they were and very naturally boycotted the childlike pedants . . . it would certainly take more than a professor and cheap glory to make *me* memorize light-bulbs or go rushing round four doors to see which had been locked by some fool who couldn't make up his own mind. And as for recognizing pictures—well, it is within my own experience that some dogs enjoy home-made movies, others fail to recognize them at all, and a third class recognizes pictures as *pictures* and not reality and rejects them accordingly, just as some dogs spurn rubber bones, some children despise Grimm, and some grown-ups would not buy a Picasso for sixpence.

But the biggest thing Science has ignored is my own series of tests on scientists. My tests have shown that scientists are slightly less intelligent than marmosets. Let me tell you briefly about a dozen of these tests.

1. Ten scientists were placed at night in the middle of a dark forest, and *not told why*. They were observed to exhibit fear, confusion, and lack of direction. Some ran in circles, some in squares, and others in curved space. Whereas ten pigeons were soon out of the woods and back in captivity, silly creatures.

2. Eighteen scientists were asked to dress themselves as fast

as possible, to win a juicy steak. One forgot to put on his spectacles, another already had his spectacles on but kept looking for them, and a third forgot he was dressing and in the middle of the process began to undress again and went to bed.

3. Nine scientists were placed in a room in which the chairs kept breaking, pictures kept falling, doors opened and shut, lights went off and on, the floor tilted, the ceiling came down, and so on. Two men dived through the window (which we had forgotten to lock), two others fainted, three got a table and tried to get in touch with the secretary of some spookery club, and the last two called out loudly: "How are we supposed to react? Please repeat the question."

4. Three hundred scientists were shown pictures of Little Boy Blue and Little Jack Horner. Two hundred fell asleep. Fifty were insulted. Forty-seven said the pictures were very bad. Two said the pictures were very good. One said he liked the smell of the paper.

5. Nineteen scientists were given pencils and paper and asked to write an historical drama in blank verse. One man said he was inhibited by pencils. The rest sulked. None succeeded. This test was somewhat staggering, with its implication that Shakespeare never existed.

6. A well-known scientist was asked to start his own car, declare from memory the contents of his pocket-book, and describe the plot of the last film he attended. He failed in all three tests, whereas sixteen morons taken at random were able to score 100 per cent.

7. A scientist was sent a bill for goods never ordered and never received. He paid it. The receipted bill was posted to him and he paid it again. The receipted bill and his second cheque were sent back with an explanatory letter, and he wrote apologetically and sent a third cheque drawn on a second bank. This cheque was refused by the bank, since he had no account there.

8. Ten scientists were given twenty dogs and asked to devise tests to prove that:

        (a) dogs are intelligent
        (b) dogs are not intelligent.

Three scientists lost their dogs at once, three others got bitten, and the rest began to fight among themselves while the dogs took notes.

9. Three scientists were told a funny story. One said it was not funny, the second said he had not been listening, and the third laughed but immediately apologized. All three apes subjected to this test laughed heartily.

10. A well-known scientist was given a cottage with very low doorways. Unable to learn by experience, he banged his head on nine out of ten doorways every day for three years, while his pet giraffe banged its head *only once*.

11. I gave a very interesting test here to fifteen scientists, and neither they nor myself can now remember what it was.

12. In the final test of this series, three dozen scientists were fed daily on oysters, crayfish, roast beef, pheasant, asparagus, and so on, with wines and fruits of every kind. This process went on for some weeks, after which they were given nothing for two days. At the end of this two-day fast they were handed a menu of a thousand delights and plainly told that they were to receive no food, just this bit of paper, and *yet their mouths watered!*

And so much for scientists, science, human sagacity, and the future of everything.

TOM HAMMERTON

A Simple Guide to Modern Music

"FROM now on music will be no longer what it was, but has become what it will be," says (according to Grove's *Dictionary of Music*) Louis Danz in his book on Schönberg. It is a sentence which will repay study. I myself, indeed, have studied it so thoroughly that my doctor has become anxious about me, and it is at his suggestion, with the object of relieving the pressure on the brain, that I canalize my knowledge of modern music in a series of articles intended—not, perhaps, quite for the man in the street —but for the man with sufficient *awareness* of the revolution which is taking place in the Sound World of To-morrow to wish to recognize the difference between tuning up and a Czech string quartet.

The chief complaint of the ignorant listener to modern music is that it sounds like noises in the head. This is simply because he is not yet familiar with modern idiom in music, which is as free from convention as its counterparts in art and literature. So has it always been with pioneer movements. The Bach public howled with derision at the first Beethoven works, and, as loudly, the public to-day mocks Bartok. Yet who can doubt that in a few years' time people will be as contemptuous of a composer who uses melodies as they will be of a painter whose nudes have ordinary chests instead of a drawer with lobsters hanging out of it?

To appreciate the Modern Idiom in music it is necessary to study the elements of

MODERN TECHNIQUE

This is not nearly so complicated as the old, classical technique which actually required a composer to be able to play an instrument and read music. These artificial limitations are now swept away, and with them the whole shackling paraphernalia of keys and clefs. Modern composers simply put in sharps and flats (usually black notes) when they feel like it, and some don't even divide their music up into bars (those upright lines like telegraph poles cut short). There is even one school of modern composers which boasts of not knowing what a written score looks like. Composers of this school hum their creations to a musical amanuensis who does the donkey-work of actually writing it down and deciding whether the notes should be egg-shaped, have a handle (up or down), be hollow or blacked in, etc. A bit of a change from those old composers who used to start with a great bank of sharp and flat signs at the beginning and keep call-

134

ing "C" "B sharp," and "B" "C flat" (if you see what I mean).

Of course, modern music has its complications too, principally in its new tonal systems. Chief amongst these are:

THE TWELVE-NOTE SYSTEM

This is used a lot by Schönberg and Berg. Grove's *Dictionary* illustrates it thus:

crab      original form
crab inversion   inversion

and adds the explanation:

". . . the Grundgestalt is considered valid not only in its original form . . . but also in inversion, in crab form (Cancrizans), and in the inversion of the crab form."

The beginner need not worry about the crabs at this stage (unless he sees them walking on the ceiling with the little hats on, in which case I can let him have the address of my psychiatrist), and need only concentrate on the "Grundgestalt" of the Twelve-Note system, which, it appears to me, is that it has twelve notes in its scale instead of the usual eight. This may be simply illustrated thus:

Fig. I. Classical or Eight-Note scale.

Fig. II. Modern Twelve-Note scale.

N.B.—Neither side counts the black notes.

It is important not to confuse the Twelve-NOTE system with

THE TWELVE-TONE SYSTEM,

a mistake which, like mixing up *Il Troviata* with *La Travatore*, will irrevocably class you with the clunks. Of the Twelve-TONE system,

Louis Danz says: "It can be likened to the change from simple (*sic*) Euclidean geometry to the higher mathematics of Minkowski and Einstein."

As I understand it, the difference between this system and the Twelve-Note system, is that it counts the old, classical, scale as *seven* notes (which it is, in a way, if you don't count that "C" at the right-hand end of Fig. I), and does count the five black notes. 7 plus 5=12 (*cf.* Hogben, *Mathematics for the Million*), twelve notes in all, which are, however, called "Tones" to avoid confusion with the Twelve-*Note* system. It is important not to confuse the Twelve-Tone system with the Twelve-Note system. (See the beginning of this paragraph.) Kyjzzyjrk further identifies the Twelve-Tone system with mathematics by calling the black notes "Squares" of the white (*cf.* his Cantata in A² for Alto sackbuts).

THE MULTI-TONAL SYSTEM

This, the *Dernier cri* in modern composition technique, has been confined, so far, purely to pianoforte works. Dissatisfied with the narrow limits imposed by the mere 479,001,600 possible combinations of the Twelve Notes or Tones evolved by Josef Hauer (Tropenlehre), Zyjrkkrjyz has written a number of works in which the pianist varies the pitch of each note continuously with a piano-tuner's key as he goes along—an originality of technique which might be expected from the master who has already startled the musical world with the "Nonet for Piano and Harp on the One Instrument" which can be played either on a grand piano turned on its side, so that during the harp passages the pianist may pluck the piano strings, or on a harp laid flat so that during the piano passages the harpist may hit the harp strings with a small felt-covered hammer. (I refer of course to Cela, not Bela Zyjrkkrjyz, his brother and also a most original composer within his own—self-imposed—limitations; *vide* his "Polka Muraille," in which he poked holes through the polka dots on a roll of wallpaper and played the result on a pianola.) Both compose in a raptus, especially in cold weather.

I should be lacking in courtesy if I did not acknowledge, in conclusion, my indebtedness both for information and the present state of my health to Zofja Lissa's "Gesichtliche Vorform der Zwolftontechnik" (Acta Musicologica, Vol. vii, fasc 1, Leipzig 1935) and "Mit bergs eigenen Schriften und Beiträgen" (von Theodor Wiesengrund-Adorno und Ernst Krenek, Vienna, 1937). My next article will deal with modern opera and contain a spectral analysis of the complicated contralto part of Ma Vlaast, the Swedish boarding-house keeper in the *Bartok Bride*. Other features will include a guide to the placing of consonants in modern composers' names, and a nasty laugh at clods who like tunes.

MARJORIE RIDDELL

Opera for Music-Haters

OPERA is all very well for those who are musical and those who say they are, but there has been to date no provision made for the opera-lover who is a music-hater. It's no good at all going to the opera if your interest lies in the story, because the synopsis on the programme is much too short to last all the evening. Would it not be possible to have an opera occasionally played straight instead of sung?

Curtain Rises   *Scene:* A Wood
Enter Princess

Princess. Alas, alas, alas, alas. I am a Princess. A Princess. I am to meet here my Prince. My father has forbidden our marriage. I am to meet here my Prince. My father has forbidden the marriage. The marriage. The marriage. The marriage. Now I am lost. I am lost. I am lost. Alas, alas, alas. Where can he be? Where can he be, be, be? (*Repeat.*)

Princess *crosses* R. *and gazes at audience. Enter* Prince L.

Prince (*to audience*). I am a Prince. Alas, alas, alas. I was to meet here my Princess. My love, my love, my love. Her father has forbidden our marriage. Her father has forbidden the marriage. And now I am lost. I am lost. I am lost. (*Repeat.*)
Princess *turns and sees the* Prince.

Princess. My Prince!

Prince. My Princess! (*Advance and embrace.*)

Prince. My love.

Princess. I love you.

Prince. My love.

Princess. I love you.

Prince. My love.

Princess. I love you.

Prince. Come away with me.

*Princess. Away?

Prince. Away.

Princess. Away?

Prince. Away.

Princess. Yes.

Prince. Yes.

Princess. Yes.

Prince. Yes. (*Repeat from *.*)

Enter Duke

Duke. I am the Duke. I am the Duke. I am the Duke. I am the Duke, I am. I am blackmailing the King, blackmailing the King, ha, ha, ha, ha, ha, ha, ha! I am blackmailing the King because I want to marry his daughter. So the King has no choice but to forbid, forbid, forbid, forbid the marriage of the Prince and Princess.

Prince (*starting*). The Duke!

Princess (*starting*). The Duke!

Prince and Princess. The Duke, the Duke, the Duke, the Duke!

Duke. Ha! I will fight you, fight you, fight you!

138

Prince and Duke *fight.* Princess *gets in the way and is stabbed.*
Falls.

Princess. I am dying!
Prince. No!
Princess. I am dying!
Duke. No!
Princess. I am dying!
Prince. No!
Princess. I am dying!
Duke. No!
Princess. I die. (*Dies.*)
Prince. It's your fault. I will kill you. I will kill you. I will kill you.
   (*Stabs* Duke.)
Duke. I am dying! (*Repeat six times.*)
Duke. I die. (*Dies.*)
Prince. I will kill myself. I will kill myself. I will kill myself. I will.
   (*Stabs himself. Totters round stage.*)
Prince. I am dying! (*Repeat four times.*)
Prince. Dying. (Repeat twice.)
Prince. I die. (*Dies.*)

CURTAIN.

This would need no music at all, and should a longer performance be desired it could, no doubt, be expanded. Should there be
any public outcry it could quite easily be turned into a comedy.

J . B . B O O T H R O Y D

Your Career as a Radio Engineer

WHEN a customer pants into the shop with his set (your delivery
van is out of order, as usual) pretend to be engaged in some operation of great delicacy. The illusion may be given by standing per-

fectly still with both hands inside a disembowelled set, your face turned up to the ceiling, your tongue out and one eye tightly screwed up. Sustain this attitude for at least two minutes before saying "Got it!" and putting the thing away out of sight.

It is not necessary to listen to what the customer says, but there is no harm in nodding from time to time. At the end you can say "Sounds like the usual trouble with these jobs," and give the customer's set a disparaging slap. "However," you say, "I'll see what I can do." This should carry an inflexion which suggests that you have taken a personal liking to the customer. He will then thank you very much and say that there is no hurry. As if you didn't know.

When he comes back in a month's time, apologetic, respectful, timidly hopeful, startle him by producing at once from under the counter a handful of pieces of metal, old valves, lengths of wire and rusty screws. Push them under his nose and say "No wonder you were having trouble!" On no account be more specific than this, as you have of course no idea what sort of trouble it was.

He will look at the oddments and say "Good heavens!"—not having any idea what you mean, but hating to seem ignorant. You are on safe ground, because if he weren't ignorant he would have done his own radio repairs.

You take up one of the bits of metal and deftly bend it double. "And *that*," you say, with a snorting little laugh, "was supposed to be your magnetic infranger."

"Good gracious! And was that the trouble?"

"Not the real trouble, no. What do you think of this?" You push a piece of aluminum and a piece of ebonite disgustedly across the counter. "I wonder you got any reception at all with rubbish like that in your thrust-figgler."

"In the thrust-figgler, eh?"

"Well, that was in the thrust-figgler"—you snap the ebonite in half—"but this"—you snatch up a hammer and batter the aluminum out of shape—"well, I don't suppose you will believe me when I tell you what *this* was part of."

"I've no idea. What?"

140

"You'll laugh when I tell you."

"Never mind."

"It was the base-nut of the collation baffle."

"No!"

You then take the customer's set down from the shelf behind you and dust it carefully, handling it as if it were made of gold-leaf. It needs dusting, as it hasn't been touched since the day it came in, except for the tying of a label on the volume control knob.

"However," you say, "I've never been beaten yet—even if I do have to work all Saturday afternoon and Sunday on a job. Four pounds."

The last two words should only be breathed at this stage. Your customer should hear them, but only so faintly as to make him hope that he has not heard them aright. The seed is sown, and the pause which follows should be devoted to reading aloud, but as if to yourself, the writing on the label. Your whole demeanour should be that of a man who is hoping to find some error in the items which would enable him to bring the figure down. Such an error should never be found, however.

"Dismantling, cleaning, overhauling, inspecting," you mutter to yourself—"one pound. Supplying and fitting new gunge-points, feed-arm, worrall-plate, variable gugwindler and burst-refiner: one pound ten shillings. Testing, reassembling, dismantling, inspecting: ten shillings. Supplying and fitting stainless three-pin fubble-nut, re-winding frayed follicle-cleat: eight shillings. Special six-hour bench-test with Ferguson's gullometer extension-arch disclosing faulty bimble-iron: seven shillings. Supplying and fitting double-strength tin-filled bimble-iron with supporting toggle, reassembling, testing: five shillings. Total, four pounds." You look up with a smile. "Can't make it any different, I'm afraid."

Your customer is not yet feeling for his wallet.

"I haven't charged you for the two fiddle-pins," you say—"we'll throw them in for good measure."

"That's very kind of you," says your customer, and puts four pounds on the counter.

As he leaves it is as well to mention that it pays to buy a good set in the long run, and that you have a "Golden Monarch" coming in very soon. If you can sell him this you have an income for life: everyone knows that "Monarch" workmanship is so exquisite that even to oil the coils costs twelve pounds ten.

Epic Conference

"ALL RIGHT. Now, after these native guides have legged it with the equipment the crocodile didn't eat, this guy Charters shows up—"

"With malaria?"

"Who? Oh, yah, yah, with malaria. And a dart sticking out of his neck. He whispers to the leader 'Bad show, sir. The jolly old canoe just drifted away by itself.' The leader just looks at him."

"And the *cheep-cheep-cheep* of the insects?"

"Yah, if you like."

"And *bom-bom-bom* on the war-drums?"

"No, no, save that. You can overdo that bom-bom-bom stuff. Then Charters puts on a twisted smile—"

"Like this?"

"Yah, yah, like that. And he says 'We may as well tear up our return tickets, eh, sir?' Then he falls in a coma."

"Say anything before he shuts his eyes?"

"Just 'Sorry, sir.' The leader looks round at the men playing Snakes and Ladders. He peeps through the tent-flap at the leopard eating this Mr. Armitage. Then he closes his copy of *Alice Through the Whatsaname*, and says 'Look, chaps, can you spare a sec?'"

"Bit informal, isn't it?"

"Sure. Like I keep telling you, when it's a disaster you gotta watch out you keep the dialogue natural. Anyhow, this Cockney guy Parker looks up from his jig-saw and says 'Cor, lumme, sir, I

was just dreamin' I was on 'Amstead 'Eath with the missus, sir.'
Human, see. Gets a laugh."

"And the coward's lip starts to quiver again?"

"No, no. He's *found* himself. Don't you remember? When he
had to fight off the boa-constrictor by himself because the leader
wanted to test him. No, he sees there's something the matter
right away, so he says 'Everything under control, sir?' Quiet, you
see. So's not to scare the men. So the leader sits at the table and
says 'You may as well come into the office, chaps.'

"So they come up to the table all sheepish. Then the leader
says 'Well, chaps, things don't look too cheery. As you will have
guessed by now, there is only one bar of fruit-and-nut chocolate
left.' The Cockney guy says 'Milk, sir?'—with a twisted smile, you
know—"

"Like this?"

"No, no. Like *this*. And the leader says 'Afraid not, Parker.
Plain.' Wryly, see?"

"Who's Reilly?"

"*Wryly*. Then he says 'Also, my second in command has a
poisoned dart in his throat, and isn't feeling too good.'

"Then he goes on 'We've no map, no compass, the rains are due
to-morrow, and old Mr. Armitage has been eaten by a ruddy
leopard.'"

"Ruddy? Isn't that a bit strong?"

"Sure it's strong! But these guys are up against it, see? After all,
they're grown men. Then the leader goes on 'All we have left,' he
says, 'is our unconquerable spirits.' They all say 'Hear, hear, sir.'
Not too loud—what we've got to avoid is mock-heroics, see? We've
got to aim at—er—"

"Realism?"

"Yah, yah, something like that. 'Well,' says the leader, 'I propose
that whoever wins the next game of Snakes and Ladders will set
out with half the chocolate and try to reach the coast. The rest of
us will wait here. If the leopards don't get us the hostile tribes will.
Or we'll succumb to the testy-fly. Or die of hunger.' 'Or old age!'
says Parker. Big laugh, see? Relieve the tension. 'Well,' says the

143

leader, 'have any of you chaps anything to say before I shake the dice?' And what d'you think one of 'em says?"

" 'Gawd, this is terrible'?"

"No, no. We got to keep it *natural*. He says 'Well, sir, this 'as bin quite a picnic, sir, 'asn't it, sir?' "

"Reilly?"

"Yah, yah, wryly. Gets a laugh, see? And *then* you can start your *bom-bom-bom*."

T. S. WATT

Noël! Noël!

"Come in, Crole, and sit down. This is going to be a long business, I'm afraid."

"Something about the balance, sir?"

"No, but of course it's most unfortunate that it should come just now, when we've quite enough to do as it is. It's a circular from Head Office, about Christmas. They've headed it 'Noël! Noël!' Most unusual affair."

"What do they—"

"I'll just run through the main points. They start off by saying that competition among the banks is becoming increasingly keen, and that a point has been reached at which it may be necessary, in order to retain our present customers and, if possible, to attract new business, to adopt methods that might have been thought unconventional a few years ago.

"The circular then goes on: 'As an experiment, therefore, it has been decided to inaugurate a Christmas Good Will Week, commencing on Wednesday, the 17th instant, during which customers at all our branches will be received in a spirit of hearty and boisterous good fellowship in keeping with the season.' "

"What exactly do they want us to do, Mr. Furman?"

"It affects all members of the staff who come into contact with the public. 'As a preliminary measure, the management, securities clerk or clerks, and all cashiers, are requested to make themselves thoroughly familiar with Chapters 28-30 of *The Pickwick Papers*, dealing with Christmas festivities at Dingley Dell. Application for copies of the book, in the proportion of one to every three of the staff concerned, should be made to Stationery Department forthwith, using form 102A'—You might see to that— 'A return is to be made on the enclosed form CGWW4 of members of the staff to whom copies of the book are issued. Initials should be inserted in the columns headed "Received," "Read and understood" and "Returned," but for column 1—"Issued"—a neat tick will suffice.' "

"Are we supposed to read it in our own time, do you think?"

"I take it so—certainly."

"Carker's going to turn nasty, I'm afraid. You remember the time I asked him to take the PAYE home?"

"Well, take him off the counter for a couple of hours and let Miss Joyce go on."

"Yes, but then the other cashiers'll go up in the air—I mean seeing Carker lounging around reading, while they're hard at it—"

"Then you'll just have to take a strong line with Carker. Anyway, all this is a mere nothing. Wait till you see 'Exclamations of Good Will.' Now, where were we? Oh yes—'*Cashiers*. It is desirable that during Christmas Good Will Week the counter should be manned by fresh-complexioned cashiers of bluff and open-hearted appearance and of a minimum weight of approximately twelve stone. Many branches will be unable to attain this ideal, but it is pointed out that officials of spare build, by standing well back on the heels, slightly bending the knees, and relaxing the muscles of the diaphragm, may do much to convey an impression of seasonable corpulence.' "

"Carker—"

" 'Attention is drawn to the fact that responsibility for the success of Christmas Good Will Week must necessarily rest mainly with the cashiers, and the utmost importance is attached to the assumption by them of a suitable demeanour during this critical period. In general, the cashiers will aim at an air of suppressed merriment. Nothing is to be gained by mechanical outbursts of forced hilarity, but a smile should never be far from the lips. Experiments made at Head Office under the supervision of the Chief General Manager have shown that the gesture of bringing the hands smartly together with a brisk massaging movement is extremely effective in creating the precise atmosphere at which we aim, particularly when accompanied by a rollicking laugh *if unforced*. Cashiers are asked to make themselves familiar with this gesture, and to employ it frequently during the week. No hard and fast rules can be laid down as to timing, but great care must be exercised so as to avoid a simultaneous execution of the manœuvre by all cashiers. This would tend to give an unhappy impression of artificiality, particularly at the larger branches.' "

"You know, Mr. Furman, I really can't see Carker—"

" '*Exclamations of Good Will*. During Christmas Good Will Week, the use of the expression "Compliments of the Season" is strictly forbidden. Fifteen alternative greetings of a more forcible type, graded according to emotional content are set out in Appendix A, and no customer should be allowed to leave the bank without having at least one of these addressed to him. The utmost care must be taken in the choice of appropriate greetings for different customers. For example, in refusing to cash a customer's cheque for lack of sufficient funds, a cashier should clearly not use No. 14—"May every blessing and good fortune, etc., etc.," delivered in a husky voice, with a hand resting on each of the customer's shoulders. No. 1—"A very happy Christmas to you!", with a quick handshake, or No. 2—"The very best wishes for a happy Christmas!", with a prolonged handshake, would be more fitting in such a case.' "

"Well, honestly, Mr. Furman, I've never—"

"My dear chap, this is nothing! Absolutely nothing! They've got a whole section on these greetings alone, and then there's a lot more about handshakes and various gestures to go with them. No. 1, 'quick handshake,' No. 2, 'prolonged handshake,' Nos. 3 to 6,

146

'very hearty and prolonged handshake and throat-clearing as though overcome by emotion,' and so on and so on. No. 15's a terrific affair: 'May heaven send, etc., etc.,' with a long handshake, 'both the customer's hands to be clasped and shaken briskly during the enunciation of the greeting, and the knuckles drawn quickly across the eyes at the moment of departure.' "

"You know, sir, I'm afraid this is going to mean a lot of activity in Errors in Cash account. Take a chap like Carker, now—none too accurate at the best of times. Mrs. Bollington comes in, say. Well, he's got to do this hand-clapping business and the rollicking laugh, relax his diaphragm and so on, get through, say, greeting No. 14, remember to give her new notes, get her statement, see that she signs her dividend warrants, and finally, reach over the counter and grab her hands for greeting No. 15. Well, you know, it's all just going to be too much for him. He's a very gloomy sort of fellow, and this rollicking laugh alone—"

"I'm sorry, Crole, but this is no time for nursing weaklings. He'll just have to get through as best he can. Now, first, I want you to get me a list of all customers with balances of over £1,000. I've not got time to go into it now, but they're each to be given a propelling pencil. You'll have to apply to Stationery Department for those. Then I want you to see the cashiers, put them through this rollicking laugh business and tell them about standing well back on the heels and so forth—at any rate, tell Carker and Payne: the others should be all right. What d'you think?"

"I'm not too sure about the complexions, Mr. Furman. Danby and Lunt—"

"Well, we can't do much about that, but you might see that the heat's turned up a bit on the seventeenth. That'll be a help. And just take Appendix A, will you, and get Miss Beale to do six copies and give one to each cashier. Who's the fattest ledger-clerk?"

"I think Pollen—"

"I'll want him on Christmas Eve, for the Wassail Bowl."

"The Wassail Bowl?"

"There's to be a party after we close on the twenty-fourth. The Assistant General Manager's coming—he's going to distribute these pencils—and they say he'll 'join an informal gathering round the Wassail Bowl (see Chap. 28) and lead customers and staff in carol-singing.' You'd better look out for him. He can be very nasty indeed."

"Yes, I know, Mr. Furman. Is that everything, then?"

G. H. M. NICHOLS

Interviews with the Anonymous

The Man with the Hoe

"Look at me," said the Man with the Hoe. "Look at me. Sixty-three, come next lambing, if I'm spared, and don't look a day over fifty. Bowed wi' centuries, indeed! And look 'ere," he went on, with rising indignation, "bowed! 'Lean forrard,' 'e says—"

"Who said?" we asked.

"This 'ere French artist chap. Milly, 'is name were—same as a lass. 'Stand 'ere', 'e says. 'Why?' I says—'there's nowt growin' 'ere.' 'That's the idea,' 'e says. 'You're oppressed, downtrodden, that's wot you are,' 'e says. 'Bend over that 'oe and look miserable.' So I does. But 'tweren't that as I minded—it were this American chap —poet, 'e were. I never said aught to 'im, but up 'e comes an' calls me all manner o' names. 'Brother to the ox, you are,' 'e says. Me, what's lived respectable in this parish nigh on fifty year! And then 'e starts askin' all manner o' questions.

" ' 'Oo loosened an' let down this brutal jaw?' 'e wants to know. ' 'Oos was the 'and wot slanted back this 'ere brow?' "

" ' 'Why, that Mister Milly,' I tell 'im. ' 'E done it—that's 'oo,' I says.

"Now I don't reckon to set up for a film star or one o' they chaps, but folks always did allow I were middlin' handsome like, an' I tell you I were fair riled agin 'im. 'You talk to Mister Milly,' I says.

'Don't you come a-blamin' me for wot 'e done!' But d'you think 'e'd let me alone? Nay! Kept on at it, 'e did.

" 'No shape more terrible than you,' 'e says.

" 'It's the way I be standin',' I tells 'im, but 'e wouldn't listen. 'When I were in Yeomanry,' I says, 'you wouldn't ha' found a straighter-backed chap in the 'ole county.' But it weren't no use talkin'. Proper abusive, 'e were. Monstrous thing, 'e called me, an' dread shape. Ay."

The Man with the Hoe paused, and regarded his instrument of toil with disfavour.

"Right poor tool, is yon," he said. "Mister Milly brought it special with 'im. I reckon it must be a French 'oe. 'Wot's this?' I says to 'im. 'That?' 'e says. 'Why, that's a 'oe. Wot do you think it is—a shovel?' 'It might be an' all,' says I. But it were cruel short in the 'andle for leanin' on."

We asked: "And what became of the American gentleman—the poet?"

"Well, arter standin' an' starin' at I as though I were a show at a tide-fair, 'e says, shakin' 'is 'ead, ' 'Ow will you ever straighten up this shape?' 'Oil o' wintergreen 'll do it,' I says. 'That'll fix 'un proper. 'Tis only a touch o' the lumbago,' I says; 'it'll soon straighten out.' But I could see as 'ow 'e weren't satisfied."

"On the whole," we said, "you preferred the Frenchman to the American?"

The man smiled a sly smile.

"Mister Milly? Well, 'e were only man as ever knowingly paid I for just leanin' on a 'oe."

One of Three

WE stopped the Wedding Guest, using our skinnier hand for the purpose.

"Careful," he said, shrinking back. "I've bruised myself a bit there. It's when I hear the loud bassoon," he explained. "Something comes over me. I just have to beat my breast." He glanced around in a furtive manner. "You haven't seen an old sea-faring man, have you?" he asked. "With a grey beard and a persuasive manner, sort of hypnotic?"

We had heard of such a one, we said.

"Don't let him buttonhole *you*," said the Wedding Guest, bitterly. "My sister's wedding, it was. I should have given her away. She used to play the cor anglais in the municipal orchestra, and she married into the strings. The bassoon was best man. I don't think the rest of the ensemble thought much of the match—they were all nodding their heads when she paced into the hall, and she was as red as a rose—at least, so I was told. While all this was going on I was perched on a bollard opposite the South Pier listening to this mesmeric able seaman. Talk about sinister! I felt exactly like a chap that on a lonesome road doth walk in fear and dread, you know, and having once turned round walks on and turns no more his head, because he knows a frightful fiend doth close behind him tread. It was just like that. Creepy! And what a yarn! I mean,

I don't mind a tall story, but this was the end. Albatrosses, and lifeless lumps, and pilots shrieking and falling down in fits, and pilots' boys who now do crazy go—and all the time I could hear the reception going forward."

"These nuptials," we suggested, "they were on the lively side?"

"Absolute uproar," the Wedding Guest agreed. "Bride and bridesmaids close-harmonizing in the garden, and bells ringing, and of course the bassoon. Everybody having themselves a time—except me. And on top of it all, after frightening the wits out of me with the tale of his own evil deeds, the old fraud had the cool impudence to exhort me to mend my ways and lead a better life!"

"And, surely," we said, "his exhortations were not wholly without effect? Did you not turn from the bridegroom's door like one that hath been stunn'd?"

The Guest nodded sulkily. "I could hardly turn up late with a feeble story about an ancient mariner, could I?"

We saw his point. Had he, we inquired after a pause, risen on the morrow morn a sadder and wiser man?

"Not unnaturally," said the Wedding Guest. "I'd missed a good party, and I had some heavy explaining to do. It will teach me not to talk to strange sailormen again, though. I'm that much wiser." He heaved a sigh. "Oh, well—'Push on, push on,' as the hermit said."

And on he pushed, looking warily about him.

L. W. DESBROW

My Cellar Book

THE gentle melancholy with which the lover of good wine turns the reminiscent leaves of his cellar book is compounded of regrets for past glories and the memories of great vintages and golden years.

My cellar-book goes back to 1930. I opened it when I laid down a half-dozen of Macgilligoody's Extra Ferruginous Tonic Wine (bottled in Blackfriars Road in 1929). I picked up the half-dozen for a mere song at the local chemist's annual sale, but they gave pleasure far out of proportion to what I paid for them. I had a bottle up when the manager of my department came to dinner, and served it with the Irish stew. Unfortunately the manager had to leave before the bottle was finished, but I could tell from the slow and reverent way in which he consumed it that my judgment had been fundamentally sound. He agreed with me that although it still showed traces of a certain juvenilism, it was pregnant with possibilities. I had the last bottle up only last year when my wife was recovering from a bad cold. It had lived up to its early promise and fully justified the confidence I had placed in it.

Parsnip wine I always regard as generous but rather frolicsome, always ready to play merry little pranks on you, but completely without malice. It is perhaps the best "all purpose" wine of all our native vintages. The best years in the 1930s were 1932, 1936, and of course the glorious 1938. I had a dozen of 1932 (bottled by my mother after six weeks in the copper). Unfortunately three bottles blew their corks in the first six months, but the remainder gave much pleasure to my friends and myself; perhaps, I might almost say, too much pleasure.

We had two magnums of the noble '38 vintage for the committee of the Working Men's Club on the occasion of a recent whist drive and dance. The wine was then "in perfection," friendly on the nose, generous on the palate, but insidious on the gait. A bottle my wife and I shared the night we had a flying bomb at the end of the road led to our removal, somewhat erroneously, as casualties suffering from acute "battle exhaustion." We have just drunk the last bottle, and I was unable to restrain myself from wondering whether we should ever see its like again. These suspicions are partly based on the fact that my mother is beginning to doubt if her wine is strictly non-alcoholic.

Many consider that in rhubarb wine our native vintages have achieved their choicest flowering. The richness of its velvet texture and the full flamboyancy of its bouquet have endeared it to generations of wine-lovers. I had some choice years in my cellar, but unfortunately the wine does not travel well, and we have had to move four times in the last eighteen months.

As all wine-lovers know, the severe attacks on the rhubarb plants by wireworm in the middle twenties had a disastrous effect on the output of rhubarb wine. The wireworm troubles are now largely over, and there have been some very good years in the "post wireworm" period. Memories of the famous "Coronation" vintage are with us yet. There were unfortunately no good years during the war; the labour shortage, coupled with the rationing of sugar, made things very difficult for the *Vignerons*. My sister-in-law, whose wine was adjudged a "first growth" at the Flower Show, 1931, always relied on my brother to turn the mangle by which the fruit was crushed. Naturally, with my brother in the Army, the burden of turning

the mangle fell entirely upon my sister-in-law herself. As a result
the output for the war years was small in quantity and, owing to
the scarcity of sugar, deficient in quality.

At my suggestion we used the whole of the 1944 output as a
basis for a fortified wine, produced by blending the native product
with two or three bottles of an interesting liquor known, I believe,
as "potheen," very graciously presented by some American soldiers
as a mark of appreciation for hospitality they had received. The
resulting blend, which I named "potbarb," suffered from imma-
turity, since the donors of the "potheen" insisted on drinking the
blend almost before I had entered the bottles in my cellar book.
I like to think that this interesting blend strengthened them in
their liberating mission, but we have lost touch with them, as we
have with so many of our dear friends with whom we have shared
a bottle of wine at one time or another.

RICHARD MALLETT

Writing

A sort of celebration of "Doting," the new novel by Henry Green

"BUT while I sit here pen in hand, I ask you."

"Oh you are" his wife moaned.

George Stubbs placed one finger on a key of his typewriter and
of the other hand a finger, for he had taught himself typing,
on another. When these were pressed the letters I and N were
expected to result.

"It's his ninth novel," he counted. "I'm sort of celebrating it.
He's made a what they say when founding a school is under
discussion."

"It's the tenth book." She could count too.

"*Pack My Bag* was autobiography, you forget that. I just looked.
I think it's the only one I never got hold of."

"I remember it's your birthday coming" she told him. "Hints I can't bear, people should say straight out."

"I'll get it from the library" said George Stubbs.

"You hope."

Having typed I and N he now typed G. There had been three or four other letters before these.

"There's the title done. All his titles are like that, all his novel titles. Participles."

"Oh if it's participles now. Anything to throw it in my face. You are a beast, George, or have I told you?" Her name was Stephanie, a large well covered woman with one of her shoes off after supper.

"My dear girl." Down hung his hands. "Why do you put on this I can only call it an act? You must have been taught about participles, no one can avoid it. Just you not taking it in isn't my fault."

"So I suppose it's mine do you mean" she repiningly wailed.

Mr. Stubbs found himself a prey to temptations. Manfully he battled against these.

"I didn't say that" he pronounced.

"You meant it, I bet you did" she insisted.

"I ought to know what I mean oughtn't I" he indignantly replied. He raised his hands again to the keys of the typewriter and produced a short straight line by tapping one of these several times.

"You forget" said Mrs. Stephanie Stubbs in quite a strong voice. "I mean all the implications. That's the way you have to read Henry Green dialogue, stiff with them it is."

"Implications" he wonderingly repeated.

"There" she accused in a thin wail. "You didn't even think I knew the word, surprised you are, George, one can see with half an eye. Oh what a beast."

"I'm a beast because I'm surprised? Don't mind me, exaggerate blue in the face." Now the first words under the already typed title were engaging the attention of Mr. Stubbs.

"Inverted commas is the first thing" he proclaimed pressing the shift key with the first finger of his large left hand. "The dia-

155

logue is the great thing, you are I must say right about that. So there they are." Raking the keyboard with his eyes he tapped a key at the top left corner of this.

The wife stooping, breathing heavily, crammed her foot into her small shoe.

"Oh do be reasonable George" she cried with what appeared to be exasperation. "You writing dialogue like Henry Green, there's such a thing as being absurd."

"I can try can't I."

"Trying doesn't mean the tiniest thing, you need an ear. Anybody'll tell you."

"I have an ear I think I may say" he declared in a satisfied voice.

"I know the one you mean" Mrs. Stubbs blandly smiled. "But even the way it sticks out is no proof."

These words were not noticed by George Stubbs, whose mind was on his work.

"I remember about participles now" his wife announced with a sort of humble triumph, then moved towards the door of this room in their flat, in London, in 1952. "*Nothing* isn't a participle, I've caught you out, George. All his novel titles were participles was what you laid down the law about, but his last one was called *Nothing*."

"Don't I know" he replied without paying much attention to his exultant spouse, who was now leaving the room. "Nor was *Blindness* if I may draw your attention to the fact" he added. "I just wondered how long it would take you to realize. I must remember not to put a comma in here, he dispenses with commas at the end of quotes" he reminded himself.

Stephanie Stubbs walked out of the door, after which she slammed this.

The husband went on typing for about half an hour, and then the wife returned carrying a suitcase.

"Well goodbye, George" she said with what might have been reluctance.

"Goodbye" he abstractedly rejoined. "Did you turn the light out in the bathroom, may one ask?"

156

On which she went out and slammed the door again.

Mr. Stubbs went on typing the first chapter of his novel. It was not till he had done several pages of this that he wondered whether she might have left him for good.

RICHARD MALLETT

Workers and Watchers

[A fancy, by an admirer of the novels of Miss Ivy Compton-Burnett, on the publication of her *Two Worlds and Their Ways*]

"I FIND it makes me uneasy to be watched," said Edwin. "I should never have believed it."

"What we can believe depends on our capacity for belief," said his brother, hitting with a sledge-hammer the spike Edwin held upright in the road.

Edwin made no immediate response, allowing the spike to be hit three more times in succession by his remaining three companions.

"Our feelings on the matter are in any case irrelevant," said one of the latter, upon the completion of his stroke. "Those people watch us for their own amusement."

"They are very easily amused," said Edwin.

A policeman joined the watching group, gaily intoning "Now, what is all this?"

" I should have thought the source of our interest was obvious enough," said Mrs Hunstantonby, smoothing the hair of the pale little boy who stood by her side.

"Will the men soon hit their spike again, mother?" said the latter, jumping up and down.

"I wish Osbaldeston would keep still," said his sister, looking coldly at him.

"So do we all, I should imagine."

"All? Do you imagine Osbaldeston himself wishes to keep still?"

"If that were so the explanation of his behaviour could be still more crudely put," said the policeman. "He would be in the grip of some nervous affliction."

Edwin set up the spike in a different place and sank upon his haunches, holding it steady.

"It is perhaps time for us to resume our performance," he said. "I have heard that a crowd may turn ugly when disappointed of the entertainment it had reason to expect."

"I never thought I should live to hear my own child abused by a guardian of the law," said Mrs. Hunstantonby, gazing intently at the spike in the road.

"It makes one wonder whether we shall not all soon be murdered in our beds," said another lady in the group.

"The suggestion that my son is in any way afflicted is offensive in the extreme," said Mrs. Hunstantonby. "That it should have come from a policeman is the crowning touch."

"That is telling him," said Edwin's brother, bringing his sledgehammer down on the spike. "It pleases me to be present when an officer of the law is in receipt of a raspberry."

Osbaldeston looked up at his mother, ignoring the spectacle of the other three men hitting the spike.

"Mother, did you give the policeman a raspberry?" he said. "Have you any more? Will there be one for me?"

Mrs. Hunstantonby made no reply, but distended her nostrils.

"I do not like raspberries," said the other child. "Outside they are too soft, and inside they are too hard. They are just the sort of thing a policeman would like, but Osbaldeston should know better."

"Why should I be expected to know better than a policeman? I think it is unfair to expect such a thing."

"Hush," said his mother.

"Well, I never did have very much education," said the policeman, with an indulgent look. "It seems not without the bounds of possibility that the boy knows better than I do, about some things."

"About raspberries?" said the little girl. "There, mother, the policeman admits it. Osbaldeston knows more than he does about raspberries."

Edwin's brother was now hitting the spike again.

"It is strange to hear such a proposition seriously advanced," he said, having done so. "The child's assertion seems on the face of it calculated to tax the credulity of even the simplest mind."

"We have simple minds down here," said Edwin.

"There are more up there, if you ask me."

"You cannot pretend that anyone was asking you," said one of his companions. "The question would have been put in a manner at once more explicit and less emphatic."

Mrs. Hunstantonby pulled Osbaldeston to her with a sharp movement.

"You must not remove things from other people's pockets, my little son," she said. "Restore that to its owner this instant."

"As I remember, you made no objection when father used to do it," said Osbaldeston, complying with a sulky look.

"Your father was the breadwinner of the family," said his mother. "I shall always regret his departure."

She looked at the workmen again, and looked away when she met Edwin's glance.

"I often think it was foolish of him to murder that man," she said. "It would surely have been easy enough to pick his pocket without hitting him on the head first."

"The technical difficulties of any calling seem simple to the onlooker," said Edwin, setting up the spike in a new position. "That is one of the professional man's exasperations."

"For example, I am sure that policeman thinks it is easy to hit a spike with a hammer," said Edwin's brother, doing so.

"I am quite positive it is," said the policeman, stepping over a rope and advancing to the group of workmen. "Nevertheless at the moment I have no wish to demonstrate my ability in that direction."

"We are to assume that he is here in the exercise of his own profession," said Edwin with a look of resignation, standing up.

"That is so. Your name is Edwin Hunstantonby?"

"Yes."

"I have a warrant for your arrest," said the policeman. "I must ask you to come along of me."

"Mother, why does the policeman say 'of me' rather than 'with me'?" said Osbaldeston.

"Hush, dear. We have already heard from his own lips that he has not had the benefits of education."

"And will somebody else hold the spike now?" said the little girl, as the policeman led Edwin away.

"A moment's scrutiny of the positions of the remaining workmen would have convinced you that your inquiry was superfluous," said Mrs. Hunstantonby. "We must learn to avoid asking unnecessary questions, must we not?"

RODNEY HOBSON

I Dare You, Mr. Cooper!

OF THE many scenes I have learned to love in motion-pictures, none fills me with a warmer glow than the dear old Bag-Packing sequence. Theme songs may come and go, bosoms rise and fall—I couldn't care less. But once let me see some clean-limbed college boy flick open an outsize cabin-trunk and lower the first half-dozen custom-tailored suitings into the hold and I lean forward in my seat, settle the hat of the lady in front more comfortably on her head and indulge in a little genuine hero-worship.

Can we ordinary people ever hope to be able to pack with the same insolent ease? I doubt it. In fact, after watching Mr. Gary Cooper toss a few things into a trunk at the local cinema last night, I'd go so far as to say a categorical "No." Never have I seen the job done better. Cooper's handling of the underwear is magnificent. In the time you or I would take to decide which sock to pack, he has stowed away twenty-five Cellophane-wrapped shirts and is already reaching for the silk cravats. Never a moment's hesitation here; not a jammed drawer or a frayed collar in the whole sequence. A first-class show.

Without wishing to belittle Mr. Cooper's performance I must say I'd like to direct him in the same sort of scene—*using my suitcase and my chest of drawers*. To begin with, I'd place my camera fairly close to him as he reached up to the top of the cupboard to get the suit-case, bringing the usual two jars of home-made marmalade with it. What an opportunity here for the taut, restrained acting in which the man excels!

For the actual opening of my suitcase I would move the camera away to the opposite side of the room. There is, I believe, a natural reluctance among film directors to dwell on details of physical injury, and I am quite prepared to string along with them in this matter. I think I would get my effect equally well by letting the audience hear the quickening tap-tap of the chisel against the lock, followed by a quick shot of Cooper's hand reaching for the first-aid box. There would of course be nothing in the script to tell him that my suit-case is best approached from the soft underbelly, where the hinges were.

In order to keep this scene down to a reasonable length I would at this point probably have to resort to what is known as a "montage sequence." As Cooper applies a rough tourniquet to his gashed wrist there is a burst of celestial music, and we flash back to his boyhood and the events which led to his becoming involved with my suitcase in the first place.

Cooper must now work fast. Not only has he got to get my suitcase open before I return with my camera crew, but he must also find some suitable cache for its payload of old tennis-shoes and pieces of grandfather clock. The last thing I want to do is lug all that heavy equipment back to my bedroom to find him guiltily trying to stuff a length of mainspring into his trousers pocket.

161

Let us assume that Cooper has mastered these two problems. All right. Now we come to the supreme test of the man. Can he, in the few thousand feet of film still to be exposed, conjure enough clothes from my chest of drawers to see him through a long week-end in Saratoga?

This should be interesting. He opens the top drawer. It yields one fully-fashioned Army shirt and a doll's nightdress. We hear the strangled sob as he thrusts them back and barks his knuckles on a toy signal-box. He tries the middle drawer. One side opens a few inches, causing the other to retract a similar distance into the fuselage. The whole then seizes up solid. We cut to a close shot of a small but highly important pulse throbbing in the Cooper temple. The bottom drawer opens at the third pull to reveal three chintz chair-covers and an Eton collar.

Here I may have to bring in the celestial music again and give Cooper a chance to steady down. This will also enable me, as director of the picture, to go into a huddle with my producer, for I am now well behind on my shooting schedule and overheads are mounting. There is only one thing to do: I call a conference of scenario-writers and commission them to write into the script a part for a lady psychiatrist, somebody along the lines of Miss Bergman. Then I nip back to my bedroom and take a quick look at Mr. Cooper. Frankly he's in pretty bad shape. His breathing is laboured and the tiniest split is beginning to show in his personality. To make matters worse, my suit-case has somehow contrived to snap itself shut. I give our lady psychiatrist an encouraging pat as she rustles past me into the room.

And not a moment too soon. Mr. Cooper has torn the middle drawer open with his own hands and is sobbing hysterically over its contents—one knee-length woollen vest.

Decent of him to turn it out for me. I'll be wanting it for my summer holiday.

In the Throes of Living

HOME AND FAMILY

RODNEY HOBSON

Second Opinion

I was pottering about in the kitchen, whipping up a spot of lunch as a surprise for my wife, who had gone to call on her mother, when the front doorbell rang. Laying aside the cauliflower I was preparing for the pot I went to the door and opened it.

A tall man in a rather good tweed suit was standing there. Obviously down on his luck, judging by the way he avoided my eye.

"Yes?" I said, a trifle sharply. I am not one of those people who spend hours on the doorstep chattering to strangers.

"Excuse me," said the tall man, "but have you an electric cooker?"

"Yes, we have," I replied. "And even if we hadn't I wouldn't dream of buying one at the door. Good morning." I closed the door, none too gently, and went back into the kitchen with a rather satisfying *frou-frou* of plastic apron.

I had just resumed work on the cauliflower when the bell rang again. I went back and opened the door. The tall man was still there.

"I wasn't trying to *sell* you a cooker," he said. "I wanted to ask your advice about mine. My name's Mumford," he added quickly. "We're the new people in the flat above, you know."

I had my apron off in a flash. "Why, of course," I said. "Do come in."

Mumford hesitated. "As a matter of fact," he began, "I'm having a bit of trouble with the Sunday joint. My wife's gone to church and left me to cope." He gave a nervous little laugh. "It's the first time I've ever tackled Sunday tiffin myself, actually."

I felt for the man. If we had been acting in an American flying picture I would have given him one of those understanding little

165

man-to-man punches in the solar plexus. As it was, I merely slipped into my jacket and motioned to him to lead the way.

"What seems to be the trouble?" I asked as I followed him up the stairs.

"The cooker appears to be on fire," he replied.

I nodded gravely. "And what kind of joint have you got?" I asked. Some, I know from my own experience, are considerably more inflammable than others.

"It's roughly elliptical in shape," said Mumford; "rather like a half-inflated rugby football."

I gave a low whistle. If I had interpreted his words correctly we were up against a piece of veal. And veal can be the very devil.

He opened the door of his flat and we went in. A cloud of thick, brown smoke met us in the hall.

We groped our way into the kitchen. It didn't take me long to locate the cooker. Motioning Mumford to stand back I bent down and opened the oven door.

The first thing I did was to snatch the smouldering oven-cloth from the back of the oven and throw it into the sink. Then, as the smoke cleared, I looked at the joint. It was a quite passable piece of beef. True, it had taken a lot of punishment, but it was not yet beyond human aid.

I ran a practised eye over the control panel on the front of the cooker. All switches were set to full boost. The top of the cooker itself was red hot. In a basket under the table a retriever was gasping for breath. I quickly snapped off all switches and moved an empty and rapidly disintegrating saucepan from the top of the cooker to a place of safety. Then, protecting my hands from the heat with Mumford's Sunday paper, I slid the joint out of the oven and carried it to the window.

"Do you think we can save it?" asked Mumford, peering over my shoulder.

I shrugged my shoulders. I didn't intend to let the fellow off too lightly.

He watched me in silence while I held the joint under the tap to remove odd traces of oven-cloth. With pathetic eagerness he helped me replace it in the pan and slide it back into the oven. Then I closed the oven door, checked dials and straightened up. Mumford made gusty noises of relief. The retriever heaved itself from its basket and tottered across to lick my hand.

"Can't thank you enough," said Mumford gruffly.

I made one or two delicate but quite unnecessary adjustments to the controls, basking in the man's admiration.

"Give it another ten minutes," I said, "and it will be done to a turn."

The chap was still obviously shaken, so I didn't leave him immediately. Instead, I gave him one or two simple jobs, such as laying the table, while I whipped up a pot of fresh mustard and brought the potatoes to the boil. Then after a quick look at the table to make sure he'd made no awful mistakes, I left him.

His thanks followed me down the stairs to my own flat. Feeling rather pleased with myself I unlocked the front door and went in. A cloud of thick, brown smoke met me in the hall. . .

JUSTIN RICHARDSON

The Aumbry

MR. CLOCKE the auctioneer has just phoned to say the men are delivering the aumbry to-morrow and is that convenient, and I

167

have just said thank you it is and I am posting the cheque to-day.

I am now writing the cheque, which is for sixty guineas, and I am asking myself what in the name of black thunder has induced me to part with my life savings for an aumbry, what brain-break-down ever made me think that an aumbry would suit this house, this nice house of my own that I used to like, and above all and urgently where am I going to put this big infliction when it arrives?

I am the sort of man that when his wife tells him there is a sale of furniture at The Gambles, Sir Malcolm Boost's place, only three miles from here, practically next door and some *heavenly* things, look here's the catalogue, there's a William and Mary secretaire and a yew gate-leg table and a Regency canterbury and a sixteenth-century aumbry and won't I take a day off and come, comes. I like the name aumbry and I don't know what an aumbry is, as if it mattered, and so I leave my business, which makes me my living and never did me any harm, and I come.

When I had reached the Boost mansion and done my simpering act while Mrs. Rigby told my wife what curtains she was going to bid for, and how she was going to cut them up and sew them back again and turn them inside out for all I care, and at last stood opposite No. 13 which was the aumbry, I want to know why I didn't say out loud "An aumbry is a dashed oak cupboard thing, with half a door missing, and great gougings here and there that might be carving or might be big kicks. It weighs half a ton and was obviously used as a hen-house. It has shelves or roosts inside and has been eaten a good deal by worms or hens. It is ugly, battered, probably knocked together three years ago from bombed railway-sleepers, and I am going home." I know all the words, why didn't I say them?

No, I must stand there and man-handle the erection and invent stories for my wife about it being an alms-chest, an almry, an aumery, an aumbry. And if it were genuine, I say I *think* this one is genuine, as if I'd ever seen an aumbry before in my life, it would be a bargain at fifty or sixty. Why fifty or sixty? Why not eight or seventeen or three? And when my wife says would it go in the hall, I don't think about it *being* in the hall but get out my ruler and take its beastly measurements and feel efficient and say yes, it would go in the hall. And it *would* take the rugs and the skates and half the dinner-service and the gloves.

Inside me also I am mouthing the word aumbry and making phrases with it. "You must come down on Sunday, Stephen, old boy, and see the aumbry we picked up." "Yes, it's an aumbry, you know. They used it for storing alms in, dishing out alms, from alms—aumery—aumbry." I am thinking about my pretty phrases and my idiotic measurements and not about the *thing* as a thing in the house at all.

And then the auction has started and in no time we are at No. 13, and someone says thirty guineas, and very soon it is fifty-nine. My wife whispers "You *said* sixty, didn't you?" as if that was any merit and I feel very knowledgeable and narrow-eyed and appraise-worthy and the auctioneer says "Am I offered sixty?" and I say, "Sixty," in a big loud knowledgeable narrow-eyed voice and wait for the bidding to go on. But it doesn't go on. There is a silence. The other bidders are dumb, paralysed, stricken, all suddenly. "For the third and last time, sixty. To you, sir."

Why didn't I rise immediately in my place and say no, not me. I can't pay for it, I don't want an aumbry: mine wasn't a bid, it was a guess; let the other people have it? Why didn't I run away? Why didn't I give them a faked name and address? Why, above all, didn't I go to Mr. Fifty-nine guineas and tell him he could have it, quite all right old boy and here's a fiver too? No, all I do is sit there and try to look like an aumbry-owner, a man who buys aumbries because he wants them, and not like a name-addict or plain sap.

And now this blight is coming to-morrow and I have checked my clever measurements and find it *would* go in the hall, but only if the staircase wasn't there. So I am to have it in my study, it would seem. Not more than two feet of it will overlap the book-shelves. If I want to look at anything before "K" in the encyclopædia all I have to do is hire a bulldozer and move the aumbry away for a moment. Too easy. And hire another bulldozer to doze it back. In a communist world everyone would have fun like this.

Anyhow, it can't last for ever. It's already three hundred years old and perhaps won't stand up to children in the holidays for more than another century or so. And we can always sell the house and say it's a fixture, we kept hens in the study and had the local woodsman fell a couple of oaks and knock us up this hutch.

"Yes. This is two—one—one—o.

"Oh, is that you, Stephen? No, wasn't in the office yesterday. Yes. Went to a sale at old Boost's place down here. What? Nothing very much, but we picked up a lovely old aumbry. You must come down and see it on Sunday."

ALEX ATKINSON

Theory

As SHE dropped the magazine on to her lap and leaned sideways to turn down the volume of the radio, Mrs. Chubb glanced across at her husband. Mr. Chubb was pursing his lips gravely over a notebook, and he hadn't spoken for twenty minutes. Mrs. Chubb frowned, and picking up the magazine turned a page with a sharp swish.

Presently Mr. Chubb began to whistle a slow tune under his breath. Then, deliberately licking the point of his pencil, he added a couple of words to the page with great care, drew a line at the bottom with a flourish, and sat back to regard his handiwork with his head on one side and an eyebrow critically raised. He looked up momentarily at his wife, but she pretended not to notice. He began to whistle again, accompanying the radio half a tone flat, and drumming on the notebook with his pencil.

At last Mrs. Chubb raised her eyes, and found him looking at her.

Well," said Mrs. Chubb. "What is it now?"

With a satisfied expression Mr. Chubb folded back the notebook and passed it to her. Then, putting the pencil on the coffee-table, he settled himself back in his chair and began to examine his nails.

"Alertly," Mrs. Chubb read, "Bruce Chubb dodged each frenzied giraffe."

There was a pause. Mrs. Chubb looked up slowly. Mr. Chubb had assumed a fixed, rather mocking smile. She held his gaze for a moment, soberly, and then read on.

"He insisted jokingly (kissing little Mabel's nose) on putting questions rather sternly to Umbopo," read Mrs. Chubb. "Very warningly, Xenophon yelled 'Zebras!'"

Mrs. Chub did not lift her eyes from the page for some time. At last she reached out to switch off the radio, and, in the silence, looked steadily at her husband, biting her lower lip thoughtfully. Under this scrutiny Mr. Chubb crossed and uncrossed his legs and cleared his throat.

"That passage," said Mr. Chubb importantly, "contains twenty-six words."

Mrs. Chubb made no comment.

"The initial letters of those words," continued Mr. Chubb, with a certain triumph, "are in alphabetical order, from A to Z!"

Mrs. Chub blinked very slowly, and then read the passage again. A glazed, far-away look came into her eyes, as though she were trying to remember the name of someone she had known at school.

"There's a theory," said Mr. Chubb briskly, "that you can learn a lot about a person's subconscious if you make them do that exercise."

"Is there, now?" said Mrs. Chubb, nodding at him expression-lessly.

"For instance," Mr. Chubb went on, "you can easily deduce from my effort that I have always been fascinated by the idea of going on safari." His voice became dreamy. He leaned back with his eyes half closed. "Umbopo, you see, would probably be a native guide. He'd know the terrain and the local dialects and all that."

Mrs. Chubb nodded. "Xenophon would be a little out of his depth, though, wouldn't he?" she said.

"Mm?" said Mr. Chubb. "Oh. Well, he was more or less *forced* on me."

"I see," said Mrs. Chubb. "And this Mabel person—I suppose *she* was forced on you too, was she?"

"Well . . ." said Mr. Chubb awkwardly. "You have to bear in mind that it isn't an easy thing to do."

Still eyeing him, Mrs. Chubb switched on the radio and took up her magazine. She began to read, but she wasn't really concentrating. Mr. Chubb, quite undaunted, pulled his chair a little nearer to the fire and occupied himself with the construction of a camel from two pipe-cleaners.

When he had got as far as the shaping of the hind legs Mrs. Chubb, reaching secretly for the pencil, began to scribble in a casual way on a blank space in her magazine. Mr. Chubb was whistling again, very busily.

"Ash blonde crooners," wrote Mrs. Chubb, with some surprise, "dance every Friday, grinning happily . . ."

ALEX ATKINSON

Dramatic Interlude

MR. CHUBB, who had been silent for a good half-hour, stirred in the big armchair and cleared his throat.

"Ah, Rose!" he said, looking across at Mrs. Chubb. "It seems only yesterday that we walked hand in hand through Sefton Park and sat awhile to listen to the band."

Mrs. Chubb looked up from one of Mr. Chubb's socks, and frowned suspiciously.

"And now, here we are," Mr. Chubb went on, with a broad gesture. "And I am forty-six and you are forty-three."

Mrs. Chubb broke off a length of darning wool.

"I remember your white jabot," said Mr. Chubb, "and the poppies on your hat. And now, as you know, our son Harry is twenty, and already shows promise as a violinist."

Mrs. Chubb regarded him curiously for a moment, and then held the darning needle up to the light.

"He is upstairs at the moment," proceeded Mr. Chubb, "shaving. His friend Hugh Symington is calling for him, is he not, and they have tickets for a music-hall?"

Mrs. Chubb deliberately put down the sock, and the wool, and the needle. Then she sat back in her chair, folding her arms, and watched him, fascinated.

"What a pity we have no great opinion of Hugh!" said Mr. Chubb. "Do you remember, Rose, at breakfast this morning, how you tried to persuade Harry that Hugh is not a desirable companion? I remember it well."

"Do you really?" said Mrs. Chubb, nodding.

"Then there is our daughter, Myrtle," said Mr. Chubb. "She is just turned sixteen, is she not?"

Mrs. Chubb did not reply. She was tapping her foot lightly on the fender, and looking straight at him. He blushed slightly, and avoided her gaze.

"Just imagine," he went on. "She has been with that firm of lamp-shade manufacturers for three whole months now! I, of course, am the chief clerk in a shipping office, am I not?"

"Well," said Mrs. Chubb, "that's what you *tell* me. Just before we go any further, though, could you give me some idea of what this is all about?"

Mr. Chubb cleared his throat again, rather nervously.

"It occurs to me," he said, "that a play about us and our family and friends could be very interesting. The heart-aches, the triumph: the laughter and the tears."

There was a short silence. Mrs. Chubb picked up the needle and threaded it coldly and efficiently.

"Would you please pass me the scissors?" said Mrs. Chubb.

"What I'm doing," said Mr. Chubb, getting down on his knees to peer under the sofa, "is working out the dialogue for the opening of the first act. Of course, it would be better if we had a maid. But, failing that, I must talk to you."

"I see," said Mrs. Chubb.

He handed her the scissors. "You have to let the audience know at the very start just what's what," he said, "in an easy, natural way."

"Do you, now?" said Mrs. Chubb.

"A man ought to have some constructive hobby," said Mr. Chubb, defensively. "Ah, Rose!" he went on, "I wonder if your sister, Helen, will call this evening? Her husband, Percy, as you know, had a fine war record and is now doing well as a greengrocer. Didn't you tell me that their daughter Jane is taking ballet lessons? And for some weeks now our own daughter, Myrtle, has been hinting that she would like to do the same. Things will come to a head this evening, you mark my words. Ah! Is that the door bell I hear?"

Mrs. Chubb rolled the sock into a ball and stuck the needle into the arm of the chair. "The coal," she said, rising decisively, "is kept in the cellar, is it not?" She placed one hand on her chest. "Ah, Bruce!" she said. "Do you remember the lovely talk we had at tea, when I reminded you that unless you filled the scuttle there and then you would be sorry?"

Mr. Chubb sighed, and bent down for the coal scuttle, and the door bell rang again.

"And if I may be permitted an exit line," said Mrs. Chubb, pausing at the door, "our son Harry is nineteen. And I am *not* forty-three."

TERENCE BERNARD THOMPSON

Otto and the March of Time

AMONG the many contributions made to modern knowledge by members of my family I give precedence to the occasion when my eldest brother Otto first timed a dream. Scientific theory, up to that time, was divided into two schools: there were people who believed that a dream was instantaneous, and others who maintained that it took time to have one. It was Otto who demonstrated beyond doubt that the second theory was correct. It was one of those happy scientific accidents which happen occasionally, like Galvani and the frog's legs, and was the outcome of a lot of unconscious teamwork.

My father was a mild man, but he couldn't stand his own family, and, looking back, I can see his point. He retired early in the struggle to his first line of defence, which was clocks. We had twenty-eight in the house, of which about fifteen were in more or less regular work. They kept a somewhat moody and personal account of the passing hours, and when anybody asked the time they had to be given a qualified answer, such as "Ten-thirty by the Tompion," or "Windmills says a quarter past." Only members of the family knew what to make of these figures, or had the length of training required to sort out the true notes from the false in the mad chiming which began five minutes before every hour and went on long after real clocks were showing five past. Some of the more crotchety timepieces refused to stick to one recital at a time (the wrong one as a rule) and worked their way through their entire repertoire. The nights were full of alarm, and occasional visitors were brought wild-eyed from their beds by the sound of heavy gunfire. They were rarely reassured by the sleepy explanation that it was only one of the grandfathers that had dropped a weight.

My next oldest brother, Carl, was a brooder. He detested bacon, and when I was little he used to make me eat his share at breakfast and take my egg instead. He was caught at this one day and given a beating, so he had to think up some other method of getting rid of the stuff. I didn't realize what it was until one day my father told me to bring him a pair of shoes which he didn't often wear. He put the left one on, and then paused and took it off again. He felt inside it cautiously and pulled out a very old piece of bacon. He looked at it for some time in a puzzled way.

"Who put this bacon in my shoes?" he said finally.

"I expect it was Carl," I answered.

"But why," said my father, "why would he put it there?"

"I expect it's because he doesn't like it," I said.

My father didn't say anything, but shortly afterwards he retired to his second line of defence, which was golf. He played golf every Sunday, rain or shine, and if the weather was too bad he retired to the clubhouse and played solo whist. He never came home until late, and then he would go to the drawer where the clock winding keys were kept and fill his pockets with them. After that he would tour the house, in darkness so as not to wake us up, and wind all the clocks that were working. He generally fell over a few times in the darkness, and if he found one of the clocks was wrong he used to put it right. If you know anything about grandfather clocks· you'll realize that this generally involves moving the pointers round the whole face, stopping to let the clock strike every hour and every half-hour as well, so that by the time he had finished the whole house was awake and reading books. All except Otto, that is, and he could sleep through an earthquake. It was in this way that he made his great discovery: through the clocks, not an earthquake.

My father came home one Sunday after playing golf and started his winding tour. He got as far as the grandfather on the upstairs landing. It was a superb piece of craftsmanship with beautiful marquetry work, but not on striking terms with Big Ben, and when he checked it against his own half-hunter, he found it was twenty minutes slow. He put it right and started to wind it up, but when the second weight reached the top the pulley-wheel must have tripped the mechanism in some way, because it dropped with a fearful crash, splintering the floor of the clock and fetching some sizable bits of plaster down from the dining-room ceiling. I came out in my dressing-gown and found my father on his hands and knees in the dark, groping about in the bottom of the clock and muttering. I switched on the landing light and saw that his left hand was full of bits of bacon, very dirty and green with mould.

"That was a loud one," I said. "What are you doing with that bacon?"

176

"I found it in the bottom of the clock," said my father.

At that moment Otto came out of his bedroom in his pyjamas.

"Interesting thing," he began. "I heard you come upstairs and start winding the clock, and then I fell asleep."

"Who put this bacon in the clock?" said my father.

"I can't imagine," said Otto coldly. "As I was saying, I fell asleep and started to dream. I dreamed I was being pursued by some people—"

"I expect it was Carl," I said.

"No," said Otto, "I didn't recognize any of them. Anyway, they chased me across the bridge in the middle of the town, and in order to escape I climbed on to the outside of the railings and worked my way along the coping."

My father was standing, still holding the bacon. I felt cold, and I wanted to go back to bed, but there was no stopping Otto.

"I reached the middle of the bridge, where there's a coat of arms in cast iron and a motto that says 'Nil Desperandum.' I was clinging desperately to the motto, when suddenly the whole lot gave way, and I started to fall into the river a hundred and fifty feet below." He paused dramatically. He had his audience by this time; even father was waiting to hear the end of it.

"I hurtled downwards," said Otto, "and hit the water with a fearful crash. I woke up."

"Well?" said father.

"It was the noise of the clock weight hitting the floor," said Otto triumphantly. "Don't you see," he went on, his eyes gleaming, "my dream took just as long as the clock weight took to get to the top and then fall down to the bottom."

There was silence for a minute, then my father turned to me.

"Tell me," he said, "why Carl puts bacon in the clocks. Just tell me that before my reason goes."

"I've told you before," I said. "Because he doesn't like it."

"I know he doesn't like it," said my father, his voice rising thinly; "but why put it in the clocks, in heaven's name?"

"I expect it's because the shoes are all full," I said.

❀

D. H. BARBER

Good Turn

"If it is wet this afternoon and you cannot do any gardening," said Edith as I set out for London one day last week, "you can get Sympson to come over and help you turn the sitting-room carpet."

"Ridiculous," I said, "there isn't any pattern on the other side."

"I don't mean turn it upside down," said Edith patiently, "I mean turn it round so that the bit that is now by the door will be by the window and the bit that is now by the fireplace will be under the piano. It is a good carpet and when we eventually go bankrupt it will fetch about eighty guineas if it is evenly worn all over."

When I arrived home about two o'clock I found that Edith had gone to the pictures, and as it was raining hard I rang up Sympson and asked him if he felt in the mood for a bit of carpet-turning. Always obliging, he said he would pop over in a jiffy and lend me a hand. It was quite a long jiffy, and I used it to good advantage by moving all the smaller bits of furniture off the carpet and stacking them in the passage. The carpet is nearly as big as the room and it is impossible to move it without moving or lifting all the furniture. By the time Sympson knocked on the front door there was nothing left in the room but the carpet, the piano, the large bookcase, the china cabinet, and the two big arm-chairs.

It would be more correct to say that only one-and-a-half of the big arm-chairs was still in the room, because one chair was wedged firmly in the doorway. When we arrived at the flat a year ago the furniture-movers seemed to have no difficulty in getting the arm-chairs through the doorway, but this one seemed to have grown considerably fatter since then. The harder I pushed the harder it became wedged. When I crawled underneath it, however, to open the door for Sympson it suddenly relented and hit me in the small of the back.

"I won't be a minute," I shouted.

"Anything wrong?" asked Sympson anxiously, peering through the letterbox.

"Nothing," I said, trying to get one of the legs of the chair out of my pocket. By pushing the chair back into the room I managed to extricate myself, and then I found that I could not open the front door because of all the furniture stacked in the passage. So I had to carry a lot of it back into the room to let Sympson in, and it soon became clear that in this I had made a tactical error. Sympson has talents of a certain kind, but as a carpet-turner I should rate him very low indeed. His feet are much too big and he is lacking in nimbleness.

As everybody knows, the only way to get the edge of a carpet from underneath a heavy china cabinet is to get somebody to lift one end of the china cabinet a couple of inches from the floor by levering it with a poker, while you jerk the carpet from underneath. At the same time the person levering with the poker has to jump quickly from the carpet with both feet at the exact second that you pull the carpet from underneath him. It requires delicate synchronization. In the end I had to do the levering myself while Sympson did the jerking from underneath, and I was jumping up and down and levering for a good ten minutes before we got the china cabinet free, and then it dropped so suddenly that a whisky decanter that had been in the family for years was smashed beyond repair.

Not since we were sappers together in the Royal Engineers have Sympson and I toiled as we toiled that afternoon. It was slow work because of Sympson's clumsiness, but there were no further major accidents, except when the bookcase tilted forward too far and Sympson was knocked almost unconscious by *Great Essays of All Nations* and I received the volume of a well-known humorous journal for 1852 on my left foot.

Our task was completed and the furniture back in its place when

179

Edith arrived home from the cinema, and Sympson and I were reclining, limp and exhausted, in the two big arm-chairs.

"I hope you've had a good afternoon in the garden," she said. "You won't have to bother about turning the carpet, because the window-cleaners were here this morning and they did the job for half-a-crown."

KENNETH DEAR

Toffees in the Third Floor Back

IF THIS should catch the eye of the bearded gentleman whose land-lady recently accused him before the Chelsea Rent Tribunal of eating toffees in bed I would like him to know that he has my deepest sympathy. I am not bearded, and I do not eat toffees in bed—or, indeed, anywhere else, for reasons which other married men will appreciate—but I have had considerable experience of landladies, and in my time they have accused me of almost everything from riding a bicycle downstairs to making a bath-tap drip to the tune of "The Red Flag" on a Sunday.

Whether the balance of one's mind has to be disturbed before one opens one's doors to the troglodytes, or whether (as I suspect) even the strongest character crumbles under the strain of enduring the idiosyncrasies of others, it is a fact that many of my landladies were somewhat unusual.

Mrs. Bridle, for example, who kept what she described on her cards as "Select Gentlemen's Apartments" off the Woodstock Road, Oxford, was haunted by the imaginary smell of frying fish. At least once a week she shattered the evening quiet of her house by charging madly up to the top storey shouting "Someone's cooking kippers! Someone's cooking kippers! Someone's cooking kippers—it's a thing I won't allow!" As she raced up the stairs her brogue-shod feet beat out the savage tempo of her words, and those of us who had lived there for a while found ourselves breaking involuntarily into an uninhibited dance as we listened.

By the time Mrs. Bridle reached the attics we all had our doors open, like troops standing by for a kit inspection, and when she had got her breath back she used to make her way slowly down to the basement, sniffing accusingly towards each of us in turn, a black look of frustration spreading over her face like treacle on a boiled pudding. This was a regular performance, as I have said, but Mrs. Bridle never succeeded in finding any food of any sort being fried, grilled, baked, boiled, stewed, smoked, or roasted— indeed, I believe the only cooking that was ever done in her rooms was by a pale young man who kept the books of a Christmas club, and left unexpectedly one December.

But whereas Mrs. Bridle's imaginative nose did no more than lead her in search of non-existent kippers, the suspicious ears of Mrs. Quaife, who kept a desperately respectable establishment near Folly Bridge, made her believe that she was harbouring under her roof a collection of potential hooligans. Her hearing was far from good, but her mind's ear could detect sounds that were completely inaudible to all other humans.

"By the way, Mr. Er—um—er," she said to me one morning (she addressed most of her tenants in that manner, for she had a bad memory for names), "please don't hammer tins in your room after eleven at night." "Mrs. Quaife," I said, "I have never hammered anything in my room, not even before eleven." "I wouldn't expect you to admit it," she said, "being as you're much more than old enough to know better." "But I assure you . . ." I began. "Say no more, Mr. Er—um—er," she said. "You know where to draw the line, I'm sure. I rely on you to toe it in future."

In time I gave up arguing with her; whether I was accused of handbell-ringing or wrestling, of bursting balloons or barking like a dog, I used to promise not to let it occur again and all was well. Exemplary behaviour was lost on Mrs. Quaife; she was happiest with a house full of repentant sinners and the confident knowledge that only her constant vigilance ensured the preservation of what she called "the cardinal's decencies."

Mrs. Bridle and Mrs. Quaife were fundamentally eccentric, I admit, but I have found even the most uncomplicated landladies capable of unforeseen effervescence. Mrs. Donovan of Bayswater, for example, who was usually as unemotional as cold porridge, almost threw me out of her house when I wore a green tie. She said it was like a red rag to a bull to her, on account of Cromwell. I hadn't the faintest idea what she meant, and I don't think she had either. Mrs. Heeping of Holland Park insisted that her boiler blew up because I turned a hot-water tap off too quickly, and Mrs. Murch of Wimpole Street shook with rage when she told me to stop getting letters from Weston-super-Mare; they made her think of her husband, she said, and her nerves were bad enough already.

But it was Mrs. Debitt of Kensington who really made me lose confidence in myself. In the presence of her three other tenants and the milkman she denounced me as being responsible for her dachshund's attack of distemper. She said she knew very well that I mixed with almost any dog that said "Hullo" in the street, and that I had undoubtedly brought a complete set of germs home with me. I pointed out, with all due deference, that I had never read or heard of a human being having distemper, but Mrs. Debitt was not impressed. "I don't say you've got it," she said, "—not yet; but you're probably a carrier."

The dog, which recovered very quickly, bore me not the slightest ill-will, but I moved as soon as possible. I just couldn't stand the way Mrs. Debitt looked at me; I felt her eyes searching confidently for the first signs of a hot nose.

Ah, well; I suppose it's difficult to live and let live when one has to live and let.

F. MAYNE

The Slaughter of an Innocent

I MUST admit that he said he did not want a policy, even a fine policy such as the one I offered him. He said, quite clearly, that he did not want a policy; but I, schooled in all the arts of salesmanship, said that he did not know his own mind.

"Very well," he said, "you may start filling up the form."

I was stunned. I had had more trouble persuading myself to take out a policy. Nor did I notice anything sinister in the wording of his capitulation.

He gave me a chair at the table while he himself relaxed into an arm-chair, lit his pipe, and seemed to settle himself in for the evening. His wife sat in the other arm-chair and took up her knitting. She had finished about six inches of a scarf.

"What," I asked briskly, "is your full name?"

"Well," he said slowly—he spoke very slowly the whole time—"that's rather difficult. It so happens that my Christian names are rather muddled. I have two Christian names on my birth certificate and three Christian names on my baptismal certificate. The extra name on my baptismal certificate is Charles, and actually everybody calls me Charlie, so that's the name I'm known by more than any other. My wife always calls me Charlie, don't you, dear?"

"Yes, Charlie," she said.

"What is the name you usually use on legal documents?" I asked.

"Well, I've never really bothered much," he said, as though

183

communing with himself. "Sometimes I put the Charlie in and sometimes I leave it out. But in this case I want to get it right. With an insurance policy one can't be too careful. If I die I don't want them to say it was somebody else who died, do I, dear?"

"No, Charlie," she said. The scarf was already appreciably longer.

It was some time before I could quieten his fears on this score. Even then he could not make up his mind. First I put in the Charles, then he asked me to leave it out, and then he told me to include it after all. Finally, with a light laugh which had just the hint of a rattle in it I tore up the form and brought out a new one. I filled in his name and address, reading out the latter as I wrote it.

"Oh, dear," he said, when I had finished. "Did you write down this address?"

"Yes," I said.

"That's a pity," he said, "isn't it, dear?"

"Yes, Charlie," she said. The scarf was now as long as it was wide.

"Why," I asked, "is that a pity?"

"Well, we are going to move to Pretoria next month and I want everything to be addressed to our new place. Would you mind altering it?"

"Not at all," I said with a laugh that sounded like a dry cough.

I tore the form up and brought out a third. When I had reached the address I looked at him expectantly. Huge corrugations had appeared between his eyes. I could see that he was thinking deeply.

"Yes?" I said.

"Now, isn't that silly of me?" he mused. "I've completely forgotten the number of our new house. Can you remember the number, dear?"

"No, Charlie," she said.

"Well," he continued, still apparently ransacking his brains, "I suppose you had better use this address for the time being. We can always change it later."

I wrote down the same address for the second time. I did not laugh in any way any more.

184

"And now," I said, fear clutching at my heart, "how old are you?"

He looked enigmatic. "I am in my thirty-ninth year."

I wrote down thirty-nine and then paused.

"Does that mean," I swallowed, "that you are thirty-eight?"

"Naturally," he said, as if surprised at my ignorance.

"Would you mind initialling this alteration?" I said, holding out the proposal form with a trembling hand.

"Wouldn't it be better to start a new form?" he said.

"I have only one more form."

"Only one more? That's not many, is it?"

"What is your occupation?" I continued.

"I'm a teacher."

I hesitated.

"You teach at a school?" I asked. I was determined not to be caught this time.

"Yes."

"At an ordinary school for ordinary boys?"

"Oh, yes."

I did not see how there could be any ambiguity here. Resolutely I wrote down his occupation.

"You didn't call me a teacher, did you?" he asked suddenly, when I had finished.

"Yes, I did," I said, without moving my lips.

"I hate being called a teacher. Couldn't you alter it to school-master? A teacher is so often a figure of fun, whereas a school-master has some status, hasn't he, dear?"

"Yes, Charlie," she said. The scarf was now longer than it was wide.

"It doesn't really matter on a form like this," I said.

"Well, it may seem a small point to you, but I'd be much obliged if you altered it."

I altered it.

"How do you want to pay your premiums?" I asked.

"Oh, monthly," he said, immediately. "It's so much more convenient."

I pretended to write it down: he could not see the form from where he sat.

"Wait a bit, though," he said, when he thought I had finished. "Isn't it much cheaper if one pays annually?"

"Yes, one does save quite a bit," I said with some equanimity.

"Well, I'll pay annually then, if you don't mind. I'm sorry to make another alteration. Perhaps you had better start a new form."

"No, it's all right," I said. "I have not written in anything yet."

For the first time since we had sat down our eyes met, but his were expressionless.

"Now," I said, feeling slightly better, "what was your last illness?"

"Well, we don't rightly know what it was. It was only the other night. I suddenly got the shivers, like an ague or fever. I lost all control of my limbs. I lay there twitching and jerking. I must have been a horrible sight. We still don't know what it was, do we, dear?"

"No, Charlie," she said. The scarf was now big enough to gag her with.

"I remember my wife saying to me, 'I wonder what it is, Charlie?'"

"What did the doctor say about it?" I asked with my eyes on the carpet.

"Oh, we didn't have a doctor. I don't believe in doctors unless I am very ill. That wasn't much, probably just a slight chill."

"Not a fever?"

"Well, a kind of feverish chill, if you know what I mean."

"No, I don't know what you mean."

"Well, if you had seen me you would understand. It's very difficult to explain."

"So I gather," I said, for quite rightly I no longer felt like a salesman.

"Tell me," I resumed, "what was the last illness for which you saw a doctor?"

"Heart failure."

"Heart failure?"

"Yes, not proper heart failure; it just fluttered. I've got a systolic murmur of the heart," he added with relish.

"You have?"

"Yes, if you keep quiet for a moment you will hear it."

Silence fell. I craned forward and listened intently.

"I can't hear anything," I said.

"You would if you were used to it like we are. Did you hear it, dear?"

"Yes, Charlie," she said. The scarf was now big enough to strangle her with.

"If you have heart trouble it will be difficult to insure you."

"Oh, don't say that. I'm beginning to feel really good about this policy."

"What doctor attended you for your heart trouble?"

"Dr. Plaistowe."

Thrown off my guard by all the clinical details, I wrote it down. He began to make wet noises with his tongue.

"I've given you the wrong name. Dr. Plaistowe treated me for my lungs and kidneys. Dr. Turner is my heart man."

"Have you a stomach man?" I inquired, screwing on the top of my pen.

"No, my stomach has not troubled me for some time. You see, I seldom eat anything, do I, dear?"

"No, Dick—I mean, Charlie," she said.

I rose with what dignity I had left and tore the form to pieces.

"Thank you for the nice evening," said the *tricoteuse*, as I went.

JUSTIN RICHARDSON

The Fathers' Race

MISS MILLINER's amplified voice has just commanded through the microphone "Fathers' Race now, please," and my daughter Goove, aided by the lanky friend Panza, is already violently helping me to take my coat and waistcoat off and pushing me at the same time toward the starting-line. I have the familiar sinking feeling common to the preliminaries of all public competitions, much heightened by the knowledge that this one has been long and carefully devised so as to make the fathers look thoroughly foolish and to cause them physical pain if at all possible, the latter being thought particularly wizard. Last year I broke a tooth.

I am now lined up with some thirty other sheepish ones and survey the field. The greybeard whom I have been appraising victoriously all the afternoon is *not* amongst us: it appears—afterwards—that he is not a father but a grandfather. On the other hand three towering and slim youths, the parents, if they are not mere impostors, of certainly nothing more than recent entrants to the kindergarten, are champing at my side with fire coming from their nostrils. One of these cads is actually wearing *shorts* and none of them has braces, like me. There is, however, a little comfort

188

farther down the line, where leaning over I remark some hopefully protuberant stomachs, and here and there the reassuring glint of spectacles. But on the whole I see that being the father of a Senior loads the dice against me and that one has to pay for having a daughter on the committee.

Miss Milliner is now telling us exactly what we are expected to do, making it sound at once easy and quite inevitable—just the way she gets small girls to learn Latin, I suppose. First, she coos, we all pass under the tennis-net stretched flat on the ground with two weighty mistresses sitting on the ends; *then* we dash off and climb one of four spring-boards sloping almost vertically up to the top of vaulting-horses; *then* we jump down and pick up a bun with a tennis-racket and *no* hands allowed please: *then* we eat the bun; and *then* we dash off to a pile of skipping-ropes and skip to the finishing-line. That's absolutely all. Oh, and will we take our shoes off, so as not to damage the spring-boards?

This is just plain death in the afternoon, making last year's shambles seem like a Dance of the Flowers. I decide that both Goove and Panza who assisted and no doubt led the committee to elaborate this mass parricide will pay richly for it if I survive. I then mechanically take off my shoes, look at a large hole in my sock, realize that I am beyond caring and resolve to go down fighting. I even get a small satisfaction from seeing that the man with shorts had shoes with spikes in them, the cheat—anyhow, jolly useful nails, and at least *that* caper has been checkmated. I also, being not without cunning myself, shift to the centre of the line, where the tennis-net, I calculate, will bulge more readily; and I take care to select a thoroughly protuberant neighbour, who will assist with the bulging. . . .

The whistle has gone, the net has bulged, I am nearly through, there is something holding me back, it is my braces, there they go and here come the spring-boards. The bulgy neighbour has got there first, but gratitude is not in me, and I just push him straight off and let him be trampled by the pursuing mob. Now I have a racket; I run to the buns, I select a bun, it won't get on the racket, I put it on with the foot with the hole in the toe, Miss Milliner

189

said nothing about feet, and the bun is now partly in my mouth. Only one other man is as yet bun-faced, but others are arriving in scores and I must eat very fast. I cannot eat fast, the bun won't *eat*, the other man has a bigger mouth or something. Heavens, he's finished already, and someone else, *and* some more, mine's gone now and here's the skipping-rope. The skipping-rope is made for a tiny child, less than a junior—a hare or even a rabbit, I should say—I bend double and hop along like a malevolent old dwarf, I am here, it is over, I am about seventh, I think. But it is over.

I am just thinking that I will pull Panza's pig-tail hard for this and torture Goove by making her wash behind her ears, when they appear together with large vanilla-iced olive-branches. "You weren't *nearly* as bad as Mummy thought you'd be," says Goove, and "You gave that old boy a wizard shove off the spring-board," says Panza, "was it fun?" "Wizard," I say. "Can you find me a safety-pin or my braces?" But this is ignored because the loud-speaker crackles, Miss Milliner is announcing the inter-Section Relay Race, and my two Seniors are off to marshal, exhort and if necessary impel respectively the Thorns and the Brambles. I find my shoes amongst a press of Briars and rescue my coat from underneath a lesser Prickle. Then with the other fathers I relapse into use as a background.

ERIC KEOWN

Life in Darkest Surrey

As CRIMES go, it was small. Small, but with an element of the bizarre which lifted it above most of the crimes one tries not to read about in the papers. Also, it was motiveless. It was plain silly.

I was the first up that morning, I cannot remember why, and as I peered out across the common to see if it was to be another case for an umbrella I saw that evil had been abroad during the night. The front garden, carved out of the common by a previous owner long enough ago for time to have sanctified the enterprise, is bounded by a picket fence, and parts of this, I realized, were missing. The pickets lay in confused heaps on the verge of the lane, like white spillikins, and little heaps of yellow powder showed where the death-watch beetle and other members of the underground had been surprised.

This was the first time the postman had found me kneeling in the lane in my pyjamas, and he seemed anxious to humour me. "A lovely morning," he said, shivering in his greatcoat, "for puttin' things to rights."

I explained we were the victims of an outrage, of one of those blind, purposeless acts of vandalism which scar the chequered progress of man. Relief spread slowly across his large red face, and he dropped to his knees beside me.

"Summun in rubber gloves, no doubt," he declared. "That be the way they set about it. And the ground too frozen-like for footprints. If we could come on a trouser-button now, or a lock of hair!"

"Or a piece of cake with a phone number iced on it," I snarled, my teeth chattering.

"Arrh, happen the first clue and it's wunnerful what comes after. Seen any dark men around, last few days?"

"Only the gipsies down by the pond, and they're friends."

"No furrin women out in the gorse with spy-glasses?"

"You read too much, Carbury," I said, taking a circular for fish-manure from him and going back into the house . . .

I was so cold that when I dropped into a hot bath the water hissed at me. I lay down in it and searched my conscience for an enemy, but I live a guileless life and am much respected. A few days before, I recalled, I'd spoken perhaps rather brutally to a small boy picking snowdrops in the orchard, but it was hard to believe he'd bother to come back in the middle of the night to mess up an old fence . . .

"You know what it is?" cried Miss Carruthers, passing after breakfast on her way to shop. "It's an ape, and a pretty big one

191

too. If my brother Herbert were here he could probably tell us the exact sort, but he's in Bulawayo, of course, so that's that. Just the kind of thing they delight in. I expect it's under the dining-room table now, planning its next move. You must go about in couples, and ring up the Zoo . . ."

At breakfast there had been three schools of thought. One held I should sit up all night with a shot-gun, since malefactors were said to return to the scene of the crime and a good deal of fence remained to smash. This sounded fine and manly, but it seemed to me that to do so without one's solicitor sitting up beside one was asking for trouble in the courts. Another put the whole bus-iness down to poltergeists, but as this was clearly due to the fact that Harry Price's book on Borley Rectory had strayed into the nursery we ignored it. The third urged it was a shame to keep the police out of an affair baffling enough to disrupt the hideous alter-nation of rearlights and dog-licences. There was something in this, and yet I had a hunch to wait . . .

"Been expectin' somethin' like it for a long time," exclaimed Colonel Pelmett, leaning hungrily out of his palæolithic motor-car. "Dam fellers are everywhere. Now Moscow's said the word, and nothing will be safe."

"Who do you think told Moscow about my fence?" I asked, because I honestly wanted to know.

"It's property, isn't it?"

"It was," I said . . .

At lunch I grew melancholy that such a nice world could house such nasty people. It was very sad, and I felt it keenly and person-ally. I was just swallowing the end of a jam roll and agreeing to call in the police when a slight sound of splintering caught my ear. Out in the lane stood a small pony, an almost circular pony with a length of rope and a stake dragging behind it. It was scratch-ing its chin thoughtfully on the top of the fence, and at each forceful stroke another of the uprights came away with a clatter . . .

The gipsies were all out when I reached the pond, except the boss. He was about eighty, or it may have been a hundred and two, and he sat staring regretfully into space, making quite beautiful

192

clothes-pegs by a bright fire. I felt I was visiting a sultan, and that a couple of goats or a bag of rubies would have been in order. He accepted tobacco, however, with a good grace, and when his pipe was alight began to tell me toothlessly of how his eldest daughter had married into the fried-fish business in Huddersfield. It appeared to be many years since she had committed this intolerable folly, but it rankled freshly in the old man's mind. I sat down on the steps of the caravan . . .

When the postman came back at teatime, bringing a circular for a new painless sort of biscuit, he was surprised to find two sturdy young gipsies banging nails into the fence.

"Happen you ain't caught him?" he shouted.

"He's caught," I said. "And there's a rope round his neck."

HOD (A. B. HOLLOWOOD)

Fire, Fire, Fire Insurance

WHEN will people realize that I can and do work with the wireless on? They burst into my room, stand momentarily stunned by the volume of sound welling from my faithful receiver and say "Oh, good, I'm glad you're not actually working because there's a man . . ." They don't understand that radio's greatest virtue is its capacity for blotting out sound, that most writers would rather work against a solid wall of self-inflicted din than suffer the nervous torture of spasmodic noises off. Radio is the most effective "silencer" ever fitted to the human ear.

They burst into my room one morning last week, stood momentarily stunned by some housewife's choice, and said "Oh, good! You haven't started yet. There's a man at the door."

"What man?" I said, blotting my copy-book and screwing the cap on my pen.

"He just asked to see you."

"What's he like?" I said.

"Tall, rather good-looking, check coat, car."

I dusted the ash from my jersey, put my feet into my slippers and climbed out of my chair.

The man was not at the door: he was very much this side of it. He shot out a hand.

"Good morning, sir," he said, offering me a cigarette, "I hope I'm not disturbing you?"

"No, not at all," I said.

"I was round this way," he said, offering me a cigar, "so I thought I'd call to see if I could help. Have your fire-extinguishers been tested lately?"

"Fire-extinguishers?" I said.

The man looked horrified as he offered me a light.

"Don't tell me, sir, that you've omitted to take the precaution of fitting your house with our fire-extinguishers!"

"Well—" I said.

"You're a longish way from the fire-brigade here, sir, you know. Wouldn't have much chance at three A.M. if it got a real hold. Better let me fit you up, sir. Here, sir, read this. It explains everything, sir."

He thrust a coloured leaflet into my hand and walked forward to the foot of the stairs.

"Say two on each floor—that's four—and one spare," he said, jotting figures into an order book. "Say five all told—yerse, five should do you."

"Did you say *five*?" I said.

He looked surprised and vaguely hurt.

"Yes, sir, that's right, five! 'Course, more would be an improvement and give you extra protection. Seven or nine would be ideal. You've only got just the two floors, haven't you?"

"D'you mean to tell me," I said, "that you're trying to sell me *five* fire-extinguishers?"

"I've just sold eight to Major Timperley, up the hill," he said. "And Mrs. Gorham—you know Mrs. Gorham at 'Brackenville,' sir?—Mrs. Gorham's got six. I've just been giving them their an-

194

nual once-over. Then there's Lady Branning, down in the village—she's got eleven, eleven of the specially large three-gallon model."

"The place must be cluttered up with the things," I said.

"Oh, no, sir, they're very unobtrusive."

"And how much are you sacrificing these things for?"

"Well, sir, the small model's six pounds including spanner and flinch-lock, and the large three-gallon model—the one Lady Branning favours—runs to eight guineas including refills, spanner and flinch-lock. 'Course, I can't let you have them for a few weeks, sir. We're rushed off our feet with orders, but if you put your name down now you'll get them at to-day's prices instead of paying through the nose. You see, sir, they're bound to go up soon because we're selling at a loss. It's the chemicals, you see, sir."

"Ah," I said, "the chemicals."

The man's method disgusted me, but I could think of nothing very shattering to say.

"Terribly easy to operate, sir. A child could—"

He broke off as a flurry of little feet crossed the hall.

"Well, sir," he said, "you just smash the knob against some hard surface, and that's it. Put anything out, it would."

"Would it put—" I said, and thought it best to leave the remark uncompleted.

"Very well then, sir," he said. "I'll put you down for five smalls and I'll see you get preferential treatment—extra-special delivery priority. There's a satisfaction-or-money-back guarantee and a discount of two and a half for cash."

I forced him back across the hall inch by inch. At one point, so stiff was his opposition and so relentless my counter-offensive, our coat-buttons were touching and I could see the pores in his blue chin. There was an anxious moment when we drew abreast of the dining-room door and I thought he would side-step through it, but I made use of my superior elbows and pinned him against the hall-stand. In another half-hour it was all over and I was back at work with the B.B.C. organ pounding at my ear-drums.

Of course I didn't *buy* his fire-extinguishers: I didn't even buy one. The fact remains, however, that I haven't had a decent night's sleep since I rejected his offer. Three nights running I've had the whole family out on the lawn just after midnight and twice I've spent half the night carrying dying coals from the grate into the garden and burying them deep under the marls of the potato-patch. Last night it took me ten minutes to knock out my pipe to my entire satisfaction.

This can't go on. If the man who called at my house last week will repeat the visit at his earliest convenience he will hear something to his advantage.

Some Arts and Belles-Lettres

DANIEL PETTIWARD

Non-Art for the Million

or How to Make the Most of Your Lack of Talent

BLACK FOR BEGINNERS

I BELIEVE I can help you to make quite a cosy little income from drawing *without your having to be able to draw*. The kind of drawing I have in mind is the black-and-white kind that goes over, contains, or—in poor Aunt Carrie's case—conceals, a joke. With an increasing number of contemporary jokes the drawing part is on a *non-art* basis, e.g. a placard saying "TOP FLOOR: IRONMONGERY— HABERDASHERY—ARTIFICIAL LIMBS AND A FREE VIEW INTO THE OVAL." To produce this the draughtsman requires no previous training in anything other than writing, ruling lines and knowing where to go for his jokes.

Non-artists are of course restricted to the kind of joke which goes with the kind of picture they can manage. One picture that every non-artist ought to be able to manage is the All-black Rectangle.

Cut out a rectangular piece of paper somewhat smaller than a postcard and submerge it in a prepared saucer containing Indian ink. Remove it and when dry uncurl it carefully, cover the less successful side with a reliable mucilage and clamp it on to a postcard, leaving a nice bit of border all round but especially at the bottom where your signature should be added, boldly, together with a joke.

Here is how the rectangle should look after being stuck on:

Darkness pictures (except in America, where they have to do with courting and begin with statements like "Yoo-hoo, Mr. Weinberger!") are usually concerned with the inconvenience of not being able to see something rather important as in "Nobody but Basil would think of bringing home a boa-constrictor during a power-cut," or "But I came all this way on the strict understanding that there was *always* moonlight on the Taj Mahal." Power-cuts have of course been a wonderful boon to non-artists, many of whom had been badly hit by the cessation of the black-out and were having to fall back on ordinary blown fuses.

WILL YOU HAVE THICK OR CLEAR

More limited in its range, and therefore less often seen, is the All-grey Rectangle shown here as it might appear in its final form. The "All-grey" can be run up in much the same way as the "All-black," only you want to put water with it:

"Yes, Mr. Clatworthy certainly seems to have got the hang of his meer-schaum at last."

Even simpler, and especially recommended for the beginner who is none too confident with ink, is the all-*blank* picture:

"That looks surprisingly like the air-pocket that played us up so on the way home from Alex, Alex."

We now pass from featureless pictures to something with a bit more bite to it, the Humorously-worded Notice. This, as I have already indicated, demands only a working knowledge of block letters and the ability to include, for greater realism, an occasional half-brick:

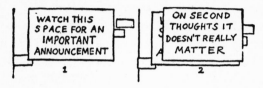

For those who enjoy something a shade more fancy and don't mind if it turns out not to have been worth while after all, there are studies of this nature:

And here is a happily-conceived little composition made up of familiar every-day objects:

As a useful exercise, stare at this picture for about thirty seconds, then cover it up and see if you can do it yourself. Not so easy, eh? That hydrant sign of yours looks like twisted wreckage.

Jokes ranging from quiet fun to high comedy at the expense of shops, restaurants and inns can be achieved easily enough by means of the Humorous Hanging Sign, which surmounts the well-known difficulty of having to draw architecture from in front.

Designs like those that follow can be used *ad infinitum,* but don't get so wrapped up in your wrought-iron work that you forget to vary the joke a little each time.

(The squirls shown here belong more properly to *semi*-art and are not really necessary.)

Genuine artists, often borrowing freely from old holiday sketches, will include any amount of half-timbering, dog-tooth moulding and fancy perspective with their Hanging Signs, but while they are at it you can be dashing off dozens of non-art versions provoking every bit as much mirth.

THE SANS SOUCI SCHOOL

In the same category is that ever green provider of innocuous merriment, the Suburban Gate. Here is a brief non-art fragment

suitable for immediate use, and, on the right, an example of the gate in action.

FAT WASPS AND FAR-AWAY SEAGULLS

For those who are not at their best with block letters or find straight lines on the soulless side there are several more animate objects which can be adapted to non-artistic treatment. A theme popular at the moment is that of two animals or insects, either discovered in the thick of some domestic contretemps or commenting wryly to one another on some glaring evidence of human folly. Non-art wasps which can, I imagine, be traced without much trouble out of reference books and shown on window panes, are especially well suited to quips about horizontal stripes not flattering the stout. Failing wasps, you cannot go far wrong with Greater Black-backed Gulls:

"And tell me, do they require these passport things for coming home, too?"

You can always get variety out of Greater Black-backed Gulls by swapping them about, banking them in other directions, or turning them, as here, into Lesser Black-backed Gulls:

"They say that cuckoo woman is always willing to sit-in for a consideration."

Fortunately, the fact that this kind of picture is rather lacking in something or other lends it a sort of fashionable *naïveté*. Also possessing a ready appeal are little birds on telegraph wires, provided you can restrain yourself from trying to put in the posts and the little pepper-castors where the wires join on:

"But this is fantastic! Do you mean to say not one of you knows what he's queueing for?"

THE GENTLE NON-ART OF CONCEALMENT

A belief which seems to persist obstinately among untrained non-artists is that human beings can only be introduced into humorous pictures if they are heavily shaded down one side and shown either sipping aperitifs in front of Hepplewhite wall-cabinets or blotting their copy-books out with the Bicester. This is no longer true. Thanks to the pioneer work of earlier non-artists, the *mise en scène* of many of to-day's best jokes consist of one or more pieces of angular non-art furniture often in process of being obtained through the hire-purchase system. As a first step students who are anxious to compete in this *genre* are advised to familiarize themselves with the outlines of the non-art armchair. Here is a popular and very serviceable specimen—note also the non-art pipe (smaller than the chair but otherwise very much the same) symbolizing domesticity:

Provided your chair is firmly planted in the foreground of your picture the public will realize in a flash, without your having to supply footnotes or four-storey cake-stands, that the action is taking place in the "lounge." Simply-framed non-art pictures, straightforward non-art standard lamps and opaque non-art waste-paper baskets can always be added to make bigger, better-paid pictures.

Artistic leanings can best be indicated by means of spots on the waste-paper basket and triangles (instead of smudges) in the pictures. Awkward gaps can always be filled in with knotted non-art flex. The only snag about lamps, pictures and waste-paper baskets is that they are very little use for putting in front of parts of people that are difficult to draw. The non-art armchair seen here in the humorous head-on position is ideal for this purpose.

"If you wouldn't mind waiting in here, madam, the Bishop should be back at any moment."

Non-art walls and fences can be utilized on the same manner for outdoor versions of the missing-bishop situation. In the quite meaningless example shown below I have also worked in the standard non-art horizon and two kidney potatoes.

For clarity's sake the top-knots in the above pictures have been drawn larger and with greater elaboration than could ever be attained in practice by the non-artist.

MASS-PRODUCING THE LITTLE MAN

Students, however, need not remain for longer than they wish in a state of having to keep the greater part of their characters behind barricades. The fully-exposed non-art Little Man, once mastered, is no harder to run off than the non-art standard lamp; which in some ways he so closely resembles. Through the persistence, in particular, of the North Circular Road Group of non-artists the public has long since become resigned to the spectacle of innumerable little men who look as if they had been sawn out of white cardboard. Here is a simple blueprint for arriving by easy stages at the front elevation of one of these:

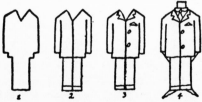

Figs. 2 and 3 can be used independently for clothes-line and coat-hanger jokes.

Faces can be made in uncountable ways, but luckily for you it is now generally appreciated that the more often you can use the same, or nearly the same, face the more people will know it next time and the more famous you will become. A reasonably individualistic but perfectly recognizable face can be obtained by using a "C" for the right ear, a backward "C" for the left ear, some more "C"s on their backs for the nose and hair and a clean sixpence for the outline of the face. Better stick to dots for eyes, and, having once chosen where they are to go, resist the temptation to put them in other places however side-splitting the result may be. A favourite place for the eyes is on a level with the tops of the ears. Ears themselves come about half-way down on the outer perimeter. Until you feel quite capable of launching out on your own face, use the specimen lay-out illustrated here. Most non-art objects automatically become humorous the moment a joke has been added to them, but it is customary in the case of faces to attempt to make them humorous in their own right. There are several accepted ways of doing this. The scheme here chosen is the Drooping Moustache method, which has the advantage of giving your little man an inscrutable all-purpose expression suitable for practically every situation. The drooping moustache fits neatly under the nose like

a slice of water-melon and dispenses with the need for a mouth.

MAIN USES OF THE LITTLE MAN

I hope to deal at a later stage with the question of little men in secondary attitudes (including little men in frilly aprons trapped at the sink), but, until I have done that, non-art students who wish to show sideways or non-upright little men in their pictures must continue to make use of armchairs and stone walls.

Where jokes are concerned only with a specific area of little man, or where they are hardly strong enough to warrant the use of the complete figure, fading out from either end may be resorted to:

"*There must have been at least two hundred other copies of the 'Daily Telegraph' in the kitchen drawer which would have served your purposes equally well, Penelope.*"

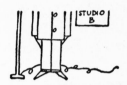

"*Fog is expected to be very localized.*"

Normally, however, your little man will be shown standing stiffly in the "lounge." Even between one chair, one lamp, one waste-paper basket and one little man the interplay is almost endless. Here, for instance, is one of the many formations you may have failed to take into account:

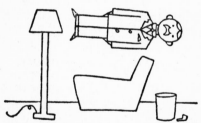

"*Would you mind seeing if it says anything in the Encyclopoedia about delevi-tation, dear?*"

LITTLE WOMEN AND CHILDREN LAST

I am well aware that by introducing my non-art little man I am creating a demand for non-art little women and children, and so, with much misgiving, I append a simple pattern from which these may be obtained. The drooping moustache being only intermit-

tently appropriate in this category a common hyphen has been
used to represent the mouth.

For those who insist, there is also

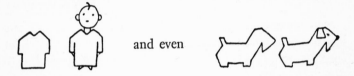

and even

It cannot be too strongly emphasized at this point that students
are *not* now qualified to record day by day, through times grave
and gay, the endearing adventures of Mum, Dad, Mavis, Percy and
"the Menace." Apart from every other consideration there is far
too much of that kind of thing about already.

SOME DISTINGUISHED LITTLE MEN

When more than one little man, woman or child is required for
a joke it may sometimes be necessary to use some simple method
of distinguishing between them. With all such methods it is most
important that your little person should retain as many as possible
of those hall-marks by which the public is able to tell him or her
from other people's little people. One of the easiest *outdoor*
methods is the one often incorrectly referred to as "Allsopp's Hat-
Discriminating System." It has been used here in conjunction with
a straight-forward sandwich-man set-up, which incidentally illustrates at the same time the extremely high concealment-value of
the oncoming sandwich-board. To obtain the maximum payment

for this joke the little men should be drawn several times over, being kept apart for as long as possible and only brought together for the grand finale when all other possible combinations have been exhausted.

A handy way to discriminate between little men *indoors*, and one which avoids tampering with either the features or the circumference of the face, is to use darkened or variegated versions of the drooping moustache. When appropriate, hair can be inked in or deleted and non-art spectacles added, to obtain still further variation.

A few of the possible permutations for faces treated in this manner are shown herewith. For the complete list see the present

writer's "The Drooping Moustache as a Stabilizing Factor in Power Politics," Pinhorn and Brazier; first published 1932.

CROSSING THE TEETH

Ringing changes on the drooping moustache is not, however, recommended as a permanent expedient. Pictures exclusively filled with drooping moustaches have been found, in practice, to produce a dispiriting effect on the public, apart from the incongruity of such adornments on characters who have not yet attained full little-manhood. The non-artist who proposes to make a habit of drawing little men in bulk should learn, first, to draw little men with different expressions and, second, little men with different professions. The main obligatory non-art expressions for little men, women and children are as follows.

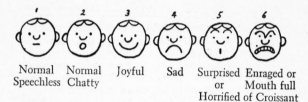

Normal Speechless	Normal Chatty	Joyful	Sad	Surprised or Horrified	Enraged or Mouth full of Croissant

Figs. 1 to 4 should be thoroughly mastered before going on to fig. 5, in which normal eyebrows (like "C"s on their fronts) are introduced, and fig. 6 which involves the use of Greater Black-backed eyebrows and caterpiller-track-type teeth. Eyes, noses, hair and circumference remain constant throughout.

THE LITTLE FOUR

The four professional non-art faces given below with a list of the main professions represented by each are the maximum needed by non-artists. The drooping moustache, if not already in use, can always replace the jaunty moustache (Fig. 2) in cases where the latter would plainly be striking the wrong note or proves to be beyond the powers of the non-artist. There is no need to bother your heads

1	2	3	4
Man of the World, Waiter, Gangster, Film Actor, etc.	Retired Colonel, Farm Labourer, Alderman, etc.	Frenchman, Conductor, Bearded Lady, etc.	American, Clergyman, Master Criminal etc.

about little women and children in different walks of life, with the possible exception noted in Fig. 3 above. Nor should any effort be made, except under the guidance of a qualified non-art master, to combine the expressions with the professions. You need only attempt a rough sketch of an enraged alderman to discover why.

Students should note that they now have a wide choice of non-art subject-matter, enabling many of the more advanced types of drawing to be successfully blended with some of the more elementary:

"And this is my husband's little den." (Traditional Old English Folk-joke)

And here is a more elaborate picture of a kind that enterprising students may care to tackle. The framed text (with deliberately small writing) is inserted to make it impossible for the editor to reduce the picture beyond a certain point:

At a recent lecture given by the author the above sketch was drawn on the blackboard, and members of the audience were invited to try their hand at suggesting appropriate captions. The first suggestion, coming from a man prominent in public life, was: "Short-sighted Civil Defence Instructor (*directing stirrup-pump team in friend's house*), 'Now then, Number 2, there's no need to stand all that rigidly to attention' (*Prompt collapse of team, except Number 2 who remains unmoved*)." Although the ingenuity of this suggestion was freely admitted, the audience as a whole was not entirely satisfied. There was a general feeling that five was not the correct number for a stirrup-pump team, and several people loudly voiced the opinion that somebody ought to be holding a pump. After some discussion the joke which finally proved acceptable to the majority of those present was: "This is our little staff, Sir William; Hotchkiss, second from left, is our illusionist." Quite a number, however, preferred "shining light" to "illusionist." I wonder if any of you can think of anything better still?

FOR THE NON-ART CONNOISSEUR

It is only right to let you know that there is an alternative approach to non-art which has gained some hold on the intellectual public during the last two decades. Its chief characteristic is that the non-artist, instead of restricting himself to subjects inside his limited range, restricts himself to subjects *outside* his limited range, his pictures normally being supplied with rather grown-up jokes like "Come on, tell us the one about Goldilocks and the three Father-Images." Provided the drawings are bad *enough* and the jokes sufficiently baffling, no one with taste and susceptibility will care to identify himself with the man-in-the-street in not thinking them funny.

THE NEED FOR NON-VARIETY

I do not propose to say any more at the moment, except to remind you that in all approaches to non-art, as in all approaches to almost everything else except cooking and one-man-band playing, the secret of success is rigid specialization. I have dealt with some of the ways in which the humorous non-artist can get into print and, with a little extra effort, increase the size and sales-value of his work: but make no mistake, the ultimate plums are reserved for the man who associates himself as soon as he can with one particular line, be it simple or complex, solitary wasps or large

212

conclaves of chatty Frenchmen, and who sticks to that line unwaveringly, come what may.

DANIEL PETTIWARD

The Pictures in My Dictionary

MOST people have their favourite pictures. Sometimes they are well-known works of art like Millais' "Bubbles" or Gainsborough's "Blue Boy" or Balbolo's provocative "Kidneys on a mauve background—1926." Sometimes they are pictures of a more personal type, painted perhaps by a well-loved hand, or of a well-remembered subject such as "Plumm Pudding sene from abuv," by Jeremy aged six. Sometimes they are pictures with no obvious appeal—a rough design, shall we say? for the proposed extension to Saffron Walden cemetery or a snow-covered fell on which has been planted a group of completely unconvincing sheep. This type of picture is cherished simply because somebody happens to have hung it on one's bedroom wall.

Into yet another category come one's favourite pictures in books. There flash before me as I write the familiar and exciting images of a very prickly Tom cowering before Mrs. Bedonebyasyoudid, of Sherlock Holmes standing aghast at the singular discovery of the Engineer's Thumb, of Peter Rabbit hiding under the greenest of

213

green cabbage leaves, and of a dozen king's daughters gazing wistfully from as many turret windows.

One set of illustrations which I keep in the forefront of my affections, although I am not above deriding them at times, is the series of pictures in my dictionary. Some of them are in parts of my dictionary that I seldom frequent and have no particular message for me, but some I know like the back of my hand and welcome like old friends. These are the pictures I keep coming across as I turn the pages on my way to discover how to spell "fulfil" or to learn once again the meaning of "exegesis."

How often, on such occasions, have I come face to face with the picture of the Quincunx! The quincunx or kwin' kungks, as it is pronounced, is "an arrangement of five things so as to occupy each corner and the centre of a square, esp. of trees and plants." The quincunx here shown consists of five little fruit trees bathed in sunlight, but we can amuse ourselves by picturing quincunxes composed of five oysters or five members of the Central Federation of Master Bakers or any other five things which if not so typical are still quincunxes so long as, by accident or design, they have become arranged, to use the adverb so conveniently to hand, quincuncially.

It will be seen that the charm of these pictures derives not merely from the drawings themselves but also from the accompanying definitions. Sometimes, too, a pithy phrase may be encountered in the immediate neighbourhood of a picture. Just above the quincunx, for example, occurs the intriguingly cryptic utterance—"Quinch same as Quitch."

On the very first page of my dictionary there is an exquisite representation of an Abacus. For those unaware of the fact, an abacus is a counting frame or table, and from the illustration and the description I am able to perceive that not only did I have an abacus on the side of my cot, but that from my earliest days I must have been, without knowing it, no end of an Abacist.

Let me interpose a word of regret here. Without wishing to complain of the arrangements generally, I would greatly appreciate it if one day some artist would depict for the benefit of posterity the likenesses of that grand opening pair, so often chosen by the

Selection Committees of dictionaries, the Aardvark and the Aardwolf.

A picture I love and would readily have enlarged and hung over my bed is that of the Aplustre. A bearded man wearing a very smart night-dress is seen rowing with great coolness in a boat from which all but the stern and the part immediately surrounding him has been shot away. It is praiseworthy at any time to row half a boat stern first, but to row it in addition with only one oar and that oar having a hairpin bend halfway up its handle and a blade like a banana-skin seems to me to constitute courage of the very highest order. The reason for the catastrophe which has overtaken the vessel is surely to be found in the Aplustre itself, a gigantic ornament of the "Present from Ramsgate" variety, which grows out of the stern like some vast malignant fungus and which, apart from unnerving the nearest oarsman by constantly threatening to catch in his hair, must have made the ship a ludicrously obvious target for enemy aircraft. The Aplustre, for the benefit of those who find it difficult to picture from my description, frequently consists of a sheaf of volutes.

As for the picture of the Aventail, no nursery should be without it. An aventail is of course "the flap, or movable part of a helmet in front for admitting air to the wearer." There, sure enough, is the wearer, caught in the very act of admitting air to himself and also relief and easement to a moustache which, by its grandiose proportions, must have suffered agonies of constriction behind the closed aventail, while adding enormously to the discomfort of the wearer by claiming every cranny of the available space.

I suppose my attachment to the picture of the Branks or Scold's Bridle is due not so much to the artistic merit of the picture itself as to the pleasant trains of thought which it induces. The branks are described as having a "hinged iron framework to enclose the head and a bit or gag to fit into the mouth and compress the tongue ." What a practical improvement on the flimsy meaningless feminine headgear of to-day! What a picture to merit pride of place on the kitchen mantel-piece!

And so by way of the pillory, the poleaxe and the porch, Stoke

Poges church, we come to what is perhaps my favourite picture of all, the Parbuckle. A parbuckle, in case you're not too sure, is "a purchase made by looping a rope in the middle to aid in rolling casks up and down an incline," and the character depicted parbuckling especially intrigues me not only because he helps to date the picture by his flowing hair, moleskin cap and drainpipe trousers, but also by the graceful nonchalance of his stance. He belongs to an era when people worked all day in picturesque attitudes for a few pence and had names like Silas Parbuckle. Nowadays, I've no doubt that parbuckling is performed by some noisy mechanical device and that the people who sit and watch it, or probably don't watch it, go on strike if they're not paid as much as a Cabinet Minister.

A picture I keep coming across is that of the Trepan, "a small cylindrical saw used in perforating the skull," or alternatively, "a powerful rock-boring tool." It always seems to me a most dangerous practice to have two such instruments with a single name. Imagine an inexperienced nurse on being asked by a harassed surgeon to pass the trepan handing him in her ignorance a powerful rock-boring tool. The possible consequences are too appalling even to consider. The likelihood of an error is not diminished by the artist having chosen to depict the trepan in a dense fog and having failed to indicate which of the two trepans the resulting "Nocturne" is intended to portray. He would have been on safer ground, I feel, had he given the trepan a miss and concentrated his talents on the salient features of the Trepang, which, as you can't possibly know, is a Malayan sea-slug much esteemed as a food delicacy in China.

The same sort of awkward mistake might well occur in the case of the Sedan Chair, which is described as "A covered chair for one or a barrow for fish." I should imagine that the two drunken-looking thugs in three-cornered hats here seen conveying a lady of quality into the heart of a mango swamp would be extremely vexed if they had been called out in the middle of a carousal to provide porterage for a pound of cod-steak.

Halfway through the S's, after a long pictureless phase punctuated only by a rather uninspiring portrait of two Spandrels, occurs the striking surrealist study entitled "Spatter-dashes." The eye is arrested by the sight of two neatly gaitered legs severed above the knee and poised in space with the toe of one shoe pointing ominously at the sentence "Spatulamancy—a method of divination by a sheep's shoulder-blade." The space which one might reasonably expect to find occupied by the remainder of the body is given over to a description of the Spatangus, "a family of irregular sea-urchins," and the Spatch-cock, "a fowel killed and immediately roasted or broiled for some sudden occasion."

I always find the picture of the viscount's coronet which brings this entrancing series to a close in the nature of an anticlimax. There is unfortunately no truth in the rumour that the oddly drawn velvet folds conceal a human face and that the picture should rightfully bear the caption—"Puzzle, find the viscount." Hence one cannot help feeling that the artist has rather missed his opportunity among the later letters. What glorious and unforgettable master-pieces might have been made of the Whiffletree or the Zobo (a creature whose lady, the Dsomo, languishes in the Supplement)! How the skill of the engraver might have been tried and have triumphed with such a subject as a Xylobalsamum or a Wykehamist! And why, oh, why no picture of the inscrutable Yggdrasil?

R. H. SLANEY

The Italicist

THE man turned to me suddenly and said "Can you talk in italics?"
I stared hard over his shoulder.
"I thought not," he said, "but I bet you can talk in CAPITALS."
I hastily looked round the bar, but no one appeared to have heard.

"Anyone can talk in CAPITALS," he said, "but italics, that's an art."

I finished my drink with a gulp that sounded like the swing doors of the saloon closing on each other, and made for the street.

"I shouldn't go out there if I were you."

I stopped and slowly turned. He was smiling. "It's raining cats and dogs, you know." His voice was friendly. "Come and have a drink. Landlord, two more please."

I returned to the bar.

"Listen to that crowd over there by the dartboard," he said, "all CAP—" I raised my hand—"all capitals. Not an italic between them. It's an art, I tell you."

He drained his glass. "Two more, landlord." He turned to me: "Listen to this."

He sauntered over to the corner and nodded once or twice. He looked at the chalked-up score and said: "It wouldn't pay to bet on the result of this game."

The players went on with their game.

He glanced round at me, then back to the scoreboard.

"It wouldn't pay to bet on the result of this game," he said, and abruptly rejoined me.

The little group of players stood as motionless as a dart that has just struck the board. Then their troubled eyes left the large "No Gambling" notice on the wall, piled a bonfire at the man's back, and sidled down to the landlord, who was peering anxiously over the counter at them.

"You see?" said the man. "Drink up. The same again, please."

When I looked again at the dart-players they were stirring a set of dominoes.

"And still talking in capitals," said the man contemptuously, following my gaze. "It's difficult to acquire, but not impossible. With practice anything can be achieved. *You believe that, don't you?"*

I nodded dumbly through the rim of my glass.

He leaned forward. *"You need another drink,"* he said slowly. He glanced over his shoulder, "SOMETHING SPECIAL," he added.

He must have seen something in my eyes. "I know," he said apologetically, "but they were only small ones."

He turned, "Landlord, the gentleman and myself need another drink. The special, *you know.*"

I began to like my friend. I told him so in very imperfect italics.

"And *I* like *you,*" he said, "you've got talent, *real talent.* You will pick it up in no time."

We sang a bit after that until I let him down by relapsing into capitals. The landlord admonished me with a genial *"Gentlemen!"*

My friend shook his head at the landlord's modulation.

I apologized profusely, and won an indulgent smile from my friend by inviting the landlord to share another bottle with us in ragged but earnest small caps.

My friend borrowed my watch to see the time. He said "Grea' heavens, my taxi! *I haven't paid him off yet.*"

I stood up and in generous capitals begged him to allow me. As he anchored me with reproving eyes, I flushed and repeated myself in subdued italics.

"*You,*" he said, accepting my wallet with charming dignity, "are a gentleman."

I bowed in acknowledgment and sat down suddenly.

Somewhere from the distant streets the muffled clamor of a fire engine reached me. The landlord spoke through a tea-towel. "Closing bell, sir." I raised my head. He looked me full in the glass: "The bill, sir. Your friend said you would settle up. *I hope we are not going to have any difficulty over it.*"

EDWIN NEWMAN

The Winkfield Award

I NEVER thought the day would come when I'd interview my old friend Dymchurch. He and I had made our modest starts in journalism together, and for a while he was no more prominent than

I, which is to say not prominent at all. Even recently he hadn't seemed to me to be doing anything out of the ordinary, and then, to my surprise, came his winning of the Winkfield Journalism Award for outstanding public service.

"It's an old story," he told me, "a cliché. I started low and worked up. Of course, I didn't realize it at the time, but looking back now I can see exactly how it began. It was my not interviewing somebody who won seventy-five thousand pounds in a football pool. That gave me my start.

"You can't plan these things," he went on. "It was pure accident, and so was the next step—not interviewing a woman who, in response to a newspaper advertisement, was about to travel five thousand miles to marry a man she'd never seen.

"Up to then, it was fairly routine stuff," he continued, "but it was the sort of experience that helps later on. You may recall that I became a war correspondent. I got to Chungking, and it was there that I never interviewed Chou En-lai. Later the opportunity arose of not interviewing Mao Tse-tung in a cave in Yenan."

"Which you took?" I asked.

"Oh, yes," he said, smiling with satisfaction. "By that time I was firmly on the road. Soon after, I did not submit a list of written questions to Stalin. War corresponding was a highly competitive business, you know. You have no idea what that did for my prestige."

"After hitting the high spots that way," I said, "it must have been difficult for you when the war ended."

"It was," he said. "I had to keep my hand in by not asking American tourists how they liked it here, and not asking G.I. brides who came back to see their families how they liked it there. It wasn't much, but it kept me from getting rusty. Then things took a turn for the better, and I was able not to interview Communists who changed their minds."

"So you were ready when the big chance came?" I asked.

"Absolutely," he said emphatically. "That's how I won the award. I told myself it was now or never, and then I went out and did not interview Tito. I don't like to boast, but I ask you, in all honesty, how many journalists, or non-journalists, for that matter, can make that claim?"

I admitted it was very few.

"Of course," he went on expansively, "there are some people who believe that the non-interview of Tito was *not* the best thing I've done. They think that came later, with my not interviewing Moussadek at his bedside. They may be right. I confess I don't know which I prefer myself. But the Winkfield people seem more impressed by the Tito thing. It *was* a bit of a coup."

"I suppose," I said, "that you feel there are no more worlds for you to conquer."

"There is that problem," he said. "But something always turns up. The big thing is to be ready for it." He lowered his voice. "You're an old friend," he said. "I can trust you. I've got something up my sleeve. I've noticed a few interviews with General Franco lately. That sounds like the beginning. I think an opportunity is building up there. It's a question of timing. I'll let a few months go by and then I'll do my stuff."

His eyes lit up, and he rubbed his hands gleefully. "It could be my greatest triumph," he said.

REV. R. LLEWELLYN LEWIS

-Back Flash

to try to arrive about two-fifths of the way through in order to come in at the beginning of the story. I am one of those people who loathe arriving at the cinema to find that the film started twenty minutes earlier. I used to find it so confusing not knowing who had done what or why, so I studied the times of showing displayed on a board at the entrance, and by careful calculation I was able to arrive just before the film began. Rather satisfactory you will agree, but then the people who make the films decided that the only way to tell a story nowadays was by means of a flashback, so now I have

In the Spring a Printer's Fancy

MANY writers make the mistake of thinking that all a printer can do is to string a lot of letters together in the order desired, put punctuation marks here and there, range the whole lot in columns and top off with a title in rather larger type. We experienced journalists, of course, know better than that, and frequently order italics (as you observe), **words in bold type,** tiny little words, or even such out of the way arrangements as whole sentences or paragraphs enclosed in a border or rule—"in a box" as we say.

This is a box

But even experienced journalists are apt to under-rate the printer's powers.

Having occasion recently to put some words in a box, I did not altogether care for the result when it was shown to me. There was a certain bleakness. "I suppose," I said, "you haven't any other kind of rule or border; something with a wiggle in it, say?" They took the box away, and when they brought it back again I was astounded.

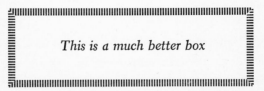

This is a much better box

I had never seen such a box, in all my twenty years' experience as a journalist. "Let it be used," I said, "subject of course to the

Editor's discretion if he happens to catch sight of it"; and shortly afterwards the great presses began to pour out copies of my beautiful box to a waiting world.

This incident emboldened me to ask the printers whether they had by any chance yet other rules or borders, and when they showed me what they had got I realized at once that I had been wasting my time. "Do you seriously mean to tell me," I asked, "that I can have this ～～～～ or this ⬧⬧⬧⬧ or even this ✕✕✕✕✕ ?" "By all means," they said. "How much," I asked, "can I have—of this ⌣⌣⌣⌣⌣⌣⌣ for instance?" "Any amount," they said. "Yards of it, if you like. Or, of course, there's this ❀❀❀❀❀ , which comes in several sizes."

"Bring pens, ink and paper," I said. "I want to create."

SPRINGTIME IN YOUR GARDEN

Now that the evenings are lengthening, the keen gardener will find plenty of work to occupy his spare time. In flower and vegetable garden alike there is much to be done, mowing has already begun in many parts of the country, and the work of trimming and tidying must not be forgotten if the treasures of full summer are to luxuriate to the best advantage.

Nothing is worse than an unsightly hedge and the shears should

by now be busily at work snipping off the winter's ragged growth to

ensure a good, even finish:

Variety is the keynote of a herbaceous border, and few will be content with a monotonous display of geum or dahlias. Mix your

favourites in bold groups and by the time the swallows come you will have a border that you can be proud of, just as printers have.

Do be on the look out at this time of the year for the tell-tale tracks

of that bane of the gardener's life, *Helix aspersa,* which comes out at dusk in formidable numbers

and may do untold damage. An ounce of soot now will save a pound of trouble later. Just sprinkle it lightly round, and your tender Alpines

will be safe from the ravages of this pest.

Here is a useful tip anent tool-shed management:

(No, no, printer—you've got the thing the wrong way up.)

Water-cans are often a nuisance unless properly stacked. Their arrangement in orderly rows is one of those tiresome but useful wet-weather tasks to which the scrupulous amateur gardener will set his hand before March is out. See that the spouts face right and left alternately as shown.

Onions should be set slanting—

I had got thus far, when the printers, who had shown a good

224

deal of interest in what I was up to (I suspect that they get tired
of interminable "e"s and "t"s and "s"s, with only an occasional
semi-colon to vary the monotony), intervened with the remark
that there was no need to confine myself to rules and borders unless
I so wished. They had other trifling decorative pieces that might be
of interest and even, they dared to say, of use.

"Such as?" I asked.

"  " they said.

Well!

"Or," they added, "  ."

While I was meditating on the thousands of words I have wasted
in my time trying to conjure up for my readers just such a dish of
fruit as this, they went away and fetched a kind of catalogue of
everything they had to offer. Kindly disregard my gardening hints
and begin again as follows.

MIDDLE-AGED WRITER THROWS BONNET OVER WINDMILL

There is not, for some reason, any electro (such words!) in the
catalogue illustrating the above incident. I fall back on this

which shows a bandy-legged artist drawing left-handed on a rock, while two waterfowl look on aghast. I like it better than another

one on the next page of the catalogue, which is either the front view of a bee, greatly enlarged, or the back view of a motor cyclist at speed. The ears are too big in either case.

Spring, I must not forget, is my theme; but, before we come to that, here is an example of what we journalists call montage:

The Brutal Sport of Pig-sticking
[*Note.—The finger of scorn is pointing the wrong way*]

When the sap is rising and all nature is astir, our thoughts turn naturally to the great outdoors, to sports and games, to quiet days by the river (though I use a smaller hook myself) and the fiercer excitements of cricket, tennis, bathing, or dancing by moonlight at Torquay and Bournemouth, all of which I could illustrate by electros had I the mind and the space to do it. Away with the dismal symbols of winter's discontent. Already the tireless chiffchaff sprinkles the woods with his reiterated call (*Printer! Where is the musical notation in*

this catalogue? Oh. Very well then). The chiffchaff is late this year, but already from copse and thicket comes the characteristic music of swans as they are driven through the undergrowth by

thoughtless urchins. The equinox has come and gone. The time for *al fresco* frisking is at hand.

There is an engraving of beehives in the catalogue that I should very much have liked to work in. But enough is enough; the vernal note has, in my submission, been fairly struck; and prudence sug-

gests that something be left for another time. Besides, the end of the page at last approaches. And so we say farewell to Cokernut Island—though not, if there is room for it, without a final flourish.

RICHARD MALLETT

Table-Talk of Amos Intolerable

"Years ago," said Amos, "I said, or I may have seen somewhere that somebody else had said—"

"No, no," we interjected.

"—that the phrase 'Far be it from me to be' now generally means 'I am.' The experience acquired since enables me to add now that anything beginning 'I make no apology for—' is, in fact, an apology, and that 'I flatter myself' means exactly what it says."

I have already mentioned how Amos would sometimes go to enormous pains in order to achieve a small momentary effect. I recall one day when he spent a tediously long time emphasizing his taste for grated cheese—purely, as we deduced afterwards, to have a plausible excuse for bringing in the following evening a small parcel which he said was a cheese-grater that he had just bought. After a time I perceived that beside this parcel on the table was another of similar appearance, but it did not strike me at once that this too belonged to Amos and had been put there unobtrusively to act as a prop in a small dramatic scene to be staged when he left. I realized this only when he rose to leave earlier than usual, making for the door with unaccustomed briskness, and paying no attention to two separate yells of "You forgot your parcels."

The battered door clacked behind him and someone was about to go in pursuit when Amos stuck his head in again and said "Give me that parcel, will you?"—as if this were the first mention of the subject.

The answer he wanted, we later realized, was "Which?" but unfortunately we hadn't been rehearsed. The man who was standing up said "Aren't they both yours? I thought—"

Momentarily checked, Amos swallowed—keeping his head stuck in the same stiff position round the door—and said "I—er—no, give me *that* one."

He still gave no hint which he meant and the other man said testily, "I thought they were *both* yours!" at the same time picking one up and scrutinizing it for marks. "Here, is this the one you want?"

With a bad grace Amos came in again and took one of the parcels. "You ought to have known," he almost mumbled, "that I should want whichever was the grater," and then he gave the whole show away by ordering another drink and getting back into his seat.

Occasionally Amos could be wounded by a critic. I remember he was once for a considerable period exercised in mind over a rather snooty review in one of the weeklies which began with the down-right statement "Mr. Intolerable, like all professional cynics, is absolutely incapable of recognizing sincerity when he sees it." Amos very much resented the suggestion that there was anything at all he was incapable of recognizing, and his first reaction was—since he acknowledged the validity of the proposition that a consistent and invariable cynic *would* fail to recognize sincerity—to declare that there was no such thing as sincerity, anyway. A little loud argument seemed to convince him that this position was untenable and he made the only other possible alternative plea: that he was not a professional cynic. In an effort to lend verisimilitude to his contention he assumed his near-cherubic look, the effect of which was spoiled by his having so often before used it to raise a laugh.

"Even I," he insisted, "have my gentle moments. If a dog came in now, I would stroke it."

At that moment—truth, as you know, does not have to be as careful as fiction to avoid questionable coincidences—a man came in with an enormous red-eyed murderous-looking Great Dane, which bared a large proportion of its fangs at the company; and Amos added, as if he were finishing his sentence, "—except that this doesn't happen to *be* one of my gentle moments."

WHEN somebody remarked that it was a very long time since we had seen a certain well-known writer of detective-stories, Amos said "Oh, surely you know what happened to him? Why, it was in the papers."

We said we hadn't noticed it. Amos leaned forward and said very solemnly *"The mantle of Edgar Wallace fell on him.* Naturally, he's been out of sight ever since."

"Odd that the person who says he would be the *last* to say something or other," said Amos, avoiding the eye of a character who had a minute or two before used this very phrase, "is so often, by definition, the first."

After a pause, he stroked his nose and added with a modest air "Though I should be the last to suggest—"

"As for me," he said shortly afterwards, when deeds of heroism were under discussion, "I propose to die in my bed, like a vindictive oyster."

"The amount of the premium placed by the average person on stupidity," observed Amos one evening when he was in a very withering mood, "may be gauged from one of his favourite phrases, which implies that it is rather a dishonourable thing—at least, that it makes one worthy of contempt—to be quite sure on which side one's bread is buttered."

Amos had got up to leave one evening during some talk about a new book that only he, of all those present, happened to have read. He paused at the door in a way indicating that he had prepared some remark about it which he was determined not to allow anybody to cap.

"I could give you a summary," he said, getting outside the door and sticking his head in, "but it would be pretty wintry," and disappeared.

His ruthlessness when he feels disinclined to be bored is considerable, though he does, sometimes, regret it afterwards. One evening, when a fat man in a small round hat showed signs of being about to monopolize the ear of the company for a time, Amos got up, went to the bar and brought back an ill-looking acquaintance who had appeared to be diffidently standing apart. Holding the arm of this unfortunate and pointing at him with his other hand, Amos said to the fat man (who was in the middle of a sentence): "Did he ever tell you about his operation?"

Then he sat down, ostentatiously looking at neither of them. It was only the noisy irruption of a seller of evening papers that prevented quite an uncomfortable silence.

He will never admit to having a hangover. "Well," he said on one occasion, the day after a rowdy evening when everyone had drunk rather more than usual, "perhaps I did feel this morning a *little* . . . I'll tell you how it was: I felt that everything I looked at, while unquestionably motionless and in the right place, had reached it—after being an inch or two above or below—just one-fifth of a second before."

I remember the way he described the methods of the author of a recently-published critical biography. "He reminds me irresistibly of a policeman, at dusk," said Amos. "He plods gloomily through the chap's work, not with any active appearance of suspicion—that would make it *interesting*—but just grimly, as a matter of routine, trying all the doors."

Detected one evening swallowing a pill (he had asked for a separate glass of water, and this had aroused our curiosity), Amos defended himself, though gloomily, with some references to H. L. Mencken. "Mencken gives you the impression," he observed, "that the average literary man will always be found keeping himself alive by means of patent medicines. I must look that up again: it's very true." This was asking for it, because there was present at the time a particularly hearty, ruddy, robust man who seldom loses an opportunity of (figuratively) beating his chest and saying how wonderful life is. Amos has always looked upon him sourly, if at all.

"Nonsense!" cried this man (whose reputation was built up on essays of an uplifting type and books of cheerful middlebrow no-intellectual-nonsense criticism). "That may be all very well for puling abnormalities, but not for writers who live a full, natural life, in touch with nature. Fresh air! Regular exercise! Health-giving sport! Less of this brooding on the sorrows of the world! That's what the average literary man needs, not medicine. Look at me!"

Amos was looking at him, but gave no sign of having heard—or, indeed, seen. "Some of us need incessant stimulants," he murmured, as if continuing his first remarks without interuption, "and in the case of others," he paused for a moment, "only considerable doses of sedative could make life a little more bearable . . . for everybody else."

I recall another occasion when Amos had been discussing this matter and another man—forgetting that he was, for some reason, in disgrace—made the mistake of expressing agreement.

"Yes," this character said, very sadly. "We all take patent medicines to keep alive. I've been taking four or five for many years."

Amos said nastily "Ah, but in your case have they had the desired result?"

"I'm holding out against the temptation to be shown over a chocolate factory," he remarked to our surprise towards the end of the evening (but not so much to our surprise as if it had been near the beginning), "until, like Johnson, I have a Negro servant."

When our looks of inquiry had mounted up to his satisfaction he went on: "I wish him to be able to say to people 'Massa's seen the cocoa ground.'"

R. G. G. PRICE

Quiet Pleasures Are the Best

MR. BADDLEBRIG was parson of the village of ——ham, and one T—day evening in Ju— as he sat in the rectory parlour with his family about him he said "Well, my dear ones, what is it to be to-night, Forfeits, Progressive Backgammon or Verses?" "Verses, Papa," said a childish treble from the window-seat, and, assent to the proposal being eagerly accorded by all present, verses became the diversion for the night. For a quarter of an hour no sound was to be heard save the scratching of pens, until, with a quizzical glance at his silver repeater, Mr. Baddlebrig announced that the time allowed for composition had elapsed and that the slip of paper he drew from the urn at his side contained the name of none other than Master Benjamin Baddlebrig himself.

With somewhat of a hangdog mien Master Benjamin read the following to the attentive ears of his audience:

HOMAGE TO JOHANNES GUTENBERG
You were the first of the lot,
J. G.
An achievement quite devilish hot,
J. G.
If you hadn't occurred
Should we ever have heard
Of Caxton or Pynson or Wynkyn de Worde?
The answer is "Certainly not"
J. G.
The answer is "Certainly not."

"The fourth line exceeds the limits of prosodic licence," said Mr. Baddlebrig severely, but at the tears which started to Master Benjamin's eyes he relented and added good-humouredly, "Even Skelton was not impeccable."

The lot next fell upon Mr. Timothy Fittle, the curate, who, with a look of embarrassed adoration at the eldest Miss Baddlebrig, recited:

OPUS NINETEEN
It was an Old Knight
And he lived in a tomb,

Revising his Will
And abusing the gloom.
To him came Merryman
Bearing a lamp;
And the Knight then complained
That the tomb was too damp.

"Capital," exclaimed Mr. Baddlebrig, slapping his thigh, "rum-punch all round. Now who have we next? Why, it is Sairey-Anne." So, with many a blush and giggle and many a prompting from her brother to "Speak up and not be a Juggins," Sairey-Anne declaimed:

A DESPERATE CRY

Oh, Flanagan, do not serve any more potheen to Rosemary. As
  her grandmother and guardian I must beg you to desist.
None of the money in her reticule is legal tender.
I have essayed to wean her from passing snide, but as long as you
  continue to serve her she is likely to persist.

"A tricksome metre, handled not without aplomb," commented Mr. Baddlebrig approvingly. Then amid intent expectation another slip was withdrawn and, after scanning it with whimsical deliberation, the Master of Ceremonies called upon—himself. Thereupon, with a modicum of hemming and hawing, he uttered the following:

PRANKSOME PRUE

Say, pardner, didya onct hear tell
Of Prudence, as was Murphy's gel?
If ya did, I'd take it kind
To give me the facks for they's 'scaped ma mind.

"Admirable, Papa!" cried the family circle. "You are the best of us all." "Innate gifts are no proper subject for laudation," Mr. Baddlebrig rebuked them gently, and called upon Miss Rebecca Baddlebrig, a somewhat soured spinster of uncertain temper, who, with a defiant sniff, proclaimed:

Who walks by the dockside
In furs and peroxide
Was once a daughter
And purveyed laughter.

After the applause had subsided, Mr. Baddlebrig remarked judiciously, "A little old-fashioned, perchance, but none the worse for that. Many such a verse had we by heart when I was at college and the earlier publications of Messrs. Faber and Faber were coming hot from the press."

The next to present a contribution to the entertainment of the company was little Jenny Baddlebrig, who sat perched on the fender, smoothing her pinafore and pouting her rosy lips. Tremulously she piped:

PENSÉE

Where the bee sucks, there suck I,
So I find the blossoms dry.
Nothing of me but will fade,
If I live alone much longer in this bee-loud glade.

All were vastly pleased by these lines, and praises were showered upon the demurely lowered head of the small poetess. When Mr. Baddlebrig decreed that the evening's festivities must shortly draw to a close there was a chorus of respectful protests; but he insisted that only one poem more should see the light before the hour struck at which the rules of health enjoined retirement. There was great jubilation when the last slip disclosed the name of Mrs. Baddlebrig, best of wives and mothers and a lady honoured as widely as she was loved. With her wonted serene composure she put down her needlework and in a low, sweet voice of crystal clearness read:

REMINISCENT QUATRAIN

Full many a noble elm and graceful oak
Did I fall out of when I lived in Stoke,
What time the cold North Wind festooned with icicles
The beards of potters on enormous tricycles.

With quietly shining faces her loved ones threw themselves upon The-Dearest-Mother-That-Ever-Was to enfold her proudly to their bosoms. Then Mr. Baddlebrig rose to his feet and pronounced the conclusion of what all agreed had been one of the jolliest evenings they had known.

COMM. A. H. BARTON, R.N.

Dogback

"IT SEEMS to be a long time since I told anyone a shaggy dog story," said Cranmer.

"It doesn't seem long enough yet," said Purbright's wife.

"There aren't any left to tell," said Purbright.

"Yet it may be," said Cranmer, "that there is one that I know which neither of you knows."

"What of it?" asked Purbright's wife.

"There's the original one," said Purbright, "about the shaggy dog which was lost. There's the pigeon which was late for dinner because it was such a nice night it thought it would walk. There's the cricketing horse; there's the horse that, to the consternation of its rider, got a foreleg up into a stirrup-iron—"

"'If you're coming up,'" quoted Cranmer, nodding, "'then I'm coming down.'"

"I don't want to hear about any of them," said Purbright's wife.

"And then there's the horrible one about the dead horse in the bath," said Purbright.

"I don't believe," said Cranmer, after a pause, "that you know the one about the knight in armour and the St. Bernard dog."

"No?" said Purbright's wife.

"On guest nights in wardroom messes I have made it last for twenty-seven minutes."

"Oh?" said Purbright.

"This knight was caught in a blizzard, without his horse, on the side of a steep Alp. Wearily he clambered upwards through the darkness."

"Did he have a banner with a strange device?" asked Purbright.

"Yes," said Cranmer. "Excalibur."

"Why," asked Purbright's wife, "—why should you do this to me just after I've given you all that lovely macaroni cheese?"

"Perhaps that's why he is doing it," said Purbright, guffawing.

"You guffawed, Purbright," exclaimed his wife, aghast. "I have never known you do that before."

"I'm practising," said Purbright. "I shall have to do it at the end of this story."

Cranmer forged on. "The knight was in great distress," he said. "His tiny mailed fist was frozen; the snow had worked its way inside his armour and was rusting his chain-mail; his banner, device and all, was frozen as hard as a board; and his helmet-plume was just another stalagmite—"

"Stalactite," corrected Purbright.

"Just another stalagmite," said Cranmer, firmly. "However, even as he was about to collapse, a St. Bernard dog appeared, as large as life—"

"And twice as shaggy," said Purbright's wife, restlessly.

"As large as life," repeated Cranmer. "With the usual small barrel under its chin. 'Mount upon my back, Sir Knight,' said the dog, sturdily, 'and we will search for shelter together.' Gratefully the knight mounted the dog and soon the strange combination was pressing forward up the side of the Alp. Hours later, the barrel long since empty, they came exhausted to a small building at the head of a pass. The knight edged his tired mount up to the door and knocked. The door opened two inches and a surly eye and nose appeared. 'Whaddya want?' they said. 'Shelter from the storm, prithee, for this poor dog and myself,' said the knight, raising his visor with an effort. 'Not on your life,' was the answer and the door slammed. The St. Bernard, which had tried to insert a foreleg into the doorway, was nipped and gave a short desperate yelp. The knight's visor dropped over his face again. 'I wouldn't do that to a *knight*,' he said in tones of muffled dejection, 'on a dog like this.'"

"Wouldn't do that to a what?" asked Purbright's wife.

"To a *knight*," said Cranmer, "on a *dog* like this. Transposition, see?"

Purbright guffawed.

In the Throes of Living

MAN AGAINST THE OTHER ANIMALS

COLIN HOWARD

Ascension and Declination of Sirius

THERE was enormous excitement when it became known that
"they" were shooting a scene for a film outside a large house
locally. After breakfast I decided I would stroll along for a look
with Marcus, my St. Bernard dog.

I have complained about Marcus in *Punch* before. He is huge,
handsome and affable. He is also incredibly stupid and super-
naturally lazy. I allowed him his usual half-hour siesta after breakfast to recover from the strain of getting up, and then summoned
him for his walk. He lurched to his feet with a sigh of self-pity, and
stumbled somnambulistically after me.

As a rule, we go only as far as the first corner, by which time
we are both tired out—Marcus with the exertion, myself with the
effort of keeping him going. When, after some argument, I made
it clear to him we were going even farther afield this morning his
reproachful eyes filled with tears.

The scene was one of frantic activity. A throbbing mobile gen-
erator roared deafeningly in a corner of the big garden. Herds of
technicians were shoving around a camera built like a self-pro-
pelled gun, unreeling tape-measures, training things like search-
lights, fooling about with yellow reflector-screens, swilling mugs of
tea, and bustling about apparently just for the sake of looking
busy. The spectacle of so much energy had a depressing effect on
Marcus, and, realizing he was about to pass out on his flipper-like
feet, I turned to take him home.

We hadn't got far when I heard somebody shouting and walking to catch us up. You don't have to run to catch up a man with
a St. Bernard. I straightened my tie. Just at first, I confess, I
thought—but it wasn't me; it was Marcus.

"Say!" said a young man with tousled hair and horn-rimmed glasses. "That's quite a dog!"

Marcus is responsive to admiration. He simpered, and even pranced a bit in a galumphing sort of way.

"We could use him," said the young man. "Would you hire him for the day for a couple of guineas?"

I said I would, and was instructed to bring Marcus back in a couple of hours. Two hours to get Marcus home, rest him up, and bring him back, was cutting it fine. We were nearly a quarter-mile from home. However, we set off. My wife was wildly excited by our news. She and I both went to work to groom Marcus for stardom.

It is not easy to groom a dog who is lying under the kitchen table in a state of physical prostration, but, with my wife on her knees on one side, myself on the other, and our heads meeting under the table, we managed to get him done, all except the bits of himself he was lying on.

Then came the terrific task of getting him back on location. We accomplished this by a little mild deceit. We pretended he had slept the clock round twice and it was now to-morrow. My wife came with us, partly because she wasn't going to miss Marcus's triumph, partly to push behind.

"We're shooting a crowd-scene—a garden-party," explained the director. He paused and tugged at his foot, on which Marcus had subsided in slumber. My wife and I deferentially prised up the appropriate portion of Marcus's body, and the director, having withdrawn his foot and found to his surprise no bones were broken, continued: "I want him to mingle with the crowd. I suggest your wife waves to him from the other side, and you release him when I nod and let him walk across the set."

At the word "walk" Marcus shuddered in his sleep.

My wife and I worked on Marcus like a couple of seconds on a boxer who has been saved by the bell. We got him to his feet, and I managed to hold him up while my wife took up her position. When the director nodded she waved and I let go of Marcus.

He fell down, bumping his nose, and went to sleep.

"What's the matter—is he ill?" demanded the director.

"No, no—it's just temperament," I laughed.

"Right, now! We're going to shoot this time!"

The hubbub was quadrupled. Men yelled "Okay!" at each other through a network of telephones. Buzzers sounded. Two lads without shoes shoved the camera slowly forward. The recording-men dangled microphones on things like fishing-rods overhead. All the extras in their smart clothes minced and smiled. The clapper-boy stepped in front of the camera, exclaimed "Scene 92, Take 1," snapped his board, and stepped back.

"Shoot!" cried the director, and nodded at me.

Marcus took a game five steps forward towards my wife, faltered, and slumped to the ground. The cruising camera bumped into him and bounced back.

"Cut!" cried the director.

By late afternoon the clapper-boy was still the only one to have made anything like an extended appearance before the camera. After the first half-dozen takes we gave up trying to get Marcus away from scratch, and let him carry on from where he'd lain down last time. He was still only a third of the way across the set.

The clapper-boy took a voice-pastille, hoarsely recited "Scene 92, Take 21," and retired to get his chalk ready for Take 22. The director grimly muttered "Shoot!" I don't think he really expected anything to happen. But it did. My wife, seeing fame and fortune slipping from Marcus, had been inspired. She had found a cat and was holding it out enticingly.

Cats and food are the only things that ever induce Marcus to work like a real dog. I believe he confuses the two. He sighted the bait in my wife's arms. When the director said "Shoot!" he shot.

If Scene 92, Take 21, ever gets as far as the can the rushes will show a dazzling and aristocratic garden-party apparently smitten by a typhoon. One will see fair women and brave men, grave foot-men and laden tea-trays, bowled over left and right by some mysterious agency moving too fast for the camera. My wife popped the cat into safety behind a wall with a split second to spare.

Marcus hurtled into the wall, which rocked a bit but stood up well. My wife and I, just for a change, went around picking up extras.

And then the sun went in and rain-spots began to fall.

"Thank heaven!" said the director devoutly. "That's all for to-day. Same time to-morrow, please."

"Ask him if he wants Marcus again to-morrow," whispered my wife.

I glanced at the director, and decided not to. I took my wife's hand, and we started to sneak away.

"Please don't forget your dog," said the director.

Marcus of course was in his usual position—flat on the ground, resting. The extras bore no malice. They realized they had Marcus to thank for another day's work. They helped us to lift him more or less tenderly into the bus waiting to take them to the station and he was driven home in style, occupying three seats and a couple of laps, and absolutely insensible. They thought he had been stunned by the wall. They did not understand St. Bernards.

Marcus is now slowly recovering from his tremendous day, on the front doormat where the extras dumped him. His film-career, I cannot help feeling, is at an end.

RODNEY HOBSON

Horse-Coper

"You understand horses," said Miss Scantling. "Do try to persuade that wretched animal of the greengrocer's not to stand on the pavement. It *will* breathe in one's face so."

"Of course, Miss Scantling," I said keenly. I happened to know that Miss Scantling had begun casting for *The Pirates of Penzance* and I was determined to hang on to my rather precarious position among the gentlemen of the chorus.

"While you're doing that," she went on, "I'm going to pop in here and change my books." She hooked a bulging shopping basket over my arm, turned on one of her splendid rubber heels and strode into the public library.

I took stock of the horse. It had the appearance of an animal that has been standing on pavements since infancy, and I began to wonder whether I was right in trying to break it of the habit. Might I not induce some fearful neurosis that would make it hate society even more than it did at the moment? It was not a risk I was prepared to take, and I decided to let the matter drop. Then I noticed Miss Scantling watching me from the door of the library. I walked boldly to the spot where the horse should have been standing and clicked my fingers.

"Coop! Coop!" I said.

I had once seen a Suffolk Punch gallop three hundred yards across a field in answer to a somewhat similar call, but its effect on the greengrocer's horse was disappointing. I tried an abbreviated version.

"Coop!" I said.

The horse looked round. It had mean little eyes and a loose under-lip. I repeated the finger-clicking, backed by a magnetic smile. Sneering, the horse turned its attention to the pavement again and snapped at a passing clergyman.

That was enough for me. I put down the shopping basket and walked right up to the beast. Laying hold of a kind of jackstay that ran aft from under its chin, I gave a sharp tug. The jackstay broke. While I was trying to tie the ends together the horse seized one of the buttons of my raincoat between its teeth and began to suck it noisily.

It took me some time to free myself, for the button was firmly sewn on and the clasp-knife I borrowed from a boy in the crowd turned out to be exceedingly blunt. I glanced quickly at the library and saw Miss Scantling in the middle of a little knot of interested spectators. She waved to me. I waved back. Misinterpreting my action, the horse threw up its head and caught me a violent blow under the chin.

I was groping my way to the back of the cart when my hand

encountered the carrots. Chiding myself for not having thought of this method before, I picked out three of the largest I could find, left sixpence deposit on the tailboard and went back to the horse. In my absence it had moved through an angle of one hundred and eighty degrees and was now facing directly across the High Street.

The owner of the first car in the queue took the delay philosophically, but a van-driver who had walked up from the back was inclined to be aggressive. Fortunately the greengrocer himself arrived a few moments later and between us we straightened things out. Then we set to work to extricate the horse's off fore-hoof from Miss Scantling's shopping basket . . .

I am free for amateur operatics this winter if anyone wants me.

RODNEY HOBSON

Hen Party

I CAN see no reason why hens should be afraid of me. But they are. Horribly afraid. Let me so much as approach a hen-run and in a flash the occupants will be forming a pyramid of quivering poultry in the furthermost corner. The weaker ones just sag to the ground in a dead faint.

So when my new neighbour Wildgoose put his head over the

fence and asked me if I would look after his hens while he was away, my first instinct was to refuse. "Be honest," said my better self; "tell him what happened when you looked after his predecessor's hens. Tell him that the very mound on which he is standing conceals the body of a Buff Orpington which guillotined itself under the trap-door of the hen-house rather than face your ministrations a day longer. Tell him," it bleated, "about the two that escaped into the woods and are now living, enemies of society, in a hollow tree and terrorizing half the county!"

"Look here, Wildgoose—" I began.

"Of course," said Wildgoose, "you're welcome to the odd egg."

I elbowed my better self to one side. "All right, old man," I said. "I'll be glad to look after the little beggars for you."

If anyone thinks I enjoyed the rest of that week he is wrong. It was sheer purgatory. Nevertheless, when the first morning of my incumbency arrived, I faced the ordeal like a man. Carrying the fragrant mess of pottage which my wife had been assembling during the week, I let myself in at the front door of the Wildgoose home with the key he had left me. The first thing I did was to open all the windows on the ground floor and turn the radio on at full boost. I didn't want the hens to think that this was anything but a normal Sunday morning.

I then went to the mirror in the hall and began to make myself up to look as much like Wildgoose as possible. I deepened the lines about my mouth, added a touch of grey to the temples and, to complete the picture, rubbed just a suspicion of rouge into the tip of my nose. I studied the result critically. It was good. I stuck my teeth out over my lower lip in a hideous grin. Perfect. I *was* Wildgoose.

I took my neighbor's noisome overalls from behind the kitchen door and slipped them on. Then I crammed his unspeakable gardening hat on to my head. With a quickening of the pulse I seized the steaming bowl of hen-food and flung open the kitchen door.

Not more than twenty yards separated me from the hen-run, but they were twenty yards crammed with suspense. One false move now and the whole subterfuge would fail. The hens were, of course, still shut in their sleeping-quarters, but I was taking no chances. I even went so far as to simulate my neighbor's shambling walk, which I had been practising behind locked doors for some days previously.

I let myself into the hen-run and made the Wildgoose kind of clucking noise. From inside the sleeping-quarters came the sound of hens surfacing from sleep. Twisting my face into the nearest approach I could manage to my neighbor's normal expression, I opened the trap-door.

There was a moment's silence. Then the leader of the herd put its head out and looked at me. This was the crucial moment. I met its gaze without flinching. The bird withdrew, apparently to re-assure the others, for the next moment they came stepping gingerly down the gang-plank, peering at me through sleep-blurred eyes.

I made more Wildgoose noises of encouragement and threw great gobbets of food among the seething poultry. The more daring characters seized avidly upon the food. But others stood about in little groups, muttering under their breath. There was a nasty feeling of suspicion in the air.

It was then that I had one of those flashes of inspiration. Bending down, I picked up the largest stone I could find and flung it vigorously into my own garden. Any doubt that may have lingered in the hens' minds was dispelled by that one simple action and the crash of greenhouse glass that followed it. I *was* Wildgoose.

I watched them for a few moments and then turned and left the hen-house, shutting the door behind me. Conscious that one or two of the warier birds were still keeping an eye on me, I took care to remain in character as I went back up the garden path. I even stopped to remove a vital part from my own lawn-mower and tread it nonchalantly into the ground. It was one of those brilliant little bits of "business" that can lift a minor rôle to greatness.

At that moment the man who lives on the other side of Wildgoose came out into his garden and spotted me. "Good grief,

Frobisher!" he said loudly. "What on earth are you doing in *that* get-up?"

I did not have to look round. I could hear the flurry of wings behind me as Wildgoose's hens clawed their way over the perimeter wire and flapped away in tight V-formation to the south.

ARTHUR P. JACOBS

The Swimming Lesson

"CAN'T swim?" shouted Harrison, with such a sharp note of incredulity that several people looked out of windows in the houses opposite. "Why, bless my soul, *every* dog can swim. Some need more encouragement than others, that's all." He glanced appraisingly at Cæsar, who returned the look with interest. Having mutually sized each other up they decided to put the matter to the test.

My wife and I and Harrison accompanied Cæsar to the boating pond in the park, and on the way I pointed out to Harrison that he was attempting the impossible. I said I had tried many, many times to get Cæsar into the water, but it usually ended by the procedure being reversed. Harrison asked in superior tones how I set about it. I said I waited until Cæsar's attention was fully occupied elsewhere, then I crept up behind him and gave a sudden push. Harrison remarked that the method was crude and certainly unscientific. Any fool should know that an animal jumps sideways when pushed from behind. He said it was an instinctive reaction and that I deserved to have a ducking because of my inexcusable ignorance of such matters.

During our walk to the park Cæsar must have been surreptitiously inviting other dogs to come along, for by the time we reached the water's edge we found ourselves at the head of a pro-

cession which stretched for fifty yards or more behind us. It was a
a quiet, orderly procession—intent upon enjoying itself later on.
I've known a crowd converging on a football ground to show similar signs of suppressed excitement.

Harrison said the great thing was to put the dog at ease; then
it became sufficiently self-confident to jump in of its own accord.
I pointed out that Cæsar always appeared to have self-confidence
in over-abundance, but Harrison didn't hear—he was down on one
knee beside Cæsar, whispering encouragement in his right ear.
Apparently this tickled the beast, for after a moment it started to
scratch itself, taking Harrison by surprise so that he toppled over
backwards. As if they regarded this as a curtain-raiser all the other
dogs moved forward into better positions around the pond. Their
tongues lolled out expectantly and several of the more excitable
ones set up a shrill yapping.

Cæsar finished scratching, investigated the recumbent Harrison,
and after sniffing at him for a second or two blew in his face. Harrison struggled into an upright position, shooed away a dozen or
more of the nearest spectators, and having patted Cæsar to show
he bore him no ill-will told him to sit down. Cæsar sat down and
winked at the other dogs; then he put his face to the sky and
howled. Cæsar's howling wasn't a pretty sound, and Harrison
turned round to ask me sharply if the dog were ill. I said no he
wasn't ill, he always made that noise when he wanted to play.
Harrison said that a bit of discipline might do Cæsar a lot of
good; then he went down on one knee again and all the dogs assumed expressions of pleasurable anticipation.

Harrison put one arm around Cæsar and pointed with his other
to the distant shore opposite. He appeared to be exhorting the
animal to deeds of heroism by making an impassioned recital of
some ancient saga. Cæsar suddenly jumped to his feet, backed
from under Harrison's caressing touch and led a yelling cohort of
canine friends around the edge of the pond on a furious sortie—
the main purpose of which was to take a look at the enemy Harrison had told them lurked on the far side. To save himself from
pitching into the water Harrison flung out his other hand and

thereby made unexpected and violent contact with a passing mongrel of immense proportions, who first gave a yelp of surprise and then made a wide circle around him, glaring back over its shoulder every few steps and hurling a mixture of threats and derision in his direction.

By the time Harrison had risen to his feet again Cæsar and his company of desperadoes had completed the circuit of the pond and were now clustered around their human friend, noisily pointing out to him that he had been in error in supposing there to be anything wrong over yonder.

Harrison discouraged a few of the more enthusiastic animals with his foot, and then singled Cæsar out from among the crowd pressing so thickly about him. Cæsar sat down again and the others sorted themselves out, with their attention divided equally between Harrison and a private fight which suddenly started immediately behind him. Harrison waved his walking-stick about like a conductor of a symphony orchestra, the individual performers of which had gone completely mad. Dogs flew from him on all sides, and when quiet was finally restored only six others besides Cæsar remained. All the survivors sat on their haunches and licked their lips in an effort to appear quite at ease.

Then, very gently, Harrison placed the stick in Cæsar's mouth. Cæsar looked surprised at this and wagged his tail. He had half expected a whack over the head, and Thor having offered him his thunderbolt instead successfully calmed his doggy fears. Harrison removed the stick, backed a few paces and put it down on the ground; then he called Cæsar and told him to pick it up. After this had been repeated several times Cæsar began to look as though Harrison had taken leave of his senses—but he cheerfully continued to oblige all the same. Until, that is, Harrison snatched away the stick from under his nose and hurled it across the pond to the far bank. Cæsar at once let out a bark of consternation, which effectively summoned the remaining dogs to his side, then led them off *round* the pond once more.

This time the mass idea seemed to approximate more to the

running of a friendly race than the making of a warlike sortie. Two dogs soon gained the lead, and when the whole company reached the other side Cæsar could do no better than hold grimly on to third place. A Manchester terrier seized hold of Harrison's stick, swung round happily and pushed the end of it into a companion's face, then made off at a brisk pace towards the distant gates. Most of the other dogs gave up the chase after a minute or two, each making its separate way homewards. The general feeling seemed to be that a good time had been had by all and there was little merit in flogging a dead horse—Harrison couldn't reasonably be expected to provide any more fun. But they didn't know Harrison.

Within a quarter of an hour he had not only retrieved his stick but was once more down on his knees at Cæsar's side by the edge of the water. He tried placing the stick a number of times in Cæsar's mouth, and then, with much bravado, threw it into the middle of the pond. Cæsar first looked shocked—then anxious. He trotted round the edge several times in a helpless kind of way, then finally rushed off howling as though the devil were after him.

It took us some time to convince Harrison that if his stick really were valuable he had better wade in after it. We finally achieved success by instilling confidence into him. As the park-keeper said when we fetched him along, the pond was an artificial one with a good concrete bottom, and in no place was it more than a foot deep. He said it had been kept shallow on purpose. In summer the kids could paddle, and the dogs weren't tempted to go swimming in it as they would have been if the water was any deeper.

D. H. BARBER

The Mouse

I FIRST saw him one evening while I was having a late supper of soup and Disraeli. Years ago an uncle left me the six-volume edition of Monypenny and Buckle's *Disraeli*, and as I have often dallied with the idea of becoming Prime Minister myself when I get a little more leisure, I have been steadily wading through it, though oddly enough the only time I feel in the mood for Disraeli is when I am eating or drinking tinned soup (I offer the choice of verbs because vegetable is mostly eating and tomato purely drinking) late at night. This I do in the kitchen of my flat, and last night I was just helping Disraeli purchase the Suez Canal when I looked round to locate a pea that had dropped from my spoon and saw that it had fallen on the floor, where a very small mouse was playing football with it.

If anybody had asked me whether I was frightened of mice or not I should have given a manly laugh and said was it likely that a man who had shot lion (or rather *at* lion) would be frightened of a mouse? But of course lions do not stroll into the kitchen in the middle of the night and start playing football with peas.

On seeing the mouse I rose hastily to my feet, my knees lifting the table approximately two inches and covering with vegetable soup a letter from Queen Victoria and some rather acid remarks by Gladstone. At this my fear turned to rage and I picked up my folding book-rest (a very clever contraption of the sort that should be provided in all restaurants now that the large old-fashioned cruet has gone out) and hurled it at the mouse, who muttered what sounded like a sneering laugh and dashed away.

I am not easily beaten, so I filled a small bowl with water, covered it with a sheet of manuscript (on which was written the carbon copy of an abortive letter to *The Times* with a very clever joke about the Lion and the Unicorn), and then balanced half my weekly cheese ration carefully in the middle of the paper. I retired to bed and found in the morning that though the cheese had sunk to the bottom the mouse was not with it.

Since then he has appeared every night at the same time, to watch me eat my supper. He does not approach very closely, and I think it can hardly be possible that he also wishes to peruse Monypenny and Buckle. Even supposing the likelihood of a mouse with literary leanings, he could, if he insisted on Monypenny and Buckle, quite easily start with Volume I on the shelf in the other room, when neither of us would disturb the other.

On the second evening I controlled myself and pretended not to notice him for a moment. Then, very quietly, I dropped a pea just by my foot. He scuttled towards it, and I seized a heavy poker which I had in readiness and brought it down with tremendous force, missing the mouse by a mere couple of inches and hitting the large chilblain on my big toe. After scraping soup from a rather stormy interview with Bismarck I retired to bed feeling that the mouse had won Round II.

On the third evening I had to change my tactics. Even the greatest generals are dependent on the weapons at their disposal, and Field-Marshal Montgomery, for instance, would not have been able to throw tanks at the enemy unless he had some tanks in stock. I was in an exactly parallel position. No peas. The last tin of vegetable soup had gone, and I had been obliged to fall back on tomato. I determined to make the great sacrifice, and

254

when the mouse appeared on the third evening, with a quick jerk of the wrist I deluged him with soup. Apart from a few spots that made the Irish Situation even more obscure than it had been previously, the mouse got it all, and retreated. I retired to bed hungry, but feeling rather like Wellington must have felt after Waterloo. If I knew anything about mice, I thought, I had seen the last of him.

Apparently I do not know anything about mice. He was back again the next night, chirpy as ever, but wearing what appeared to be a red fox-fur coat instead of his usual chinchilla.

Since then I have decided simply to ignore him. Sooner or later, however thick-skinned he may be, it will no doubt dawn on him that he is *de trop*.

ANTHONY ARMSTRONG

Pig-Keeping

WE DECIDED to keep a pig. We learned that first of all we had to register the pig with the Ministry of Food and then register ourselves for monthly allocations of pig-meal. We learned that we had to undertake that the pig would live regularly on our premises and be fed and tended by ourselves or by a living-in member of our household. ("Fed," it was explained, meant "being served with food at feeding times.") We learned that we had to make a declaration of intention to slaughter, and when the hour struck apply for a licence to slaughter. We learned that slaughtering was only to be done by a slaughterman approved by the Food Office, the nearest being twenty miles away. We just about decided not to keep a damn pig after all.

Then we thought of rashers of bacon by the half-dozen, of ham, of lard, of . . . We bought the pig—and are now what you might call Capigalists.

My son and I and our Mr. Friar built a sty. The pig arrived. That, by the way, is the correct order of events. The reverse constitutes a Grave Problem. The sty was built at the farthest end of the garden, because. As a result we couldn't get the trailer in which the pig arrived anywhere near the pig-sty, so we had to carry it. The pig, not the trailer: a trailer hasn't got two convenient ears and a tail. The pig squealed in high falsetto chords all the way, till we felt like three approved slaughtermen. It wasn't from pain or even fear, though—sheer resentful indignation tinged with reproof.

The pig was installed in the sty and in its first five minutes ate two cabbages the size of footballs, supplied by my two daughters and causing bitterly jealous argument. ("Daddy, it ate *mine* first!" —"Daddy, it liked mine *best!*")

Next came the naming of the pig, which in our household means voting-papers and cold war, culminating in a rough-house something like free democratic elections in Eastern Europe. The name emerged as "Penelope." The real choice had been "Pygmalion," but certain vital facts about our pig had for the moment escaped us, and the emendations, "Pygfeemalion" and "Galantea" were over-ruled. The runners-up were "Low Pressure," because she was always in the trough—closely followed, because she looked like a Rumanian Cabinet Minister, by "Mrs. Pauker." "Gadarene Gertie"—my contribution—was howled down.

Now the basic idea of pig-owning of course is that for some months you keep a pig and then for some weeks the pig keeps you. There are, however, certain misconceptions about the business in the lay mind. One is that you just feed a pig on "scraps that come out of the house." Try mentioning that to your wife some time. Grey with insulted fury, she'll explain to you that if you think she's such a bad housekeeper that anything eatable is thrown away . . . Well, you soon see her point, probably long before she's stopped explaining it. At meal-times the phrase "I wouldn't give that food to the pigs" occasionally recurs to your mind with quite a new interpretation.

Another misconception is that a couple of meals a day during which the pig eats itself silly and treads in the rest is all that's required to fatten it. Our Mr. Friar soon disabused me. Our small sounder is being cosseted as never animal was before. It has a few tasty odds and ends, turnip and whatnot, thrown in first thing in the morning before it gets up. During this, its breakfast is being boiled up. Mr. Friar doesn't actually wear a chef's cap and taste the brew at intervals, but he comes very near it. At midday it has a cabbage, not from the old bed we eat ourselves, but from the better bed, the ones we don't even send to the church Harvest Festival. It has another pailful of, I must confess, extremely savoury-smelling "goo" at four P.M. And last thing at night it has another cabbage as a snack before retiring—its night-cappage, as it were.

In between it is expected to lie down and grow, not rush around the sty exercising its hams and rashers away to nothing. Luckily a pig has, situated somewhere about a foot back from the shoulder and six inches down, a kind of switch or button, which on being scratched with a stick slowly folds the legs up under it and makes it collapse with a satisfied grunt. Mr. Friar likes one or other of us to stand by during meals to work the undercarriage button when the pig is ready.

Mr. Friar watches the pig with an eagle eye. He says it's getting a nice straight pig now, a good square pig, he says. One morning he reproachfully mentioned that it looked a bit hollow-sided and accused me of having failed to give it its snack of cabbage the night before, when it was his afternoon off. He even moved the whole chicken-run one day to another part of the garden. I understood the pig was being upset by the chickens. The continual clucking and the occasional pæans of feminine triumph over a dear little new baby egg were disturbing its afternoon nap and interfering with the gammon-growing. If they still talk loudly enough to annoy the pig I expect we shall have to give up keeping chickens.

Meanwhile I have made my own personal contribution. I picked a peach which was going bad and so had been spared by my daughters, and solemnly gave it to Penelope. She ate it—stone and all—with a noise like a bilge pump; so early next year, we hope, we shall be offering visitors a slice of genuine peach-fed ham.

I say we hope. But already I can see storm-clouds. And the moment we have obtained our licence to slaughter they will break. "Daddy, you can't *murder* Penelope!" "Daddy, I forbid it!" "Daddy, she's the darlingest pig: I love her!" "Daddy, you're *horribly* cruel!" And we shall by then have undertaken to surrender fifty-two weeks' bacon coupons.

F. MAYNE

My Last Ride on a Horse

It took place in Rhodesia. I had left my cosy little flat high up in Johannesburg and was visiting a farm for what is usually called a holiday. There was fifteen miles of it. I was on the horse for fifteen miles, three miles out and twelve miles in. There was a party of three and there was I. They rode horses. The horse I was on was a mare, a special kind of horse. I don't know much about horses as this was the first time I had ever been on one, but I could see that the horse had no business to last another winter. My host told me that I was given the horse because of my inexperience. It was quiet, he explained, and would not toss me off and run me over. I could see at a glance that my host was right. The horse could not toss me off unless I lent it a hand. The saddle, too, was just the thing for a beginner. It had knobs on so that one could not slide off.

I got on all right. I realize that this is not usual. It should have been necessary to lower me on by pulleys or to hound the horse into a trench. I got on, and didn't fall off the other side, and I was facing the right way, because I know what a horse looks like, although I didn't know they went so far down in the middle. Almost immediately I was aware of a sharpish pain underneath somewhere, but I affected not to notice it. I didn't see the use. The horse offered no resistance. It hadn't any. It looked at me with one eye. The pathos of it all struck me to the heart's core. We were both caught in a web of which we had not shared the making. I felt a shudder. I don't know whether it was I or the horse. I would like to be able to record that I saw contempt or irritation in the horse's eye. Anything would have been better than that look. Its emptiness went straight to my stomach and stayed there. I couldn't help wondering if those Aztec chaps would have thought that I was a god if they had seen me on the horse.

We, the party of three and I, started off. At first I had company and was able to talk about the horse. I noticed a peculiar noise like a fret-saw whenever the horse tried to get air. My host knew a lot about horses and even more about the horse. He said it was nothing much; it was just broken wind, heaves or roaring—they are all the same. He said that the horse used to suffer from strangles, and that frequently ends up in broken wind, heaves or roaring. He also said that three or four grains of arsenic once a day in a mash would cure it. I felt that the dose was too small. He admitted that the horse was not in the best of health. It had an incurable derangement of the optic nerve, which he called glass eye, and when it got tired it suffered from colic or gripes, which is cured by a few ounces of laudanum, with two ounces of turpentine in a pint of linseed oil. It suffered from the ossification of certain cartilages due, so he said, to the wearing of high-heeled shoes. It also suffered from corns and saddle galls. These, I knew already, were contagious. Then there was the clicking or forging caused by the horse knocking its feet together as it walked. One way and another it made quite a noise. I asked how old the horse was. He said he could not remember.

We had only gone about a mile when I found that I was going to be alone. The horse gradually gave ground until it was about thirty yards behind the party of three. I tried to force the pace. I made clicking noises in my throat for a few hundred yards, but then found I couldn't keep it up. Something seemed to be wrong with my throat. I wondered if I had caught the heaves. With the party of three slowly receding I began to feel intense. I would not have minded solitude; it was the thought of being alone with the horse. I did not want to hit the horse with the little stick which my host had provided. I remember reading somewhere that one horse-power represents the amount of work done when 33,000 lb. is raised 1 ft. in 1 min., and equals 746 watts. I don't know what a watt is, and I'm a bit hazy about a lb., but I didn't want to take any chances. It didn't say anything about the age of the horse. I had no qualms on humanitarian grounds. I wasn't feeling so human. Besides the horse wasn't one either. I began to press my heels gently but firmly into that part of the horse's side which is between the ribs and hips. It turned and looked at me with one of its glass eyes but, beyond that, did nothing. My position was growing desperate. If the party of three got lost the horse might go on walking for ever. I didn't want to end my days, or even one of them, on the horse. In rapid succession I hit it with my little stick approximately on the fetlock, the withers, the frog, the gaskin, the hock, the pastern, and the splint bones. Finally, I gave it a crack on the head. This time I did not miss, but it still plodded on. It did not even bother to look at me with one of its glass eyes. I now perceived that I had very little control over the horse. One might even say that it was a runaway horse, only it wasn't running.

I need not have worried about getting lost. The party of three suddenly rounded a bend in the path and were lost from sight. A terrible cry broke from the horse. It was something between a whinny and a neigh, only worse. It sounded rather like my Uncle Samuel who imitates elephants. I was nearly left behind. I think it must have been the knobs on which I was impaled, and the reins which I was clutching hard, which took me along. The horse was actually running. I began to regret my wasted youth. I kept on changing knobs. I tried to make it stop by pulling on the reins, but, although it raised its head upwards, sideways, and backwards, its legs did not change pace. It had got the bit under its tooth. Only when we turned the bend and the party of three swam into sight did it resume its normal plod as suddenly as it had stopped it. I was flung against the horse's skull and it took me some time to get back on my knobs. The horse was making an awful noise now. It was roaring like a waterfall.

My host turned and congratulated me on my seat. He asked me why I did not keep up a steady pace instead of proceeding in fits and starts. He asked *me*. He noticed that I was admiring the distant prospect by the way I was screwing up my eyes. He named the Chmani-Chmani mountains in the distance. They looked a bit like my saddle. He said something else. I could see his lips moving. There was another bend in the path. The horse was getting ready to imitate my Uncle Samuel.

I focused what was left of my mind on one o'clock. By one o'clock I should no longer be on the horse. By one o'clock everything would be the same as it was last night. I might have changed shape a little but it would not be hereditary. Perhaps a lion would eat the horse from under me before one o'clock. I began to scan the bush. The Chmani-Chmani mountains seemed no nearer, but they looked enchanting. I've always been fond of scenery.

By the time we were on the way home I thought my worst troubles were over. I had not gained any control over the horse, but I was growing numb and had adapted myself in some measure. We were approaching a stream and my host, who was now convinced that I was quarrelsome, yelled to me not to allow the horse to drink. We had just passed a bend, so I heard him. The party of three splashed through the stream leading by forty lengths. I thought of stopping the horse, waiting until the party of three disappeared, and then taking the stream at a run; but the horse was not thinking along the same lines. He trudged across the stream and a surge of exultation swept through my upper half. I was nearly through. But just then the horse plunged its face into the stream and began sucking up water like a vacuum-cleaner. It had merely been making for the shallow opposite bank so that it could drink without having to hold its head up too high. I heaved at the reins with all my strength for my host's warning had filled me with a nameless dread. I struck the horse savagely all over with my little stick. My anxiety to stop it drinking caught me unawares. I had relaxed my grip on the reins, and I was watching the receding waters with such intensity that I did not notice the disappearance of the party of three.

They came back for me in the stream, which was gambolling over my withers and between my hocks. I was waiting for it to carry me off to fairyland. They said that they had noticed that I was no longer on the horse. I had noticed it too, but I was in no hurry to get back there. I was much more comfortable in the stream. They forced me to my feet. I was hoping that I was so badly injured that I would have to finish my journey on foot, but only one of my knees was back to front, and they pushed my scalp back into place. My host was growing irritable by now. He hinted that I had let the horse down. He spoke of it as a sacred relic.

From now on the horse began to give full play to its personality. Its broken wind was now in fragments. If there hadn't been a stiff wind blowing down its throat I don't think it would have made it. It began to trip over pebbles. I think it tried to avoid them. Its knees began to give way and it would often buckle up and teeter over to one side of the path. I was often hard put to it to keep up. Then the colic or gripes came out, probably due to the stream it had drunk. Great spasms shook me. My host asked me if I found the horse too much for me. He said it as if in jest but I knew he didn't mean it that way. I said, not without a tinge of resentment, that although I naturally had a plentiful supply of laudanum and turpentine on me, I had run out of linseed oil. It must have been the saddle galls eating their way into my soul. I didn't even have the Chmani-Chmani mountains to look at any more.

The path was straight right down to the farmhouse, and they were eating lunch when the horse arrived. It was one o'clock. I dismounted and found myself kneeling beside the horse, which was spitting out its tooth.

ANTHONY ARMSTRONG

Hen

THE impending reduction of the poultry food ration to infinitesimal proportions has, according to the newspapers, caused nationwide indignation and precipitated a storm of protest. It means, I gather, that hardly anybody in England will be able to keep hens any more.

Well, if I'm one of the nation—and I suppose I'm in process of being nationalized along with everything else important—the newspapers have made an inaccurate statement in estimating the nation's width. And if there is a storm of protest, here's one little wave that's not beating furiously against the cliffs, but is rippling placidly along with a contented smile.

For I personally shall be only too glad to get rid of our hens. I speak as one who, returning to Civvy Street after five and a half years, finds that his household has gone in for hen. It is keeping hen in a derelict corner of the garden. Not only that: I am having to feed hen.

And that's the trouble. For if there's anything to set me against hen, it is having to feed it.

I will pass, retching slightly, over the subject of the actual food. The sweet simple corn, those little golden nuggets which used to shower down upon the poultry run, like Zeus keeping a date with Danae, is no more. Instead hens have to exist on elderly boiled potatoes mashed up with a frightful secret weapon called "balancer meal," which smells like dead crusader. (Maybe it *is* dead crusader.) Yet the morons actually seem to like it.

Which brings me to the real reason why I object to feeding our hens. It is their almighty, terrifying, dyed-in-the-feather stupidity. It just makes me wild. (To be fair, they may think I'm equally stupid to *get* wild.) In fact after only a few months of feeding hens I've come to the definite conclusion that these birds are about the stupidest creatures ever created. Even the ant, which has a habit of walking up a six-inch blade of grass and down the other side instead of going an eighth of an inch round, would be considered bright beside the hen in spite of the difference in size of brain.

For what happens when I go to feed the hens? In the first place they cluster round the gate of the run so that I can't get in, and this in spite of the fact that the food is invariably tipped out in a trough at the other end. Any hen that had the sense to wait over there would not only be first at the eats but would have saved its breath by having the food brought to it instead of racing to the gate, and then racing back under my feet as I carry the food to the trough. It would also avoid being painfully trodden on en route, which happens every time to at least three of them.

Then again what happens when one of them gets a big lump, can't swallow it and so retires from the scramble round the trough to tackle it in peace in a corner? All the food is exactly the same —that is, equally revolting—yet about half a dozen others stop eating what they've got and go after this one hen with the big mouthful. They don't get it, because she runs round and round with it; on the other hand, she can't eat it because they don't give her time. If she does put it down for a moment and one of the others manages to snatch it, the game of chase is merely resumed, but with a different "he." And this chase may go on for a quarter of an hour till one of them manages to choke the lump painfully back, with the usual air of surprised incredulity at having done so; and they return to the trough, to find the remaining hens have cleared up the rest of the food while they've been disputing over one exactly similar mouthful of it.

Or sometimes, as you open the gate and go in, a hen gets out in the excitement. Can it find its way in, though the door out of which it has just come is wide open? No. It will race wildly round the outside of the run, passing the open door each time but flinging itself madly at the wire netting at every other unlikely place, and finally entangling and nearly strangling itself. You have to go out, unwind wire from the gasping, purple-faced idiot, give it first-aid and then lob it over the netting like a grenade.

Other nitwits, who are among the first to greet you at the gate with the bucket of food, follow you excitedly to the trough, snatch a mouthful or so while you are tilting it out in the trough, and then leave it in order to race excitedly after you as you take the empty bucket back. You slam the door in their faces, while they eye the bucket hungrily and are likely to cluster there for hours waiting for food.

Then there is the hen that likes to think itself shy. In point of fact, it's only suffering from arrested mental development—arrested, that is, before it started any development whatever and going along quietly with the cops to a life-sentence. This hen rushes up with the rest and rushes back with the rest, but the moment the food is tipped out it goes all coy. It eventually comes up to the trough, where all the others are scrabbling like mad, and then shies off with a scared and puzzled look. After which it hovers on the outskirts watching you hard and obviously wondering when you are going to dish out the food. When at last the others have cleared the platter and are moving off to digest, it comes cautiously up again and investigates the empty trough. It then stands there for a mournful half-hour ruminating on the reason why you haven't fed the hens that day and what all the fuss was about.

Well, I could go on for hours, but already I'm feeling better. And a thought has just occurred to me. Hens are still stupid enough to lay eggs and let other people take them. That *is* a point. Yes, they've definitely got something there, and I think after all you can count me in as an operational billow in the storm of protest.

H . F . E L L I S

Story without a Moral

"THE trouble is," said the pigeon, "that every time I take a step my head jerks backwards and forwards. Look! Jerk, jerk, jerk, jerk. I tell you, Doctor, I can't stand it." Dr. Clavicle, the eminent Harley Street consultant, pressed the tips of his long nervous fingers together and looked with interest at his unusual patient. For a moment the words "You had better go and see a vet, my good woman," trembled on his tongue, but curiosity, a certain weakness he had always had for the bizarre, restrained him.

"You find this—ah, reflex distressing?" he asked gently.

"Well, wouldn't you?" said the pigeon. "Nid-nod, nid-nod, every step you take."

"Hum!" said the doctor. "Yes, yes. No doubt. You realize of course that thousands—I may say *all* pigeons suffer from the same complaint? If you have been inclined to brood over what may perhaps seem to you an embarrassing idiosyncrasy but is in fact a perfectly natural intra-muscular reaction—"

"You lot all get colds," interrupted the pigeon rather rudely, "but you don't seem to enjoy them any the more on that account. As for brooding"—and here for a moment a sort of ruffle, that might but for the feathers have been a blush, passed over her face —"I ought to have mentioned before that I'm not—not married at present."

"Quite," said Dr. Clavicle. "I see. Well, now, we must see what we can do for you. How is our general health. Good? Good. And in ourselves, our mind? No special worries, apart from this little, ah—Exactly. Sleeping all right? Taking our oats—well, no, of course; that is just a little expression we use. Taking our—our grain and so on satisfactorily? Good. Now then, just follow the tip of this pencil round with the eyes. Only the eyes, please. Try to keep the head rigid. What's that? Of course, yes. I beg your pardon. Just the right eye only then, please. Good. Thank you. Now the left. Hum! Now open the —um. Thank you. No trouble there, no trouble at all."

"It's about my head," began the pigeon impatiently.

"Exactly, yes. I'm just coming to that. Now this—er, oscillation of the head and neck of which we complain. We are not troubled by it, I take it, when at rest? Or in the air? Just so. Purely a peripatetic phenomenon."

"Eh?" said the pigeon.

"Only when walking," explained the doctor. He stepped to the window and stood for a few moments with his back to the room, deep in thought.

"Suppose we give up walking for a little while?" he suggested suddenly, wheeling round on the pigeon. "Just till we get over this. Concentrate on our flying, eh? Then perhaps later on—v-e-r-y gradually at first of course—we may be able to resume the use of our legs without distress. The neurosis will have—"

"Can't fly all the time," said his patient. "A pigeon must eat."

"In that case," said the doctor briskly, "there is only one thing to be done. We must put the neck in a splint."

It was a delicate operation, but Dr. Clavicle was used to delicate operations, and in a very few minutes the splints were in position and the bandaging neatly secured.

"There," he said, stepping back. "Is that quite comfortable?"

"No," said the pigeon. "It's hellish."

"Ah, well. A little discomfort at first perhaps until we get used to it. The strangeness will soon wear off. Now, will you walk home, or may I call a—that is, shall I open the window?"

"I'm late," said the pigeon. "I must fly. But—er, what do I—how much is the—?"

"Just leave whatever you feel inclined as you go out," said the doctor urbanely. "*Good* afternoon."

"Hum!" he muttered to himself a moment later, lifting a shapely white egg from the window-sill in practised fingers.

"Not married, eh?" But he was not shocked. He had seen too much of the seamy side of life in the exercise of his profession to be conscious either of surprise or disapproval.

Two days later the pigeon reappeared, made a crash landing on the doctor's desk, picked herself up and angrily demanded her fee back.

"Tut!" said Dr. Clavicle. "I've blown it. Is anything the matter?"

"*Oh, no!*" cried the pigeon furiously. "*Oh, no!* Everything is *perfectly* all right. I came to you because I couldn't walk without jerking my head about. Well, it's still true, only now because I can't jerk my head about I can't walk. Any fool ought to have been able to see that that would happen. I can't even take a couple of steps. Watch."

"Steady," said Dr. Clavicle. "You're in the ink-pot. Dear me, yes. It's purely a matter of balance of course."

"Whatever it is, I won't stand it," said the pigeon. "Can't walk. Can't even bend my head down to eat. The only way I can get a mouthful is to lie on my side and scuffle round in circles. I tell you I've been the laughing-stock of Trafalgar Square."

"Well, well, that's easily remedied," said the doctor, and with a few quick, deft movements took off the splints. "How does that feel?"

"My word, what a relief!" exclaimed the pigeon, and she took a few quick steps up and down the desk, her head going to and fro like anything. "Lovely to be able to walk about again. Always was fond of walking—from the egg, as you might say."

"No discomfort?"

"Discomfort!" repeated the pigeon. "Not now you've taken that frightful contraption of yours off."

"Splendid!" said Dr. Clavicle. "A most satisfactory cure."

"Cured?" said the pigeon thoughtfully. "Why, yes—I suppose I *am* cured. What an amazing thing!"

"Nothing amazing about it. A perfectly straightforward case. If we become conscious, too conscious, of some perfectly normal function, operation, reaction or what-you-will of our bodies, there

268

is always a danger that it may become a worry to us. We brood on it. In the end it may cloud the whole mind and even in extreme cases unseat the reason. A famous judge, as you may have heard, became so conscious during long hours in court of the workings of his internal organs, heart, liver and so on, that he was compelled in the end to leave the Bench. I have known hundreds of cases. And the remedy, my dear madam—"

"Miss," said the pigeon.

"—the remedy is to deny that operation to us for a while, to stifle it, so that very soon we long to have it back. We realize it is necessary to us. Instead of being a nuisance it becomes—"

"You could hardly do that to the judge's liver," interrupted the pigeon. "However, I see what you mean. It may happen with quite ordinary habits, I suppose, of which one is normally unconscious, such as putting the tips of your fingers together?"

"Putting the tips—? Hum!" said the doctor, thrusting his hands into his trouser pockets.

"Don't let it worry you," said the pigeon kindly.

"Worry me, my dear madam!" pished the doctor. "We medical men are hardly likely—"

"They're together again now, you know."

"Tchah!" said Dr. Clavicle.

"If you *do* find the habit getting on your mind at all," said the pigeon cheerfully, "just lash your hands together behind your back for a day or two. You can easily rest your head on the plate when you're eating. And now I really must be going. No, please don't trouble. I'll walk."

"Nid-nod, nid-nod," cried the doctor fiercely after her retreating figure. "I don't know how you can stand it."

✤

COLIN HOWARD

The Deaf Adder

READERS who remember Marcus, my huge, handsome, lazy, stupid St. Bernard, may be interested and incredulous to know that he recently had an idea.

Ideas are not things that come readily to St. Bernards. Their heads are not built for ideas. They bear a strong resemblance to that prehistoric monster that employed its head solely as a battering-ram, and kept its brains in its tail. Only of course a St. Bernard's tail is very little more intelligent than its head. This idea was certainly the first idea Marcus ever had in his life. I cannot think how he recognized it.

The idea had to do with the easing of life for St. Bernards. For some time past Marcus had been growing steadily more disgruntled with life. It is his belief that life should consist of sixteen hours of sleep, six hours of rest, and two hours of intensive eating. His only hobby is chasing cats, which he either loathes or considers edible—I am not sure which. However, the local cats do not suffer much. It will be seen that Marcus's day does not leave much time for cat-chasing.

But—and here lies the root of Marcus's moody dissatisfaction with life—he is occasionally called on to work. His work comprises a sullen amble after breakfast as far as the nearest corner and back. A real dog would look forward to this walk for hours beforehand, trembling with expectation. To Marcus it is sheer, brutal slavery.

Roughly, then, his idea was this: "If I were deaf I couldn't hear them when they called me for my walk, and they wouldn't be able to shift me, because nothing can shift me. So I will pretend to be deaf."

I do not claim Marcus thought it all out as neatly and briskly as that. He must have spent a good many weeks working out the advantages of deafness, and several more gloomily repining because he wasn't deaf. That he should pretend deafness was a flash of inspiration that probably seeped into his enormous head in a matter of days.

After all this thinking, Marcus presumably spent a month or two quietly recuperating under the kitchen table. The floor under the kitchen table is his favourite day-bed because he honestly believes he cannot be seen there, and therefore cannot be made to work. On the rare occasions that he rises, the table rises too. Highly-strung visitors, faced with this frightening apparition, have been known to go away and tell people we keep a howdah'd elephant in the kitchen.

At last he put his plan into execution. My wife came to me, much perturbed.

"Poor old Marcus has gone deaf!" she exclaimed.

"Deaf?" I cried. "But he could hear perfectly well last night."

"Well, he can't hear a thing now. Come and speak to him."

I came into the kitchen and addressed Marcus. Into his mournful eyes came the glazed expression of one who is jolly well not going to hear. I ought to have understood immediately; but who would credit a St. Bernard with having an idea?

"Poor old lad!" I said. "Perhaps it'll pass off. Coming for a walk, Marcus?"

Marcus, with masterly histrionism, gazed at me with eager devotion, as though he would have given his last bone to have heard what I said.

After a good deal of persuasive shouting we left him where he was, and he went to sleep smiling.

It was some days before we noticed Marcus was only partially deaf. He was still able to hear anything connected with food, such as a plate set on the floor to be licked, or a courteously-worded announcement that his supper was served. We went on talking to him about food and not talking to him about anything else. While this lasted he was the happiest St. Bernard in Great Britain. He wouldn't have changed with Rip van Winkle. But we realized a certain inconsistency about his deafness one Sunday when I was carving the joint. A tiny scrap of meat slipped from the fork and dropped on to the carpet. The dining-room is one room and a passage away from the kitchen, where Marcus, tired after his rest, was asleep, but he heard it fall. A blurred, tawny avalanche hurtled out of the kitchen and into the dining-room, and had wolfed the scrap almost before it had landed.

"Hey!" I said. "I thought you were deaf?"

Marcus's jaw and tail both dropped. He went back into character immediately, but the seeds of suspicion were sown. He lay down to rest—it is, as I have said, a long way from the kitchen to the dining-room—and to try to work out some logical means by which he could still hear anything to do with food but could remain deaf to all else.

He failed to find an answer, so he did without one. He continued to hear on one subject only. My wife, who is the most charitable person alive, and a constant film-goer, at first attributed this to schizophrenia. When we had finished arguing about the pronunciation, she went on to assert that this proved what she had always maintained—that Marcus had a mind somewhere. If he hadn't, she said, how could it be split? She wanted me to psychoanalyse him.

But even my wife grew suspicious of the selectivity of Marcus's hearing when, in one short hour, he failed to hear three commands to come out for a walk, one bellow to put that milk-bottle down at once, a number of hysterical appeals to get out of her way for goodness' sake and let her get at the stove, and a stern lecture on the sanctity of the bread-board; but heard without difficulty a cat in the next road, the arrival of the butcher, and an invitation to finish a pot of fish-paste that had gone off.

When she was convinced of his guile she agreed with me he had to be cured. But how? The course we took was not, perhaps, entirely sporting. Marcus had gone deaf; *we* went silent.

When Marcus was around, we went through all the actions and expressions of speaking without uttering a word. Marcus began by being lazily puzzled. Very soon he was really worried. Had he overestimated his will-power and gone *really* deaf?

The horrible part of course was that, for all he knew, we might be talking food all day long, discussing dainties we had put out in the garden for Marcus, asking him if he fancied a few biscuits? The thought of what he might be missing was torture to him. He would lie staring agonizedly into our faces as we mouthed silently at one another—trying, I will swear, to lip-read.

As he never got called for meals, he had to look out for them himself, and he hardly dared close his eyes in case he missed one. I doubt if he got fourteen hours' real sleep out of the twenty-four, and he worried himself down to about three hundredweight.

We kept it up for a few days. Then we decided to restore Marcus's hearing to him. I said aloud: "Come on, Marcus! Time for your walk, boy!"

An expression of beautiful relief spread over his vast face, taking about one minute to do so. He wasn't deaf after all. He bounded to his feet. He frisked to the gate like a mettlesome carthorse. He joyously took one of the longest walks of his career—almost half a mile.

Heavens, how he slept that week!

He was not troubled again with his deafness. Neither were we.

COLIN HOWARD

Memory Holds a Seat

SOMETIMES I wish I had never gone to that circus, or at least that I had never given the elephant that bun.

It was a bun I had bought because it was the only thing left in the shop, and although it was cigarettes I was after I did not like to come out without buying something. I took the bun to the circus with me, hoping to meet somebody I could give it to on the way, and standing outside the big-top waiting for his entrance-cue was this elephant Chota. Chota reached out for my bun, and I thankfully gave it to him and patted his trunk and said "Hullo, old boy!"

The elephant started. He popped the bun into his mouth and eyed me meditatively, wondering where he had met me before. I do not normally greet strange elephants so warmly; I was merely delighted to be rid of the bun. Then Chota gave an unconvincing trumpet of recognition, and embraced me fondly. I followed the workings of his mind. He thought his memory must be slipping, and elephants are sinfully vain of their memories. He didn't want me to go around claiming he had forgotten me. So he put on this Well-well-fancy-seeing-*you* act.

I unwrapped myself and went to my seat, and Chota stood racking his brains trying to place me. When he came into the ring he glanced anxiously around for me and waved his trunk at me in a friendly way. He wasn't going to be caught twice. A mighty murmur filled the tent as everybody told everybody else that the elephant never forgets. My neighbour looked at me in silent respect, obviously attempting to picture me in a sola topee, lounging in a howdah and potting at tigers.

By the end of the show Chota had succeeded in deciding that he remembered me. From that conclusion it was a short step to his conviction that I was his dearest friend. Half-way home I heard something like a lorry with four punctured wheels behind me. I turned. Chota was following me. I nervously waggled my stick at him.

"Go home!" I said. "Bad elephant! Go home at once!"

He didn't. He stood gazing at me with a world of dog-like devotion in his little eyes. I went on, and he came too. I nipped inside my house and slammed the door, and Chota stood outside in the roadway and trumpeted his love for me over the garden gate.

I rang up the circus and told them I had inadvertently taken away an elephant of theirs, and would they please come along and

274

fetch it. While I was waiting for them the doorbell began to ring. I thought it was Chota, and didn't answer it at first. When I did, there was a policeman there. He wasn't wearing a helmet. Chota was.

"That your elephant outside in the road?" he demanded.

I explained it was simply an elephant that had followed me home, and that the circus would be along any minute to collect it. He said he would wait and make sure they did—he seemed to feel a delicacy anyway about resuming his beat without his helmet.

The elephant's keeper arrived. He climbed on to Chota's back, tossed down the policeman's helmet, and endeavoured to steer a course for home. Chota petulantly plucked him from his perch and returned to serenading me.

Chota's keeper climbed out of the privet hedge and said he would go back for reinforcements. The reinforcements consisted of the other elephant—Chota's partner in their speciality act. She was the decoy. She laid a coaxing trunk on Chota and tried to wheedle him into coming home with her. Chota explained he had met an old friend. The decoy—an elephant herself, she understood an elephant's natural feelings—at once withdrew. She was returned to the circus in exchange for a tractor and ropes.

A full-dress tug-of-war between an elephant and a tractor is an awesome spectacle, but it is not an exciting one. There is too little action about it. Both parties dug their toes in and provided the long-sought answer to the old one about what happens when an irresistible force meets an immovable body. The irresistible force and the immovable body both win; it is the ropes between that lose.

The circus then agreed to allow me to retain Chota for the night, which was not a thing I wanted at all. The objections of the policeman were overruled, and, on receiving an assurance that Chota could be regarded as a fixture until morning, when he would be hungry and would return for his fodder, he obligingly fetched four red lamps, one of which he placed at each of Chota's corners.

Unhappily the circus underrated Chota's powers of endurance and his devotion to me. In the morning he showed no sign of going home to breakfast. I did notice, however, that my privet hedge had vanished. He camped on the pavement all day, ignoring the black looks of pedestrians, who had to walk round him. The circus, which was billed to appear in the next town, had to cancel the performance and give an extra show where they were. I believe Chota's partner, who had to do the act without Chota, was rather a flop.

The circus remained a further week, playing to dwindling houses. The proprietor then said he could not wait for Chota any longer. He said it was costing him thousands. The only solution was for me to buy Chota. I said I could not afford to buy an elephant, and I did not need an elephant anyway.

"I can't afford to *give* him away," he said. "Tell you what—I'll raffle him at a guinea a time. I take it you wouldn't object to giving a guinea for an elephant?"

"I might not win him," I argued.

"You will," he said.

I did.

The circus moved gratefully on. I was left with an adoring elephant for my shadow. I will not say he followed me everywhere, but he followed me everywhere an elephant could, and waited outside where an elephant couldn't.

The possession of an elephant helped me in neither my career nor my social life. Financially, it crippled me. I stuck it for six months, and then presented him to a zoological society. I had to take him to his new home myself, or he would never have gone. I said good-bye to him, and left him with a great lightening of spirit.

Chota gave me two minutes' start, then strolled through his bars and came too. At the bus-stop I felt a loving breath on my neck and, turning, found Chota helping me wait for the bus.

In these days there is only one way for a man to be able to afford to keep an elephant. I resigned my post in the City and took on my present job of elephant-keeper at this zoo. The curator informs me that an elephant is liable to live for anything up to seventy years, so I look like being here for quite a long time yet.

Eccentrics and Individualists

H. F. ELLIS

Reactionary Affair in the Toy Dept.

VOICES—other than children's—are not often raised in the Toy Dept. I therefore withdrew my attention from a Constructional Outfit, priced at eleven guineas, and forced my way through a clump of pandas to the scene of the disturbance.

"What's the idea of this damned affair?"

The voice was loud, the face red, the hat hard and brown. He was accustomed, one could guess, to shout inquiries from the saddle at tenants standing in cottage doorways. And he would tell you, given half a chance, that the farmer's boots were the best manure for the land. However, he was not talking about boots at the moment.

"What's it *for*, eh?"

The assistant was nervous but suave.

"That is Old Mother Goose's Cottage, sir."

"So it says. I've got my eyesight, thank God. But the damn thing goes round and round. I'm asking you what's the point of it, man."

I doubt whether the assistant had troubled himself much about the point of it up to this time. Those who work in Toy Depts. grow used to seeing some sort of contrivance going round and round at Christmas-time; and if it isn't an electric train eternally passing a wayside station it may as well be Old Mother Goose's Cottage with a fairy on the roof. But he explained, reasonably enough, that the idea was to enable all sides of the building to be seen. "It is lighted up inside, as you will notice," he added, "showing Peter Rabbit, Donald Duck, Rupert and other favourites, in characteristic attitudes. The kiddies—"

The old man rapped him smartly on the waistcoat with the head of his cane. "Mother Goose," he said, "was a native of Boston, Massachusetts—and don't you forget it."

"Is that so, sir?"

"Dead and buried two hundred years before Peter Rabbit was ever thought of," said the old gentleman, triumphantly. "So now then."

"The kiddies like it," said the assistant rashly.

"Like it!" cried the old man with a sudden burst of fury. "I came in here to buy my grandson a mechanical toy, and all you have to offer is this damned contraption—marked 'Not for Sale.' Freddie! Come out of that, boy! D'you hear me?"

A small red-haired child, who had got his head through the flaps of a wigwam, came out of it and eyed his grandfather with gravity.

The old man removed his stick from the assistant's waistcoat and pointed it at Mother Goose's Cottage.

"What d'ye think of it, Freddie, eh? What do you say to that?"

Freddie watched the cottage round three times before making up his mind.

"It's potty," he said.

"There you are, you see," said the old man. "Got any kites?"

"Kites will be over in the Sports Department," the assistant told him, not without relief. "*Through* the archway and—"

"Don't stand there giving orders to *me*, sir," the old man roared. "I'm asking you whether you've got any kites. If you have, bring one. If you don't know, go and find out. And what's more," he added—while all over the department customers stood rigid with astonishment, some trailing wooden carts from nerveless fingers, others frozen in the act of returning stencilling outfits to their shelves—"be quick about it."

Not for ten years had any of us heard an assistant in a Toy Dept. addressed in such a forthright manner. I confess that to cover my own embarrassment at such behaviour I read the rules of "Extinguo—the Hilarious New Atomic Warfare Game"—twice through without taking in a word. Then we all heard the assistant say, in quite a small voice, "I'll make inquiries, sir," and a sigh— whether of relief or disappointment, who shall say?—swept through the room.

Pondering this incident as I idly tested the wheels of a model ambulance I found it difficult to account for the survival of so feudal an outlook in the middle of the twentieth century. The man, himself hardly to be ranked as high even as a small country squire, appeared unaware that the day of the petty tyrant was over, that the hectoring and bullying of those whom he chose to consider to belong to a "lower station in life" was not tolerated in the modern state, that, in short, he was making a thundering ass of himself. I felt it was high time somebody told him so, only I did not feel that I was quite the person to do it. And in any case the assistant had by this time returned, with a kite.

"If you will pay at the desk, sir," he began, but catching sight of the old gentleman's face, took the proffered notes and hurriedly sped away. So, I reflected bitterly, is democracy betrayed.

"Impudent jackanapes!" bellowed the old gentleman after him, by way of thanks.

So loud and so uncompromising a cry as that could hardly fail to bring one of the shop's heavier guns on to the scene, and very soon a tall figure, with the bearing and address of a Harrovian, could be seen making its way through the throng.

"Perhaps I can be of some assistance, sir," he said, making more of a statement than a question of it.

"I doubt it," said the old gentleman. "What are you?"

What are you! A question that only magistrates in police courts are allowed to ask!

"I happen to be in charge of this floor at present," said the Harrovian briefly.

"Then I advise you to sweep it," said the old gentleman. "It's filthy."

"Forgive me if I point out—"

"Be off!" said the old gentleman fiercely, and the Harrovian, raising his eyebrows, went.

"Potty!" said Freddie, for the second time.

When this remarkable pair had departed with their kite, I remained for some time leaning against a rocking-horse, lost in thought. It had indeed been a sorry day for the new Britain. If a loud voice and an overbearing manner were to be allowed to carry the field with no more opposition than a pair of raised eyebrows, the forces of reaction would very soon begin to rally their scattered strength. At the same time, the unworthy thought obtruded itself that the old gentleman had at least got what he wanted and got it quickly. I therefore stepped briskly across the room to a young man who seemed to be disengaged and tapped him on the shoulder. I may or may not have accompanied the action with the words "Here, you!"

"I want," I told him, "a doll that shuts its eyes when canted over backwards. And I want it now."

"Hadn't you better wait and see whether Mummy pops one in your stocking at Christmas?" he replied, civilly enough.

"I told you to wear a hat, Tony," said a girl who seemed to be with him. She had the New Look, but the one she gave me was comparatively old-fashioned.

"I beg your pardon," I began in some confusion. "I'm afraid I made a mistake—"

"A hereditary failing, no doubt," said the young man.

Looking back, I find the young man's remark hardly less puzzling than the old gentleman's behaviour.

❊

C. R. I. ESTRIDGE

Toujours le Guide

WE WERE approaching the castle. I was saying "On your left you see the castle of Gruyère." I sat down again, for what more could I say; I had never seen the castle before in my life. If it hadn't been that I remembered how they'd said ". . . and the castle is called Gruyère" as they pushed me into the coach with my packed luncheon, I shouldn't even have been able to say that. I should have had to use the old formula "On your left you will see a six-teenth-century castle. Apart from its picturesque position on top of a hill it is of little importance," and pray that the horrid little man in the back seat had lost his place in the guide-book.

Suddenly I remembered what else they had said as they pushed me into the coach. "You stop there for two hours. You spend an hour going round the castle." The coach drove relentlessly on up the hill leading to the castle and into the old square. The coach stopped. The old Swiss driver got out and made his way towards the hotel, where doubtless a glass of white wine and a fine meal were waiting for him. I got up and said in a knowing way, "We stop here." Now if you have ever had the fortune to be a guide you'll know that there is nothing that a coach-load of people like better than to be told a fact which is perfectly obvious. My re-mark was greeted by delighted mutterings throughout the coach. Everybody was smiling except the little man in the back seat, and I could hear "We stop here" being bandied about as though it had been the latest saying of an Oscar Wilde. I waited for silence, rather like a comedian after a good joke, and then let drop another pearl of wisdom. "I now take you round the castle." Now of course everybody has a weakness for castles, and a coachload of tourists in Switzerland is no exception. I couldn't have pleased them better if I had said "On our return you can all stay at the Grand Hotel." For the Grand Hotel was on the lakeside "and ever so expensive, dear, and of course we wanted to save our francs."

I got out. Everybody followed suit. That's another thing you learn if you are a guide: you're part of a giant follow-my-leader game. I could tell you about the time I got out of the train at Paris—but that's another story. I looked around: painted on a wall I saw "Visitez le Château—60 cents." The little man with the book asked me "How much is it?" He was from Bradford. "Sixty centimes," I said, as though I'd known all my life. I led the way up to the castle. The rest of the coach-load of thirty followed. The old women washing at the fountain looked up, without excitement, and continued their washing. We reached the entrance to the castle where there was an old man selling tickets. "Bonjour, monsieur, je suis le guide," I said. "Ah, bonjour, monsieur, ça va?" he wheezed. "Ça va bien," I said. And there it had to end. I had told them in London that I spoke German, so I had been sent to the French part of Switzerland.

We went through the gate and there we were in a grass-covered courtyard, surrounded on all sides by the walls of the castle and, far above, old wooden galleries. On one wall was painted a huge picture much worn by time. I took up my position to one side of it and stole a hasty look at it while they closed in on me. In one corner cowering amongst some trees was a shepherdess and approaching from all sides were armed horsemen. "This painting," I started, "was done in the latter part of the sixteenth century." I could see I was impressing them and I hadn't even begun. To my left I caught a glimpse of an American taking notes on a pad supplied by some airways line; this nearly unnerved me, but I took a grip on myself, adjusted my badge more firmly in my buttonhole and continued, "It is believed to have been painted by a minor Swedish historian while staying here to investigate the ancient history of the place." When you are a guide you learn that half-measures never work; I was warming to the task now. The American was scribbling away contentedly. I continued: "Experts differ

284

slightly as to the context of the scene depicted, but I think the most widely held view is as follows." Well, perhaps it wasn't widely held yet, I thought, but by the end of the season it would be. "The incident took place in 1246, when a young shepherdess was caring for her sheep in the woods near the castle—you saw them as we drove in, didn't you?" "Yes," they all said happily—they were thinking how observant they'd been. "The lord of the castle was hunting with his men-at-arms when suddenly he caught sight of the beautiful shepherdess and there and then decided to make her his lady. This he did and he brought her back to the castle with him, causing much jealousy amongst the lords and ladies already in residence. Later on you will see the room where the shepherdess slept." (This was quite safe; the Swiss always keep one room in their castles with a bed in it.) While finishing the story I had been looking for the next port of call; seeing a door near by I led the party towards it. In we plunged. Easy—this was obviously the guard-room.

By the time we had gone round they had a good idea of the history of a castle I had visited a few years before in Scotland. I led them down again to the little village, being careful to avoid the stall selling English guide-books. "This is the best place for tea," I said, pointing towards the only hotel, and in we marched. "Bonjour, mademoiselle," I said. "Je suis le guide." "Enchanté, monsieur," she said and brought me a bowl of cream and four large meringues.

Over tea the American said to me: "Did it take you a long time to learn up all those facts? The folks back home will sure be interested." "Oh, yes, simply ages," I said, and thought of my instructions for this particular trip: ". . . and the castle is called Gruyère."

ERIC KEOWN

Sale This Day

IT WAS a dull sale at the big grey house on the hill. I'd only dropped in for half an hour on my way back from the downs, to find they'd got as far as "LOT 507, garden-roller by reliable maker, slightly defective." And then my heart stopped. For, looking over someone's shoulder, I read: "LOT 510, wickerwork bathchair with tiller steering, good as new."

I don't see that I need make any apology for having always felt, deep below the surface but never satisfactorily banked down, a great flame of longing to possess a bathchair. When you consider there are men of authority in the world who collect match-boxes, a desire to own this most delightful and innocent of all vehicles requires no defence. There are, of course, many pleasant things one can do with it, high among them being, I think, to smoke a cigar in the *tonneau* while someone younger than oneself is pushing the machine up a hill, but what I personally had always had in mind was to fit it up with a sail. A sort of spinnaker, I sometimes thought.

I got a fright from a bull-necked man in the front row with a dangerously indolent look in his eye, but he threw in the sponge at seven-and-six, and half an hour later I was out in the street with the most beautiful bathchair you ever saw, the kind that old gentlemen looking like small dromedaries in bowler-hats used to tow gloomily along the South Coast. Having some miles to go I set off down the hill at a smart pace, when it occurred to me that here was one of those rare opportunities to get my own back on gravity. The road was well metalled, the gradient reasonable, and I found that by pressing my old gloves on the tyres I could brake comfortably. The sensation of freedom was glorious, and I wished that some competent poet were with me to nail it in words.

I was still going nicely when a startled cry from the pavement drew my attention to a man named Evans to whom I had once given a cat. I waved heartily in return, and the consequent release of pressure on the right-hand wheel shot me across the road like an arrow towards the only other vehicle in sight, a milk-cart. The milkman had evidently been an athlete in his youth, and his horse was by no means without presence of mind. What might have been a very gruelling pint-to-pint became no more than a stirring memory, once I was out of earshot of the milkman and again sailing down the middle of the road.

The hill growing a good deal steeper, I braked harder with my gloved hands, and at that the smoking palms gave way. From this unhappy moment the curve of acceleration rose so sharply that big decisions became inevitable. I could either jump overboard, at heavy cost to the National Health Service, or I could go on, entering the ancient borough in the valley below, if all went well, in about two minutes at something approaching the speed of sound. Seeing a massive pair of gate-posts on the port side, however, a third course suggested itself, and leaning right out of the basket as if it were a racing dinghy going into the wind I swung the tiller hard over. "Four Beeches," the house was called, I don't know why. There was a short drive leading up to it, and this I took like a rocket. Two alternatives then came up for consideration rather quickly. One was to try conclusions with some brick steps and become involved in a Richard Hearne act through tall French windows, the other was to swerve to the right along a sandy path that led round the house. I chose the latter, once more employing a technique common enough in Fireflies and such craft but less often applied to racing bathchairs; and a moment later I repeated the manœuvre, at the corner of the house.

A childish fancy that my troubles were over was soon dashed. The path now widened into a small square, and across it sat the owners, arranged as if for a family group except that they were all asleep, basking in the early sun. I was still going far too fast to avoid everybody; and it was purely in a spirit of gallantry, which I hoped he would understand, that I picked out the master of the house and drove straight at him, skilfully avoiding the women and children. On the whole I came out of it better than he did, for I remained seated. He was a large man with a very red face, and as he lay in a rose-bed with his eyes still shut he clapped his hands loudly and shouted hoarsely for his bearer. Wondering if it was quite wise to do so, I helped him to his feet. It took him a little time to assess the situation, starting from cold, as it were, but when he did no shade of welcome crossed his rugged features. His womenfolk observed us breathlessly. I laid unheard-of apologies at his feet, I laid them in rows before his family, but still his jaw bulged powerfully. I told him of the sale, of Evans and his cat, of the long-jumping milkman and his thoughtful horse, of the many terrible decisions which had been forced upon me. His ham like fists were white at the knuckles as at last he found words.

"Why the devil did you buy the infernal thing?" he roared.

I took a deep breath.

"It has long been my ambition," I said, in a simple, manly way, "to rig a bathchair with a sail. Even, perhaps, with a spinnaker."

Never could I have imagined such a change in such a man. Instantly he became a mountain of geniality, seizing me by the hand and letting out vast guffaws of pleasure.

"Now you're talking!" he shouted.

"Now you're not!" whispered his family, as they crept into the house.

"Of course your spinnaker notion is stuff and nonsense," he rumbled, "but I don't see why she shouldn't carry plain Bermuda if we put plenty of lead in her keel . . ."

It was surprising, to say the least of it, to be sitting in my bathchair beside this remarkable man, while he began eagerly to draw in the sand.

❋

ERIC KEOWN

Passing Strange

JAMES chased the final crumb of cheese to the edge of his plate, emptied his tankard and called for the bill. It was this last action that weighed with me most.

"If you've half an hour to spare," he said, "I'd be glad of your help."

"I really ought to get back," I muttered, "and just now I'm not in the mood for haggling over snuff-boxes or meeting a man who knows a man who—"

"It's nothing like that. It's a practical experiment to do with my novel."

"Oh, your novel. How is Lady Honoria Trimm?"

"As comfortable as can be expected. She's having a baby on page 105 and is reading about the Pre-Raphaelites with her feet up for the next three or four chapters. What I'm working on in the meantime is her brother Edward's proposal. I believe I've found a brand-new location for this, on two passing escalators."

"Well?" I asked.

"It's vitally important to get the timing right."

"Why?"

"Because whatever I put in a novel a hundred lunatics with minds like cheap alarm-clocks chip in from the steam-room at Harrogate and the forests of Assam to say it's impossible. This time all the answers are going to be ready."

"I can't see it matters."

"I didn't expect you would. Now all I want from you is to jump on the up escalator when I jump on the down and impersonate a smashing brunette called Anastasia de Grotchkin. As we pass I shall say my piece across the L.P.T.B. mahogany, and all you have

289

to do is reply: 'Sir, you forget I am a de Grotchkin. You shall hear from my brother!' The question is, can it all be fitted in, or must I cut?"

"Why must I be so idiotically haughty?"

"It's a longish story," said James, handing me a small cigar. "You see, this Edward is an impulsive lad, not much liked. He lost two fingers leading his college side in the stool-ball game against Girton, he lost all his money looking for pirate gold in the Pacific, in fact he's led a thoroughly dangerous and reckless life. Anastasia he ran into playing the zither in an absinthe-dive in Cannes. He followed her to a similar outfit in Budapest, he trailed her all over the Balkans, diving all the time, but whenever he had her nicely teed up for a proposal there was always some act of God and the girl got away. Floods, fires, famines, germs, gunmen. I could give you all the details—"

"Skip them," I urged.

"Anastasia doesn't really like Edward. He's lost touch with her completely, but now suddenly he sees her coming up on the other escalator. You see what a whale of a situation it is?"

"I'll buy it," I said wearily, so we took a taxi to Leicester Square Tube station, where escalators abound. James bought two tickets and we parted, fighting our way through a dense wall of citizens. On my way up I took a stance on the inside, and turned to find James waving madly as he bore down towards me.

"Anastasia!" he cried, sweeping his hat into the eye of the man next to him. "My darling! Where, oh where, have you been? Have you forgotten those happy days munching *apfelstrudel* in the Zoo at Przymsl? I love you, Anastasia! Won't you marry me?"

By this time he was rather more than broadside on, and I suppose I had still three seconds in which to play my part. But something died inside me at that moment. I was fond of James, I had no wish to let him down, but the best I could do was to bubble and hiccup in a quite meaningless way. The whole incident seemed to leave a queer impression on the parties round, who could be heard murmuring above the rumble of the machinery. A little damped, I crossed over to the down escalator and started off again.

I noted James was coming up. This time, however, he was out of love.

"Trust you to put up a black!" he roared in passing. "You always were a thundering great oaf. You always will be!"

"Sir, you forget I am a de Grotchkin. You shall hear from my brother!" I replied firmly. An old gentleman standing below me looked interested to hear this. I decided to give James one more chance, and seeing him mounting the down escalator I got on the up. As he approached he smiled forgivingly.

"Anastasia!" he cried, and said his lines as passionately as before. It was just then I spotted my Aunt Emily directly behind him. She and I had not spoken since a noisy row over a dog ten years ago, but ten years are big enough to swallow a toy poodle and though she was fully four-fifths gorgon I was fond of the old trout.

"Aunt Emily!" I shouted, looking necessarily right through James. "How are you? Is it true Agatha has done it again?"

James swung round in a fury and his elbow caught Aunt Emily in the mouth. She was by no means the woman to take this lying down, and she hit James a powerful crack on the ear with her umbrella. The last I saw of them was a tangled mass sweeping knottily towards the Northern Heights. I gave up my ticket and walked quickly out into the street. For the first time I observed my original old gentleman still beside me.

"Excuse me," he said, "but I was so much interested to hear you're a de Grotchkin. Is the countess well?"

For a moment I hesitated, but really I felt too exhausted to go into it all.

"She is beginning to show her age," I said weakly.

"And Boris, poor fellow?"

"His sciatica, alas, is mounting."

"And little Tanya?"

"She is a big girl now," I said sadly.

"Then you must please dine with me to-morrow," cried the old gentleman pleadingly. And like an ass I said I would.

J . C . SINGTON

This Landlord

THIS morning when I came down to breakfast I found my land-lord's legs sticking through the ceiling. All that was visible of him was a pair of seedy carpet slippers and two lengths of rather dis-tasteful trousering. This is a new method of annoying the tenants, and I do not think I like it. This morning we had mostly plaster for breakfast and that is one reason why I am looking for some new digs. The way this landlord is carrying on the house is not fit to live in.

The first time I noticed anything peculiar about the man was the day the hot water geyser exploded. I had gone upstairs that day, as I usually do, to have a bath. I had already asked the land-lord if I could have a bath because he does not like people having baths and has to be told about them first, and I was not antici-pating any trouble provided that I kept the bath-water from over-flowing on to the washing. As soon as I reached the top landing, however, I saw that I was not going to have a bath. Standing out-side the bathroom door, instead of the usual five people waiting to get in, was the landlord, surrounded by dense clouds of steam and giving every appearance of being in a nasty frame of mind.

At first sight I thought he was producing the steam himself, but then I saw that the source of the trouble was two live jets proceeding from underneath the bathroom door, the whole giving the impression of one of the minor eruptions from Mount Etna. Now I am not one to stand around and gape, and thinking that the landlord had a sick fancy to play about with some steam (he does some funny things) I turned round and started back to my room to wait till he had finished. I did not get very far. Taking the intervening stairs in one bound, the landlord alighted beside me and demanded whether I knew the price of geysers. I have never pretended to know the price of geysers and the question came as something of a surprise. Fortunately I was not permitted to answer. Descending the stairs crabwise, the landlord began to explain that he had not had a new geyser put in for nothing, a statement which I was prepared to accept. Without waiting for me to comment he went on to describe the setting up and installation of a geyser until, by the time we reached the ground floor, I could if necessary have installed one myself. Happily my room is on the ground floor, so I side-stepped into it as we passed and locked the door. After a threatening silence the landlord went back to the bathroom to brood.

That was the beginning. After that our relations grew worse. The landlord took to lying in wait for me as I went out and jumping the question of when I was going to pay the rent. After three weeks I found that the furniture in my room was slowly disappearing. I let one or two pieces go just to make sure and then branded the rest by boring two small holes into each on the underside of the wood. The other tenants got pretty sick of me in the next few days going up to their rooms and inverting all their furniture, but I beat the landlord and ended up with more furniture than I had to start with. I even reclaimed some of the landlord's own, which made him so mad that he set the dog on me, an ugly animal with protruding front teeth, but fortunately it did not bite. For a fortnight I lived in comparative security.

The climax came when the landlord discovered that my electric meter had been shorted out of circuit. I had gaily been using the electric fire for two months without realizing that the thing had been running on air, and I came in one day to find the landlord crouched in deep contemplation beside the meter. Thinking at first he was looking for mice I went down on all fours to see if I could help. I soon saw I was mistaken. Thrusting a long piece of flex under my nose as if it was Exhibit "A" at a murder trial, the landlord demanded whether I knew the penalties for defrauding the electricity company. I have always disliked people who open the conversation by asking cryptic questions, and I replied somewhat briskly that I did not. "Very well," said the landlord. "The police do, then." He seemed to expect a reply to this remark, so I waited for a moment and then suggested that the man upstairs might know as he was a lawyer. "In that case," said the landlord nastily, "you ought to get to know him better." At this point the meter, which had been simmering quietly for some minutes, blew up. There was an impressive white flash and tongues of flame began to edge round the carpet. The landlord, trying to give the impression of being an air-raid veteran (he spent the war in Vancouver), plunged headlong to the carpet and began threshing about like a salmon. It was some seconds before I realized that the reason for this odd behaviour was his trousers, which were burning nicely. I extinguished the flames with my shoe and retired to a distance to watch events. The landlord was not looking particularly pleased. Wisps of smoke were beginning to curl up from the carpet and the meter looked as though it had had a direct hit. Slowly the landlord rose to his feet, smouldering. "I've had enough of this," he remarked, clutching hold of the lamp standard. "Enough of what?" I inquired, edging behind the sofa. "You'll see," snapped the landlord, and flung out of the room. The next day I received a short note. "You are required to leave," it said. "Your room has been let to another tenant." I transferred this to my next-door neighbour, who left without a murmur the same night, and the situation now is that the landlord and I are not speaking to each other. How it will all end I do not know. A few more of these stunts and I shall start losing my temper.

❧

ERIC KEOWN

A Blow for Freedom

It was a dull and brutish day. The library of the club was stuffy, morgue-like and full of retired tea-planters paddling gingerly in their football pools. Since an injudicious lunch my metabolism had proceeded inharmoniously. I felt despondent about the inner meaning of being.

"Mr. Bingle!" keened a page-boy, taking no natural pleasure in this privileged rupture of the silence rule. He looked very sad. It came home to me with poignancy how black the hours must be when most of them are spent trailing up and down stairs bawling for Mr. Bingles who are probably in Aberystwyth. My heart went out to the little lad.

"Mr. Bingle!" he cried again, but without hope.

I beckoned him over to the chair in which I lay prone.

"Someone has need of me?" I asked.

It was good to see his eyes brighten. Perhaps I was his first triumph.

"Wanted on the 'phone, sir."

"By whom?"

"Dunno, sir."

I strode with him firmly down the stairs. My prompting had been nothing but humane. I looked forward to being Mr. Bingle.

"There y'are, sir," said the boy, proudly pointing to a box.

"Find out who it is." Prudence sets some limits, beyond which I felt lay Mrs. Bingle.

"It's a Mr 'Arris, sir," he whispered.

"Ha, Harris," I said.

"You've been a long time, Bingle," came a voice sharply, a voice to which I failed altogether to take.

"I was polishing my nails in the slumber-room," I said.

"You sound very funny. Sort of muffled."

"It's always the same with double pneumonia."

"Double—?"

"Pneumonia. Spent the night on the Embankment. Been out with the boys."

"Look here, Bingle, I don't like your tone."

"That's what they all said in Harley Street this morning."

The man at the other end, whom I judged to have a lumpish diamond in his tie, could be heard making a great effort at restraint.

"How are things going?" he rasped.

"Very slowly," I told him.

"You know how anxious we are to get this affair settled?"

"So am I," I said warmly. "I'm sick and tired of it."

"Buckwheat considers it extremely urgent."

"Buckwheat is a damned fool," I said.

"Really, Bingle!"

Did I nevertheless detect a note of respect, even of anxiety, which had been quite lacking from his original remarks? I rather thought I did. It seemed to me Bingle had been playing his cards badly. He appeared to be in some kind of key-position, and yet to be permitting this Harris to walk all over his face. A practical sympathy with Bingle and his dependents seized me.

"I honestly don't know if I can be bothered to go on," I said.

"Bingle, your attitude amazes me!"

"It doesn't me," I said, "I've been going into the profits."

"We've been over all that before."

"Let's go all over it again. If you put my slice on a butter-dish it wouldn't show."

"Buckwheat and I feel we are being more than generous, Bingle."

"But even if it were ten times as big, after the offer I've had to-day from America I don't see how I can afford not to ask you and Buckwheat to take a running jump at yourselves."

There was an ugly hydraulic sound at the other end, wherever that might be.

"America? Not Gumstein?"

"That's neither here nor there," I said. Nor was it. I refreshed myself with a little snuff, of a blend first concocted for the pleasure of Queen Victoria's mother, and waited.

"Bingle, old boy, I wonder if you're free for dinner?"

"I'm dining with a gorilla at the House of Lords."

"Because we mustn't be hasty about all this, must we? You know how much Buckwheat and I value your services."

"You bet I do," I said.

"Suppose we double your whack?"

"I could go back and finish polishing my nails."

"Come, old boy, a joke's a joke."

I have known that for a long time.

"Look here, I don't know what old Buckwheat'll say, but will you carry on if we treble?"

"I might," I said. "If I have it in writing by to-morrow morning."

"I say, you are a tiger, Bingle!"

"Aren't I?" I said, and hung up.

And now I suppose I must look for another club.

DONALD MATTAM

Documentary

The Second Day of Christmas

DARLING BASIL,—What an *original* present! One receives so many hum-drum gifts at this season that it was positively refreshing to unpack that tremendous crate and find—a tree! A pear tree, according to Father. I can hardly wait till it fruits! (Father says that it takes ten years, and that this specimen is three years old. We

may see it fruit *together* . . .)   All my love,
                                                    ELAINE

P.S.—Father has just flushed the partridge. A nice plump one, he says. Two presents in one! (Or, rather, one present in the other. Thank you so much.)   E.

The Third Day of Christmas

. . . Are the two turtle-doves really for me? They're *too* sweet, and, in confidence, I prefer them to the partridge, though Father enjoyed his share of the bird enormously. Doves are *calmer*, aren't they? We had a lot of trouble dislodging the partridge, as a matter of fact, and the tree still takes up most of my bedroom.

Are they a new kind of dove, by the way? I think they are, but Father says it's just the moult.   Affectionately,
                                                    ELAINE

EXTRACT
The Fourth Day of Christmas

. . . The foreign stamps were responsible for the catastrophe. The box was unpacked by my maid under the impression that it contained some form of Parisian millinery. When the millinery flew out and pecked her she fainted, I am sorry to say, on two of them. The third French hen broke a rather valuable stained-glass window and escaped. I shall no doubt be able to thank you more effectively later on, but she *was* a good maid . . .

Advertisement, local paper, dated Fifth Day of Christmas

WANTED URGENTLY

BIRD-MAN with wide experience. Interest in arboriculture a recommendation.—The Towers, Pons Episcoporum.

EXTRACT
The Sixth Day of Christmas

. . . About the Collybirds you must have been grossly misled. They are merely wild specimens (and why I say "merely" I do not know; their wildness was devastating) of a black fowl which infests the neighbourhood. Father was displeased and had to engage a bird-man at some trouble and expense. The five gold rings you elected to send on the Fifth Day of Christmas displeased him still more; he sent the bird-man packing. Why *five*, by the way? More binding than the usual *one*? All the rings are, in any case, over-large, though I am doubtless at fault in thinking that all are slightly worn?

I shall not be able to write again for some days, I fear, as all the aunts, uncles and grand-parents are with us for the New Year and life is going to be rather complicated.   Cordially,
                                                            ELAINE

TELEGRAM

Dispatched Thirteenth Day of Christmas
EXPECT LORDS LADIES TAXI MUSICIANS MILKMAIDS PASSENGER BIRDS GOODS RINGS REGISTERED POST TREE BRITISH HAULAGE FURTHER ATTEMPTS COMMUNICATION WILL BE REPORTED POLICE AND I MEAN THAT ELAINE

F. O. VANN SPENCER

A Tuba for Mrs. Trumble

THE way Mrs. Trumble emerges from her house reminds one of a cuckoo springing from a clock; it troubles me slightly. What troubles me more is the fact that Mrs. Trumble is a watcher. She is a good watcher; she can watch anything or anybody, and her ability in this respect is matched only by her judgment in knowing *when* to watch.

Mrs. Trumble watches me often, and I find it irritating. She can watch me clean windows, or trim the grass, or wipe jo loves Md in chalk off the fence better than anyone I know, and I rebel inwardly against her habit of sliding out from her house to give an infuriating half-nod before she slides in again.

If she nodded to me I could perhaps tolerate her; but she doesn't, she half-nods to herself. What's more, she half-nods in a *knowing manner* as if she suspected before she came out that I should be cleaning the windows, or mowing the lawn, or rubbing chalk off the fence, and had merely satisfied herself by confirming it.

Just how she can know when other people are about their local actions without indulging in a steady wait behind long curtains— a practice in which she hasn't yet been caught out—baffles me.

I could forgive Mrs. Trumble (I think) if it were known that she was engaged in some private experiments involving the use of extra-sensory perception, for then we should realize that she was compelled in the interests of science to interrupt her work and carry her washing-up mop with her to the gate for a check-up, as she has done on many an occasion with me.

My wife is particularly bitter about our inability to move outside the house without being scrutinized.

"It isn't that she wants to see what you're doing. It just worries her not to know for sure," I say. But my wife refuses to be comforted.

Clearly, Mrs. Trumble has to be made to realize her anti-social behaviour. It is to this end that I have a plan based on the use of an old tuba now resting in the attic; I await only a promised red tunic from a friend. The whole scheme is a gamble of course. If I fail I lose all, and shall most certainly have to consider moving.

With the red tunic I shall wear one wellington boot, balanced by a plimsoll and cricket-pad on the other leg. Thus clad, I shall

300

be wheeled by my wife in the baby's perambulator through the front door out to the privet hedge, there to wait.

When Mrs. Trumble appears I shall lift the tuba to my mouth and gently play as if by nature wrought.

It will be enough if only traces of bewilderment register on Mrs. Trumble's face. On the other hand, if she nods . . .

D. H. BARBER

Triplets

"COLONEL and Mrs. Jumper," droned the man at the door, "Mr. Segby-Ash and Miss Peggy Segby-Ash, Bishop Stoot and Lady Cicely Stoot. Mr. Sympson."

It was a political dinner, and I had arrived early myself. A mistake in tactics, because the mob that followed me had gradually hemmed me into a corner of the room, where I had hardly space to lift my gin.

Sympson shook hands with our host and smirked at our hostess, and then disappeared in the direction of the bar.

"That was Sympson," I said to Brigadier Hogg, who was holding his cocktail above his head like a banner with a strange device, to prevent its being crushed against his waistcoat.

"Was it?" he said. He was absorbed in the task of trying to lever his elbow between two fat back-benchers, in order to get his glass on a level with his lips, and did not seem particularly interested in new arrivals.

I turned my eyes once more towards the man at the door, who was still announcing guests in great numbers.

"Commander Flit, Mr. and Mrs. Gooch, Miss Svelte and Miss Carmen Svelte, the Right Honourable Percy Drooping, Sir Peter and Lady Collarby-Starch. Mr. Sympson."

I gazed in astonishment as the Collarby-Starches drifted away and made room once again for Sympson. There was no mistaking him. He shook hands with our host with the same egregious expression and bowed in the same fake-Regency fashion to our hostess. Perhaps his made-up tie had worked a little farther round towards his left ear, but that was all.

"Sympson has just come in again," I said to Brigadier Hogg.

"Don't be absurd," said the Brigadier irritably. "Why should he come in twice? I reckon you've had too much pink gin."

He had managed to lever his elbow between the two back-benchers, but they had closed in on it and he still could not get his glass near his lips. I tried to help him by giving one of the back-benchers a gentle push, but, apart from upsetting most of the Brigadier's cocktail over the other back-bencher's shoe, achieved little.

The Brigadier gave up all hopes of refreshment and joined me in gazing at the man at the door.

"Mr. and Mrs. Gallup," he was saying, "Miss Pansy Trott, Major and Mrs. Griddle, His Highness the Bam Wanjar of Ghool. Mr. Sympson."

The Brigadier looked at me oddly.

"There's Sympson now," he said. "Only just got here. You've no head for spirits, as I've often told you, and ought to stick to beer."

Dinner was announced before I could reply, and I crept uneasily into the huge dining-room and found my allotted place. I had decided to stick to water for the rest of the evening.

Sympson sat down opposite.

"You'd think," he said, leaning across the table, "that by this time they'd have invented a fool-proof flash-bulb. A pal of mine on the *Daily Wire* very decently offered to do me a bit of good by including me in a picture of the Minister for Denationalization receiving his guests, but his flash-bulb failed twice, so I had to make three separate entrances. I hope nobody noticed."

"I don't suppose anybody did," I said, gratefully accepting a glass of white wine from the waiter.

❦

The Lowing Herd

THE compartment throbbed with the sound of men sleeping. In the corner facing me Colonel Rackstraw snored in short bursts, raising his right hand to the salute at the end of each salvo and then letting it drop on to his evening paper with a crack like a whip-lash. From Marriott seated next to him there issued a series of high-pitched warbling notes which, with a little careful editing from Mr. Ludwig Koch, could have gone straight into the Home Programme as Bird-song of the Month. In the far corner our vicar was droning away at an organ voluntary, interspersed with some half-remembered banns of marriage from the previous Sunday.

In desperation I opened the fashion magazine I was taking home for my wife and sought refuge in the world of *haute couture*. Almost immediately a sentence sprang at me from the printed page. *"Boleros,"* it said, *"are running like wildfire through the Paris collections."*

I looked at the colonel. Would he ever forgive me, I asked myself, for allowing him to sleep on in ignorance of such things? It was not a risk I was prepared to take.

I leaned over and shook him by the arm. He trumpeted loudly, saluted twice in quick succession and opened his eyes.

"What's up, Hopcroft?" he muttered thickly.

"The news looks pretty bad, sir," I said. "It says here that boleros are running like wildfire through the Paris collections."

"Boleros, eh?" The colonel made a gallant attempt to bring me into focus. "Thin end of the wedge when those fellows start running amok. First-class fighters, mind you, but a packet of trouble as soon as they're out of the line . . ." His voice tailed off and he began to nod.

"Don't you think Marriott should know about this?" I said loudly.

The colonel opened his eyes and stared vaguely at Marriott. Marriott chose that moment to start on a *reprise* of the seagull noises which had practically emptied the compartment at Clapham Junction.

"Yes," said the colonel, "I think he should." He nudged Marriott in the ribs. The bird-song stopped and Marriott woke up.

"Anything wrong?" he mumbled.

"Quite a lot," said the colonel tartly. "Hopcroft here tells me that boleros are running like wildfire through the Paris collections."

"Are they, by Jove!" Marriott blinked at us. "We had a plague of 'em once under our floorboards. Little beggars had eaten clean through a couple of joists and were starting on the third. Boleros, eh?" He undid another button of his waistcoat and closed his eyes.

The colonel nudged him again. "Better tell the padre," he shouted.

Marriott opened one eye and peered at the vicar, who had just embarked on a tremulous *vox humana* passage. "I quite agree, sir," he said. He shook the vicar by the knee and woke him.

"We thought you ought to know, padre," said Marriott, "that boleros are running like wildfire through the Paris collections."

The vicar yawned. "I can well believe it," he said sleepily. "We find an alarming number of foreign coins in our own offertories."

He settled back in his corner and closed his eyes. In a few moments the compartment throbbed with the sound of men sleeping.

❀

G. D. R. DAVIES

Skilled in Skinning

How many readers, I wonder, can say off-hand in what work of
fiction Ned Land appears? Ned was a Canadian of course and a
harpooner by profession; and what I chiefly remember about him
now (for it is a long time since I read *Twenty Thousand Leagues
Under the Sea*) is a remark he let fall on the subject of sharks.
"The shark," said Ned (I quote from memory), "is an awkward
fish. He has to turn over on his back before he can nab you."

What put Ned Land into my mind was an advertisement I saw
in *The Times* the other day, as follows:

"COLONIAL DEVELOPMENT CORPORATION requires a FISHERMAN
for WEST AFRICA, experienced in tropical shark-fishing with nets
and long lines with chain snoods; also skilled in skinning, fleshing,
curing of skins, net-making, fixing and preservation of gear."

Ned Land of course was not in the least afraid of sharks. Put a
harpoon in his hand, fit him out with one of Captain Nemo's self-
contained diving-dresses, and he would walk up to any shark you
liked and look it straight in the eye.

Without seeking to emulate the Canadian's peculiar sang-froid,
I felt that I was fully equal to encountering one of the ugly elas-
mobranchs at the end of a long line. The more I looked at the
advertisement the more intriguing it appeared. At last I put on my
hat and made my way to the offices of the Colonial Development
Corporation in Dover Street, W.1. It was not that I was dissatisfied with the job I had already; but I thought I should like a
change.

The commissionaire at Dover Street directed me to a door
marked "Private." I knocked and went in. "I've come about that
shark-fishing job," I said.

I am pleased to record that the Corporation made no attempt

305

to temporize or to shuffle me on to another department. The man whose office I had entered simply closed the file he had been reading, selected another from a metal cabinet, seated me courteously at a little distance from him and, after indicating that I was at liberty to consume any tobacco I might have about my person, asked me what experience I had of shark-fishing.   ·

"Not a great deal," I said modestly, "but I would propose, if appointed to the post, to catch them on the end of long lines with chain snoods."

"Chain how much?" said my interviewer rather abruptly.

"I should also," I said, "introduce an element of surprise by an occasional use of the net."

The Corporation man looked at me carefully, and then read something in his file for rather a long time. Presently he looked up and said: "What would you use for bait?"

An acquaintance with the works of R. M. Ballantyne enabled me to answer like a flash: "Salt pork."

"H'm," he said. "Salt pork, eh?"

"Precisely."

"Not fresh pork?"

"No."

"Why not?"

There was a short pause. "Of course," I said, lighting a cigarette and absent-mindedly placing it behind my ear, "if nets are used the question of bait does not arise."

"No," he said. "What kind of a net would you employ?"

"A very strong one. Now, as regards fleshing and skinning—"

"Your hair's on fire," he said.

We put it out with the help of a bucket of sand. Disconcerting as the incident was, it yet did something to put the interview on a less formal footing. After a few witty exchanges on the subject of free wigs he put his file away, drew his chair closer to mine and said: "Well, look here, old boy: about this shark business. I may as well tell you that I've never seen a shark in my life."

"Not even in the City?"

While he was laughing at this *mot* I sat smiling calmly and waiting for him to regain control of himself. I felt I was now in full command of the situation. Eventually, pulling himself together, he said: "Well, now, old man, tell me frankly: are you any good at catching sharks?"

"I wish I had a sovereign for every shark I've caught," I replied coolly.

"Pretty expert, eh?"

"You might say that, I suppose."

"I *do* say that, dash it," he said warmly. "You're too modest, old boy. Er—skin 'em pretty well, too, of course?"

"You may take it," I replied, "that I am not altogether unskilled in the art of shark-skinning."

He laughed again at that—he was a much more risible man than I had at first supposed. "Not altogether unskilled, eh?" he said. "That's a good one! Well, I don't see that we need look any further for the man to fill this post. Bit of bad luck for the sharks when *you* walked into this office, eh?"

We both laughed a good deal over that one.

"Seriously, though," he said, "I wish you'd explain to me what these chain snood things are. I've been wondering about them ever since we inserted the advertisement."

"Well," I said, "it's a very simple device really. I believe it was the Phœnicians who invented it. The chain," I said, "is wound into a helical spiral with the links overlapping, and attached transversely to the bight of the line, running *under* the fin-fouler and back *over* the eye-swivel of the threshing-gear. Then when the shark—"

"I see!" he broke in eagerly. "The bight tightens round the cylinder, engaging the cogwheels in the standing part, and its jaws automatically close on the salt pork! What an ingenious arrangement!"

"I see you are an engineer yourself," I said cautiously.

"You flatter me," he said, ringing a bell on his desk. "But tell me one thing: supposing you used *fresh* pork, do you think the shark might take it—with a pinch of salt? Perkins," he said to the commissionaire who had entered, "please show this gentleman out. He has mistaken this building for the Ministry of Food."

I took my hat and left. The last I saw of him he was doubled up over his desk and laughing like a hysterical dogfish.

MICHAEL WHARTON

A Slight Case of Psychiatry

"M TO R?" said the man at the door.

I hesitated.

"M to R?" he repeated in a jeering tone. "In other words, does your surname begin with any of the letters of the alphabet generally found between M and R? That is to say, M, N, O, P—"

"My name's Pinwright," I said.

"Right. This way then. And take that grin off your face."

Not a very auspicious beginning. I should explain that I was visiting the Employment Exchange at Lumpchester to register as a Self-Employed Person, over seventy years of age, and with an income of under two hundred pounds a year. I had long read with admiration those thrilling advertisements in the newspapers calling for greater efforts in our industrial drive, and it had occurred to me that I might be of some use in spite of my disabilities. I had previously filled in a form in which, under the heading "Other Remarks," I had suggested that I might be given the job of driving the municipal steam-roller. It had always been an ambition of mine.

In the inner room a grey-faced man with rimless glasses faced me from behind a long table, on which was a large and very complicated-looking form. Half a dozen other men of various shapes and sizes, obviously psychiatrists, sat on chairs at the back of the room.

"Good morning, Mr. Pinwright," said the man at the table. "Please sit down." I did so and at once fell heavily to the ground. "No chair," I explained as I got up, dusting my trousers. "That was Intelligence Test number one," said the man. "Now for number two. Over there you will see a bath full of water. Here is a teaspoon. What do you think is the best way of emptying the bath?"

I hesitated, suspecting a trap, looking now at the bath, now at the teaspoon, now at the examiner. "Who filled the bath, anyhow?" I asked, hoping to gain time. "I see the teaspoon has 'British Railways' on the handle. That shows it must be a new one."

The examiner looked rather annoyed, and one of the psychiatrists, who had been doing something with log tables in the background, suddenly said: "This man's I.Q. is only seventy-five. That means, strictly speaking, that he ought to go to an approved school."

"Hm. He's a bit old for that, unfortunately," said the examiner. "Is he a good mixer? What about the Chief Psychiatrist's Report? Dr. Albumblatt?"

Dr. Albumblatt, a squat beetle-browed figure, leaned forward. "I have examined Pinwright," he said, reading from a typewritten sheet in a guttural voice. "He is a schizoid type, is web-footed, and has trouble with his aspirates. There is marked avuncularism, contradicted, unfortunately, by a Scrooge complex. Alpha Rhythm, two point six five plus. Annular Reaction Nil. His patellar reflex is intermittent, and there is a tendency to aorta of the maxillary antrum. His batting average last season was nought point nought two. The Electro-encephalogram shows marked strygismus, or hooting in the brain, though this may be due to a faulty connection in the apparatus. The—"

"Thank you, Dr. Albumblatt. There's just one other thing. Would you say Pinwright had any criminal tendencies?"

The psychiatrist shrugged his shoulders. "Who can say? Perhaps. Perhaps not. Perhaps. Perhaps not. Per—" "Thank you," said the examiner firmly. He threw himself back in his chair and for some time stared at me fixedly. By this time I was beginning to wonder, not so much whether I should be given a job as whether I should ever get out of the room alive. But at last the chairman said "Have you a sense of humour?"

"I'm not sure," I said.

"Well, if you're not sure," said the examiner, "we'd better give you a test. All right, Travis, put him through it."

One of the psychiatrists put a record on a gramophone, while the others watched me narrowly.

"Who was that lady I saw you with last night?" boomed a voice, and another voice replied "That was no lady—that was my wife."

After a pause I laughed slightly. Dr. Albumblatt made a note. The examiner looked doubtful. "Better try him with another record," he said. "Sorry, that's the only one we've got left. The last man we interviewed broke all the others laughing." "All right, then, put him through that one again."

Again the voices boomed through the room, but this time I started laughing as soon as the record stopped, producing an ear-splitting guffaw, doubling up in my chair and slapping my knee uncontrollably. I was beginning to wonder if I had gone too far when I noticed that the psychiatrists had just seen the point of the joke themselves. While they were delightedly explaining it to one another I slipped away.

About a fortnight later I received a printed card which read "Dear Sir,—Your application for priority anthracite is being considered, and you will be informed of our decision in due course."

It seems possible that some interdepartmental confusion had occurred somewhere. But even that hardly seems to explain everything.

G. D. R. DAVIES

A Quantity of Beans

It ALL happened a good many years ago; but to me, coming suddenly and unprepared on the bizarre story in the sober pages of *Carver on Carriage by Sea*, every detail presented itself as vividly as it must once have done to the illustrious Carver himself. Not many of us have time to read him right through nowadays— it is not a book you can slip in your pocket—and I make no apology for bringing the strange case of *Notara* v. *Henderson* before a wider public.

It was in the year 1872 that, as Carver puts it, "a quantity of beans had been shipped in a steamer at Alexandria for Glasgow . . ."

In the historic harbour of the Pharaohs the good screw steamship *Sternfirst** lies alongside the quay. All day the ship has been a hive of activity; now, under the soft Egyptian stars, she lies quiet, and no sound disturbs her calm but the bubbling of the night watchman's hookah and a regular, monotonous thumping from the engine-room, where the Chief is beating a native stoker over the head with an iron firebar. In his cabin the captain is writing a letter to his owners. "My dear sirs," he has begun, "we sail at dawn to-morrow—"

The silence of the night is broken by a raucous hailing. The captain pauses in his work and looks out of the porthole, then

* That was not her real name.

resumes his writing. He has just added the words "weather permitting" when there is a knock at his door and the mate, a hulking, black-browed giant of a man, enters the cabin. "Beg pardon, Captain—," he says.

"Well, Mr. Gable?"*

"There's a boatload of cargo alongside, sir."

"Cargo, Mr. Gable? What sort of cargo?"

"Beans, sir."

The captain twirls his moustache. "Beans, you say, Mr. Gable? Then stow 'em in the hold."

"The hold's full, sir."

"Full, is it? Full, eh? Then put 'em in that sort of loft place at the bottom of the first flight of stairs."

"In the 'tween-decks, sir?"

"Those are my orders, Mr. Gable."

"Aye, aye, sir." The mate goes out and the captain turns again to his interrupted task. "All our cargo," he writes, "is safely in the holds, with the exception of a parcel of beans which I am stowing in the 'tween-decks . . ."

The voyage was uneventful until, some weeks later, the *Sternfirst* arrived, not at Glasgow but at Liverpool. Carver does not think it necessary to comment on this slight error; both places, after all, are large, greyish cities on the right as you go up the Irish Sea. Anyone might have done the same. No time was lost in putting to sea again; but "on coming out of the Mersey," says Carver, "the ship was injured by collision with another steamer and" (this is the crucial point) "the beans were wetted . . ."

Mersey River . . . a moist, grey dawn breaking over the mud flats; a thin mist curling over the turgid waters; sirens hooting as the big ships glide slowly down the river. Aboard the *Sternfirst* an ordered activity reigns; the mate, hoping to distract the men's attention from the recent navigational contretemps, has set the starboard watch to polishing the funnel, while the port watch are busily holystoning the hatch-covers. An apprentice, whom we will

* An *alias*.

call Charteris, is at the wheel; the captain himself is on the bridge, scanning the horizon with a telescope.

Suddenly there is a cry from forrard: "Steamer on the port bow!"

"Steamer on the port bow, eh?" says the captain briskly. "Bless my soul, so there is! Mr. Charteris!"

"Aye, aye, sir?"

"Avoid that steamer, Mr. Charteris."

"Port or starboard, sir?"

"Don't bandy technicalities with me, sir," says the captain hotly. "This is no time for a display of nautical pedantry. Get out of that ship's way!"

"Aye, aye, sir," says the boy doubtfully, beginning to turn the wheel.

"Not that way, you fool!" cries the captain. "Turn it anti-clockwise! You men in the front end! Get ready to push that steamer off! Full astern! Lower the anchor! Man the lifeboats!"

But it is too late; all the captain's seamanship cannot prevent a collision now. The two ships pass side to side, scraping a considerable quantity of paint off each other and breaking one of the *Stern-first's* portholes. From his bridge the master of the other ship shouts words that bring a blush to Mr. Gable's cheek and cause the captain, speechless with rage, to throw his hat on the bridge and jump on it. . . .

It is not known at what stage it was discovered that the beans had got wet, nor who made the discovery; it might have been Apprentice Charteris . . .

"Excuse me, Captain . . ."

"Well, what is it now?"

"I've just been looking at the beans, sir, and—"

"Looking at the beans! Looking at the beans! D'you think I've nothing to do but listen to a left-handed, red-eared, dog-faced, ullage-swilling spawn of a plumber's mate telling me he's been looking at the beans?"

"No, sir."

"Then go and—"

"Please, sir, the beans have got wet, sir."

The captain's face, at first bright crimson, changes slowly to puce and then to mottled purple; his mouth opens and closes, but no sound comes forth.

"Please, sir," says Apprentice Charteris, "do you think the beans ought to be dried, sir?"

The captain sits down heavily and strikes his head several times against a brass-bound sea-chest. His hands pluck feebly at his collar. Finally he speaks.

"Yes, Charteris. By all means, my boy. Certainly the beans must be dried. Just step along to Mr. Gable's cabin, will you, and ask him, with my compliments, if he'll lend you a few of his hand-embroidered, monogrammed lace handkerchiefs to dry 'em with. Will you do that?"

"Aye, aye, sir," says Charteris, mystified but obedient; and off he goes. Presently a scuffling is heard, shouted orders, and the sound of a body being dragged up the companion-way; then, after a short interval, a regular bumping under the ship's keel. A faint smile overspreads the captain's haggard features as he takes his pen and writes in the ship's log: "Tuesday, 11 A.M. Keelhauled Apprentice Charteris."

As Carver succinctly puts it: "No steps were taken to dry the beans."

The latter end of these vegetables is veiled in obscurity. We know that they had (in Carver's own words) "suffered much additional damage" by the time they were discharged; we know too that the Exchequer Chamber, which heard the case, held that "the beans ought to have been dried." More than this we are not told. Carver himself, after recording the above-mentioned judgment, simply puts a row of dots, and starts off again:

"Plaintiff was the owner of seventy-two chests of indigo . . ."

But that, I surmise, is another story.

ERIC KEOWN

Loose Leaves from My Autobiography

Most duels, I suppose, have arisen from some nonsense about a woman, or simply because one man has unequivocally called another a cad. My duel with Clarence Snailwell was of quite a different kind.

We were staying at the time with Hugo Fitzhugo in his mouldering manor house in Essex. He was a bachelor, who, though of ample means, believed that nothing good had happened since 1485. He lived uncomfortably in a knightly dream which left a rather simple expression on his face, devoting himself to the acquisition of a formidable collection of primitive weapons which hung in menacing clusters round his damp-stained and unplumbed walls. The only part of the house in good condition was the cellar, and consequently the annual feast of lampreys, swans, neat's tongues and suchlike which he gave to commemorate the, to me, somewhat shady tactics of the Black Prince at Poitiers was pretty well attended by his older and thirstier friends.

It was towards the close of one of these indigestible banquets, which rarely broke up before dawn, that I became embroiled with Snailwell. Being a man who would very willingly rob his grandmother, as, in fact, he was later discovered to have done, he was a sentimental idealist, and while we cooled our heads together at an open window he referred in absurdly flattering terms to the beauty of the sun, rising over the distant marshlands. I replied that it reminded me of nothing so much as an overripe blood orange. He insisted that the harmonies of dawn were perhaps our chiefest joy. I told him I found the whole business, not excluding the disgusting noises of the birds, in the worst possible taste, and I added that I considered Nature to be the arch-vulgarian. Our dispute took heat until, in a silence in which you could have heard a boar's head drop, he flung the dregs of his flagon in my face.

This was of course the very thing for which our host had for many years been hoping. Leaping upon the table he cried that choice of weapons lay with me. I looked long round the Great Hall.

"It shall be cross-bows," I said haughtily . . .

Our weapons were extremely heavy and had to be wound up like grandfather clocks. Snailwell and I stood back to back on the wet lawn, swaying a little in the cold morning air.

"March!" cried Fitzhugo, and— when we seemed to have been walking for some time—"Fire!"

I was the first to pull my trigger when we swung about. There was a dull twang as if somebody had kicked a cistern and the arrow flew uncertainly for a few yards before plunging into a rose-bush. When Snailwell fired nothing happened at all, because, as we afterwards found, mice were nesting in the mechanism. It was very disappointing.

"A draw," ruled our host. "And Clarence chooses weapons for the next round."

"Boomerangs," said Snailwell, without a moment's hesitation.

At this there was a rush to the house which left him and me alone, facing one another awkwardly with our hands still full of old iron.

"A singularly lovely sunrise," he cried defiantly.

"A botch of cheap pinks bungled by an amateur," I answered.

We were given three large boomerangs each and again told to march. At the command "Fire!" my opponent was first into action. His weapon, however, flew backwards out of his hand during a preliminary flourish and caught one of our fellow-guests a blow in the stomach. The man, a stockbroker named Bellamy, fell head-on against a statue of Pan and suffered a mild concussion. My own opening stroke was more successful. That is to say, the boomerang went forwards for a little way. It then came back with incredible speed, giving one of my seconds a nasty gash on the shin. Snail-

316

well's next effort flew straight into the sun and was never seen again. Mine went off like a homing pigeon towards the peach-house, which it met with a very satisfactory sound. The third volley left our hands at the same moment, locked in mid-air half-way down the pitch, and showered the spectators plentifully with aboriginal splinters.

It was now decided by Fitzhugo that so indeterminate a contest could only be settled by recourse to battle, and Snailwell and I, hotly protesting, were thrust into complete suits of armour and told to get on with it. His was topped by the conventional coal-scuttle of heraldry, mine with a sort of washing-up basin trimmed with fishing-net. Our weapons were spiked iron balls attached to short poles by heavy pieces of chain, and neither of us found them very handy. Vision was much restricted, and movement all but impossible. Occasionally we succeeded in lifting the ball high enough to tap the other lightly, but as our armour was designed to withstand a battering-ram it all seemed very hopeless.

In this manner we teetered about the lawn, Snailwell hissing at me from under the coal-scuttle and I hissing back at him through a crack in the washing-up basin. It was extraordinarily exhausting. We were still at it when the gong went for breakfast, and a rush of feet told us that once again we were alone. Unfortunately at that moment I was in the act of scoring on Snailwell's hauberk, and as a result of this we both went down. Not, however, on the lawn but into the lily-pool, where we lay side by side in about two feet of green water.

"There has never been a lovelier morning," gurgled Snailwell, through a mouthful of tadpoles.

"Done in icing-sugar for the Chantrey Bequest," I gasped, pulling a frog out of my jambard.

I think we both slept for a little after that, and then we were awakened by a muffled "Strewth!" behind us. It was the postman. He was a bustling, muscular fellow with an instinct for fifteenth-century mechanics, and he seemed pleased to learn that anything

317

he liked was his. Together Snailwell and I walked up to the house in silence. At the top of the terrace we paused.

"Snailwell," I began.

"My dear old boy," said Snailwell.

C. A. E. GREEN

It Sways to Advertise

"I'LL TURN round in a minute, sir!" cried the sandwich-man in the teeth of the gale. "I daren't let go o' these railings till I get round the corner."

I nodded approval—he was putting up a magnificent fight. Rigged with boards fore, aft and aloft, rolling and pitching in the wind, he reminded me of yachting days. At last he heeled over and staggered into the lee of a doorway. I congratulated him warmly.

"Why not lower your top board until the wind drops?" I added.

"I can't," he panted, clinging to the door. "It's joined to the lower board at the back, all in one piece."

"So it is. It must be very trying in this weather."

"Just as I've started a big campaign too."

"Indeed?"

"Yes. I'll tell you how it works if you like. D'you see what's printed on the back of me boards?"

"I do. It reads 'GUESS WHAT'S ON THE OTHER SIDE.'"

"That's right—me own idea. Makes you curious, don't it?"

"Oh, I don't know," I replied carelessly.

"It's what we advertising men call a eye-catcher," he went on. "Now, when the public reads 'Guess what's on the other side,' they have a guess and hurry past me to see if they was right, same as *you* did."

"Not at all."

"And then they see this," he said, turning round at last.

He revealed the words, on the front of his boards, "THEY'RE CRUNCHY." He ground his teeth by way of demonstration, and I turned away with a shudder.

"Then you ask me '*What's* crunchy, chum?'"

"Do I?"

"Yes," he said, turning back his cuffs, "and with that I darts out me hand and gives you this little twist of paper, containing one free tablet, with compliments."

He did a little bow, which brought his top board forward with a sort of flailing action. The tablet fell to the pavement.

"Don't eat *that* one, sir," he exclaimed, stamping his boot on it. "Where's your hygiene?"

"I was picking up my hat," I replied savagely, flapping my fingers to restore the circulation. I think it was about here that a querulous note crept into my voice. I watched him moodily.

"So then you ask me—'What are they called, chum?'—and I gives you this leaflet."

"It all seems frightfully involved," I commented, sneering as the wind blew it away.

"Dash it!" he said. "There's another one gone! Anyway, it says on this leaflet—'Obtainable at all chemists.' So you go into one and ask for an ounce of these tablets. Guess what happens next?"

"He gives me an ounce of your confounded tablets, I suppose," I said, fixing him with a glassy stare.

"Ho, no."

"Why not?"

"Because he ain't got any."

Now a moment's thought will convince you that an ordinary slashing stroke with an umbrella is wasted on a sandwich-man. A lightning thrust on the flank, between boards, might just reach a vital part, but I dismissed this as too chancy in a gale. I decided instead to resume my journey home.

"Wait a minute," he cried, struggling along beside me.

"Go away," I shouted. "People are looking at us."

"Let 'em wait," he said. "As I was saying, when the public keeps on asking him for these tablets he sits down and writes out a quick order, and next time you go in—"

"Kindly release my arm before I do you a mischief," I said in icy tones. "This is my station."

The scenes here at rush-hour are unexampled for sheer ferocity. Already a host of would-be passengers were closing in on us. There was a brief, silent scuffle, but before I could tear myself free we were hemmed in and carried helplessly in a solid mass past a frantic ticket-collector. I was touched by my companion's quiet dignity.

"I'm sorry about this," I murmured, as we glided down the moving stairway together. "I should have been more patient. My fault entirely."

"I don't mind," he said. "It's all good publicity."

"All the same—"

A train came in and the doors slid apart. I tried to retreat, but it was too late. The crowd surged forward, and my friend's top board struck the roof of the doorway and crashed down upon us with a loud booming sound. At the same time the rear board rose and cut a sickening swathe among the passengers standing inside. Everything went black, and I seemed to be floating endlessly through an agonized swirl of writhing humanity.

The train was moving out by the time I wrenched my hat up to eyelevel again. I just caught a glimpse of him through the windows. It made me realize what a wonderful thing advertising is. His boards had jammed horizontal, like a table, surrounded by a border of livid faces, all guessing what was on the other side. I think they guessed right, too, or else he had told them already.

At any rate they were all grinding their teeth.

ALEX ATKINSON

Them

I DON'T know how Humblestone feels about it, but I look back with pleasure on the chat we had on the five forty-five the other night.

I was reading comfortably about life on Venus when he bent forward and tapped me on the knee with his cigarette case.

"Well," he said, "how d'you think they're doing now?"

I folded my paper, and I stared straight back at him. "Splendidly," I said.

He nodded. Then he said dubiously "But what about that thirty thousand fee? Where are they going to get that from?"

"Out of stock," I said, and he laughed in a grudging, indulgent way. Then he looked cautiously at the third occupant of the compartment, a man in a bowler hat, and lowered his voice.

"Eldridge was telling me," he said, "that another transfer would ruin them."

"Yes," I said. "But what about Hamper?"

"Hamper? Who's Hamper?"

"Hamper," I said. "*You* know Hamper."

He looked puzzled for a moment and then he nodded doubtfully. "Mm," he said.

"Hamper told me," I went on, "that, in view of the way the thing was handled in nineteen forty-three, Jackson may be the one."

"Jackson?"

"Jackson or the man with the piebald horse. What's his name?"

321

Humblestone blinked slowly at me, and then he said "Yes. But there's training. That's not going to be easy. That ankle won't be fit to run on for a month. They're going to be wide open down the middle."

"Easy as pie," I said. "What about all those dumb-bells they had left over?"

"Dumb-bells? Who?"

"All those dumb-bells," I said. I turned to the man in the bowler hat. "Bundles of dumb-bells," I said, "and what do they do with them?" The man in the bowler hat shook his head, and Humblestone looked at him sharply. "Threw them in the Thames," I said, "without so much as a by your leave."

Humblestone licked his lips, and frowned. "Who did?" he said.

"*They* did."

"I never heard about that."

"There are a lot of things you never hear about," I said. "What about the way they hung up flags with little hens painted on them? There was something behind that. You're not going to tell me," I said, "that those refrigerators were left empty *by mistake?* What about Saturday? You've only got to read your papers," I said. "Who moved Harry? Who *moved* him?" I leaned forward and tapped him on the knee with my cigarette case. "It can be dropped from low-flying aircraft," I said. "Or it can be brought over in innocent-looking parcels. And another thing," I said, "they can go without water for longer than you think. *Much* longer. Take France, now, just for the sake of argument."

"France?" said Humblestone, gropingly.

"Or packets of salt," I said. "Take packets of salt. Where are you going to bore your hole, just for a start? There's altitude to be considered."

"Would you mind telling me," said Humblestone, reaching for his dispatch case, "just what the hell you're talking about?"

"Them," I said harshly, opening the door for him. And I bundled him on to the platform, and slammed the door, and put my feet up on the opposite seat, beaming.

As the train moved off again the man in the bowler hat cleared his throat, and came to sit beside me.

"Do you really believe, then," he said, "that they'll risk going to the country before October?"

COLIN HOWARD

Port-Fed Stilton

I BLAME myself entirely. I should never have allowed it to taste strong drink.

I scooped a large spoonful out of the middle and poured in a half-glass of port. The stilton coughed and spluttered, and I left the port to soak in. It didn't. It was still lying there, markedly untouched, the next morning, a placid little pool. It stayed there for a week, growing scum, and I resolved to resort to forced-feeding. I jabbed an elementary drainage-system through the stilton with a skewer. The stilton absorbed the port slowly and reluctantly.

It was after the third dose that I noticed the stilton's slowness and reluctance were wearing off. The fourth dose went down like lightning and the stilton was clamouring for more.

I am telling no lies when I say it polished off the rest of the bottle in under two days. The second bottle lasted only three days altogether. There was something compelling about that stilton. It was difficult to say "no" to it. It struck me that good port was wasted on a stilton that soaked it up at that rate, and I went out and bought it a bottle of the cheapest port-type British wine I could find.

I never did it again. I gave the stilton just a half-glass, to see if it would notice the difference, and it did. You may say a stilton cannot glare at you. I can only say you have never seen a stilton in the grip of the craving for alcohol. Trembling, I sucked the port-type wine out with a fountain-pen filler and rushed down to the cellar and got up a forty-year-old hunting port swathed in cobwebs, that I had been keeping for my golden wedding.

The stilton smacked its lips over it, and put the whole bottle away before bedtime. In the night I am almost certain I was awakened by bumpings below and a hoarse, hiccuppy voice singing "A Little of what you Fancy does you Good."

The next day it was not thirsty. It was in a sullen mood, and seemed glad of the cool napkin wrapped round it. But the day after it was itself again, and raised hell because there weren't any cobwebs on the bottle of vintage port I had got in for it.

Before long I was ordering its port by the half-dozen. The stilton was running me into more money than I cared to tot up. It was galling to think that, while it lolled there swigging its port, I could no longer afford even a mild-and-bitter for myself at night.

I saw there was only one thing for it. I should have to eat the thing up and regain my liberty.

It was a job for which I needed help. I belong to a rather serious literary society, and I asked them in one evening to discuss the influence of Spinoza on Nietzsche over a cup of coffee, with light refreshments of biscuits and cheese on the side.

The evening was a great success. We finished off the stilton to the last, soggy crumb, and stood round roaring out the chorus of "We Won't Go Home Till Morning" while Miss Hornby, our Hon. Secretary, did a skirt-dance on the table. Professor Applestall bagged a policeman's helmet on his way home, and the Misses

Duncan returned two doorknockers and a dust-bin anonymously the next morning.

What I say is, there's nothing like a nice bit of cheddar.

ERIC KEOWN

Cheers from the Pavilion

THE arrangements for my hundredth birthday, which have been under consideration for some time, are being pressed forward feverishly since I read the other day of an old gentleman who, on being asked what had caused him to survive so long, replied that he had no idea. His answer grieved me profoundly. I am absolutely determined that whatever gaps in my mind remain unplugged I shall not be short of reasons why I am a hundred.

I passed my twenty-first birthday sucking lozenges for a sore throat in the company of three dozing monks and a salesman for electric-shock machines, in a third-class carriage rattling very hotly through France. As a celebration you can say it was wasted. At the actual minute of my birth, the timing of which had been accurately noted and reported to me on the slender chance that the fabric of history might some day wish to absorb it, I did make a halting attempt to share with the nearest monk the excitement of my brand-new majority. At the first mention of *vingt-et-un*, however, he left the carriage hurriedly, under the impression that I was offering to engage him in a game of chance; and after that the rest of us went gloomily to sleep. Between the twenty-first and the hundredth no other birthday merits attention. If you consider the score of the Ice Age or see a play by Mr. Priestley you will realize that the intervening years are deceptively telescopic and that with your hundredth birthday waiting impatiently round the corner you have scarcely time left to put on a clean collar before setting out to meet it. I made up my mind there and then, as we halted at a small station called Eau Potable, that mine was going to be an out-standingly jolly affair. I intend that the reporters and telegraph boys and the nice girls from the B.B.C. and all the beagle-faced men from the insurance companies shall talk of it afterwards in whispers. It will be quite a party.

Television, or whatever inbecile process television has by then yielded place to, will probably begin it. For this I shall sit in a rocking chair, wearing a big white false beard with three or four woolly peninsulars running down into my mug of warm milk. Warm milk will at this stage be pressed relentlessly on everybody present, but especially on the reporters. I shall grin mildly at the cameras and gurgle about how wonderful science is and about how I once saw Edward the Seventh knocking the ash off a cigar in Pall Mall and about how I have always been careful to keep a tonquin bean in my waistcoat pocket during easterly spells and about how I otherwise owe everything to two daily tablespoonfuls of dandelion-juice sucked through a lump of caustic soda. All this will ring so many cracked old bells with the reporters that they will ship their pencils and forget to ask me what part, if any, beer and tobacco have played in my preservation.

This is the moment, I think—though I admit the arrangements still change kaleidoscopically from time to time—when, flinging my beard through the window, I shall walk across to my desk and, pulling out a revolver, shatter the ceiling-light in my study with one cunningly directed bullet. I have long been wanting to do this, and it seems to me to be worth waiting a little longer. With my present degree of skill I couldn't guarantee to sock the light before the whole ceiling collapsed, but I still have a few years in hand for practice. This simple gesture will put the reporters on their toes, if not on the flat of their faces. And if I do happen to shoot one or two of them in the process, well, there has never been any shortage of reporters, and, as I should be the first to ask the police, if a man cannot get away with murder on his hundredth birthday, when can he?

I shall now produce a bottle of whisky from my desk and, filling a pint-sized tumbler, drain it off at a gulp. It will only be coloured

326

water, of course, as I shall want to keep my head clear for the early phases of my birthday, but it is sure to make an impression on those present, and the real whisky which will be passed round simultaneously is sure to make another. At this point my nurse or the hired hand or whichever of my great-grandchildren can still put up with my increasing foibles will appear, to urge me not to place too great a strain on my limited physical resources. My answer will be to seize a horse-whip from the wall and advance on them with the veins in my neck bulging disgustingly. The telephone ringing, I shall go back to the desk and assure the caller that I will see him damned before I will play polo on my hundredth birthday. And this, as I see things at the moment, is the time for a challenge to the leading member present of what might be called the more serious press to a duel with carving-knives on the front lawn. Being persuaded, but with abounding reluctance, to go back to my chair, I shall now be subjected to an eager battery of questions. Brushing these aside, I shall say something to this effect:

"Ladies and Gentlemen, there are only two things I regret. One is that I have been obliged to earn my living, and therefore to expend in an unseemly fashion a great deal of energy for which without the slightest difficulty I could at all times of my life have found far more exhilarating outlets. The other is that after the coming of anæsthetics, antiseptics and improved sanitation, the invention of all of which was most disgracefully delayed, a law was not generally passed obliging all scientists to be strangled at birth. If that humane measure had reached the Statute Books the world in which I have just knocked up the century now under discussion would be a much more habitable place. I owe my longevity solely to a considered policy of always sitting down whenever it has conceivably been possible to do so, I regard the cooking in this country as still no more than embryonic, and I am leaving my entire fortune to the founding of a Chair of Pure Inaction at Cambridge University."

We should then all be ready for a goodish lunch, the menu for which is under constant review but must await local conditions before taking final shape.

WILLIAM THORNTON

Yes, Mr. Hackenstraw

IN THE very early morning I knew it was going to be a bad day. I knew when I'd had my first cup of tea and I went to shave and found the wash-basin full of anthracite. I went and looked in the slow-combustion stove and, sure enough, I could see where I must have poured in the shaving water.

I took the anthracite out of the wash-basin, piece by piece, and shaved in cold water, and drank another cup of tea. I always make the early morning tea. Sometimes I do it without any trouble; sometimes I pour a caddy full of tea into the kettle while I'm thinking of something else. I took my wife a cup of tea and told her about the anthracite. I had to tell her twice before she seemed to take it in, and then she said we were lucky to have any solid fuel at all, the Coopes hadn't had any since the end of November. Shortly after this conversation I left for the office, feeling not so bad.

I felt bad again when I was sitting at my desk waiting for Miss Podmarsh to bring in the letters, and when she came in I could see she could see I was in a bad temper.

"What's that kettle doing there, Miss Podmarsh?" I snapped.

"I don't know, reelly I don't, Mr. Hackenstraw," Miss Podmarsh said, climbing up the filing-cabinet to get the kettle.

"Well, remove it!" I shouted. "It doesn't look good." I passed my hand over my eyes, partly because I didn't want to see Miss Podmarsh looking at me reproachfully and partly because I had a feeling this had all happened before—dozens of times.

"Yes, Mr. Hackenstraw," Miss Podmarsh said.

She went out with the kettle, and for a long time nothing happened in the office of Hackenstraw and Company, Advertising Agents. Then I put down a switch and said into a little black box thing on my desk: "Miss Podmarsh, bring me in some journals carrying our latest SLYMM-LYMMS ad."

"Wahp, Mr. Huckenstrahp," the black box said, and after a bit Miss Podmarsh came in with this month's *Lady and Leisure*, which is a magazine I rather like to read whether it is carrying any of our ads or not.

"Put it down there," I say calmly without raising my eyes.

"Yes, Mr. Hackenstraw," Miss Podmarsh says.

"Oh, Miss Podmarsh," I say, "I think I left my brief-case in the outer office as I came through this morning."

"I didn't see it, Mr. Hackenstraw."

"I'm not asking whether you saw it, Miss Podmarsh. I'm merely observing I think I left it there when I came through this morning."

"Yes, Mr. Hackenstraw."

"Kindly go and see if it is there."

She goes out and I hum a little tune to myself. I feel my exchanges with Miss Podmarsh have hit a new, smoother level. Dignified. The box on the desk buzzes. I put down the switch. The box says "Swahp hahp, Mr. Huckenstrahp."

"What?" I say.

"The brief-cahp. Snahp hahp!"

"All right, Miss Podmarsh."

After this I try to read *Lady and Leisure*, but I can't settle to it. I'm worried about that brief-case—not that it had anything in it. I wouldn't carry a brief-case at all, only my wife has a kind of obsession about them. The first thing she says when I get home is

"What about your brief-case?" and I give it her and she takes it and mumbles over it and says she'll put it in the hall ready for the morning. I don't dare think what sort of a state she'd be in if I didn't have it with me; so I ring the bell and instruct Miss Podmarsh to buy one in the lunch hour.

"Yes, Mr. Hackenstraw," she says.

Now I can settle down and look at *Lady and Leisure*, which is a paper I enjoy, as I said before. It's a paper that takes your mind off things. Soon I'm engrossed in an article called "Seven New Ways with Tinned Tomato Soup." This is so good I have to ring for a sandwich, and then I go on to the page that is really my favourite: "Pauline Prune's Page," where she answers her letters. Everyone knows they're written by members of the magazine staff, but that doesn't prevent their being works of passion and imagination.

These letters take you out of yourself. There's a lady who wants to know what hair-style Miss Prune thinks would offset short legs and very large feet, and there's another whose grandfather laughs at her fiancé because he keeps his money in a purse and what ought she to do about it. But the best one this month is from a lady who—but I'd better quote it in full:

"DEAR PAULINE PRUNE,—I have been getting very worried about my husband. We have been married sixteen years next July and now he is getting a very queer habit. He's always in a hurry in the mornings, and although he kisses me good-bye he seems to be very forgetful of other things, e.g., for the last few weeks he has been going off carrying the kettle in mistake for his brief-case. When I ask him about his brief-case he just points to the new one he has just bought, as if nothing had happened. What would you suggest I should do about this? Our small box-room is nearly full of brief-cases, and buying new kettles all the time is running away with my savings. On the other hand friends say that to tell my husband might easily be very dangerous, like with sleep-walkers who should not be awakened.

Yours sincerely,
(Mrs.) K. P. H.

It's wonderful the way they think of these things. I feel a lot better, and when Miss Podmarsh comes in I give her such a smile she nearly falls over backwards.

ERIC KEOWN

Noises Off

You want to feel well when you stay with James because the chances are you will find yourself at the wrong end of a tombola or else facing backward girls at basketball. I felt frightfully tired, and said so.

"You can be as peaceful as you like," James said. "I thought we'd take a little drive before lunch."

"Fine," I agreed. "You've certainly picked a good spot in which to eke out your glutted existence." It was true. As far as the eye could peer Nature had spread herself in a big way. Nothing had been spared to make the prospect a success, and for once the dirty finger-prints of man were not to be seen.

"And what a healing quiet," I added. All at once the calm was shattered by a giant voice which seemed to come from nowhere in particular. It was Jove talking out of the soles of his boots.

"*Attention, please! Will Sergeant J. P. McGlurkin come at once to Hut 40B?*"

James's face had gone the dull purple which in happier days one might have associated with port.

"Brutes!" he growled.

"What the devil was that?"

"Training camp the other side of the hill. New C.O. insists on having it festooned with loud-speakers."

"Have you protested?"

"Have I protested? The War Office empties at the mention of my name. But this chap says the efficiency of his—"

"Attention, please! Will Corporal O. P. Glottis go to the M.O.?"

"Let's drive," said James.

"Have you no redress?" I asked, as the car swung out into the lane.

James smiled gently. "I thought I'd take you up Bundle Hill," he said. "The bluebells are a knock-out."

At the top of the hill he turned sharply across smooth grass and stopped in the shade of a great beech-tree, on the edge of a precipice.

"What's all that down there?" I asked.

"That? Why, that's the camp," said James, fumbling under a sack at the back.

"James!" I cried sternly. "What are you up to?" For he had produced a large trumpet and was busily screwing it into a socket in the roof.

"The things I promised through this at the election," he said. "It's just as well I didn't get into power." He now plugged a small mike into the dash. "You'll find it more entertaining if you stand away a little. Just tell me if it's live?"

He coughed lightly and the trumpet barked thunderously over the camp.

"Very much so."

"Good."

"Attention, please!" cried Jove. *"Will Private B. Hoskins go at once to the Equipment Office?"*

James instantly went into action.

"Give ear, chums!" he roared. *"We've changed our minds. Will Private B. Hoskins be good enough to join Sarge McGlurkin for a bitter with the Adj.? Who will also be glad to see Corporal Glottis as soon as he's done up his shirt."*

Life in the arena below seemed curiously arrested. It was like looking on to an anthill as the first wave of D.D.T. rolled in. James made the V-sign through the window.

"Attention, please!" yelled a furious Jove. *"Whoever has tapped the loudspeaker circuit is to report immediately to the Guard Room."*

332

"*Wash that out, boys!*" James parried. "*On second thoughts he must be such a brave chap we're putting him in for a big gold gong.*"

The ants, several hundred of them, were standing absolutely rooted.

"*Attention!*" roared Jove. "*Will all officers please come at once to Headquarters?*"

"*Achtung, kinder!*" thundered James. "*Will all privates with ginger moustaches of a span of more than one foot kindly gather on the square for their weekly Kiss-in-the-Ring with the R.S.M.?*"

The ants began to move, spasmodically, then one or two broke into a run.

"*We are very happy to announce that the Sergeants' Bluebell Ramble is at last being resuscitated. It will leave the Mess at 1430. This will in no way interfere with the Pink Elephant Sale in the Naafi at 1700.*"

Jeeps began to dart rather rapidly about the camp.

"*Hark, larks! The subject for next week's poetry marathon will be as follows:* 'The Smile On the Face of the Colonel.' *Entries should be written on all three sides of the paper and inserted at sundown in the Commanding Officer's In-tray.*"

All below was now in a pleasing state of chaos.

"*You naughty, naughty boy!*" bellowed James. "*Come to the Mess and be smacked!*"

He got out and, unlimbering the bits and pieces, shoved them carefully under the sack again. As we drove quickly down the hill he grinned happily.

"That should stir things up a bit," he said.

"It certainly should," I agreed.

"Poisonous things, loud-speakers."

"Foul."

"I shall ban them directly I get into office."

"Here, James! What on earth are we going in here for?"

"Oh, didn't I tell you? We're lunching with the C.O."

❀

M. W. HIVES

That Still, Small Voice

JACOB MORGAN paused and clutched at my arm.

"I feel a trifle dizzy, man," he said; "the heat of the sun is like to shrivel me up. Rest I must have and where better to resuscitate my failing limbs than in the shelter of Glynis Parry's cottage yonder."

I knocked at the weather-beaten door and Mrs. Parry opened it and listened as I explained.

"Come in you. Come in and welcome. Poor old Jacob that has never missed a Sunday chapel. Bring him in and put him on the sofa."

Jacob lowered himself on to the horse-hair, and within a couple of minutes Mrs. Parry had her four daughters and her two neighbours in enthusiastic consultation.

"A damp cloth around his head," said one. "That is the remedy. For look you how his face is all fired up."

"No, water it is he lacks," cried another. "Bring you a glass and let our Megan race to the chemist for bicarbonate."

"The poor old man should be by rights in bed," advised another. "I tell you his looks have not the healthy bloom, as I should know, having buried two and sat with more than I can tell."

"Let us try a little sulphur; his blood it is that heats and races too fast for his poor old brain. And look you there is still some liquorice in the cupboard that has not been used for long enough."

And then spoke Dilys Parry in a moment of comparative silence; a shy, wild young thing but all her wits about her. "There is still a little brandy in the bottle, mother," she whispered. "Maybe a little drop might help the poor old man."

But her voice was lost in the dreadful babel that broke out with

334

renewed vigour and filled the tiny room with lilting accents. Jacob Morgan heard that whisper, though, and raising a gnarled hand he spoke with resonant authority.

"Quiet you," he commanded. "Quiet all of you and let young Dilys speak again."

MICHAEL WHARTON

A Word to Parents

THERE is a proverbial saying in our part of the world—"As owd as Ormondroyd's." It refers of course to the famous boilermaking firm of Ormondroyd and Uggshaw. In fact nobody knows how old it is. They say that Queen Elizabeth, on one of her tours of England, slept in one of our largest boilers, and that Mary Queen of Scots was imprisoned in one of the smallest ones. One thing I do know, and that is that ever since anyone can remember there has been an Old Man Ormondroyd—grim, black-booted, worsted-suited, indigo-waistcoated, gold-watch-and-chained—presiding with stern yet kindly despotism over the machicolated buildings that crown the windy heights of Cleckersyke Clough. Thank you. As everyone knows, most of the Ormondroyds have tended to disinherit their eldest sons, usually for marrying mill-hands, governesses, or beautiful slave-girls, but occasionally for running away to Paris to become artists. In one case, owing to a mistake by a railway booking-clerk, one of the young Ormondroyds ran away to Sheffield instead and became an extremely wealthy steel-magnate—but he was of course disinherited just the same. At Ormondroyd's tradition is everything. Parents who are thinking of apprenticing their sons at the famous old firm often complain because Ormondroyd's even to-day preserves so much of its individuality—even eccentricity. "Look at Mutterthwaite's," they say. "Look at Grampus and Hardcastle's. Fully rationalized. Up-to-date. Turning out boilers by the thousand. How often do we get a boiler from Ormondroyd's? Once a year perhaps. And even then it is turned out not for the commercial market but for the private collector, usually in America. If I sent my son to Ormondroyd's would he really get a fair chance of learning modern boiler-making?"

The answer is of course that Ormondroyd's are not aiming at quantity. I remember the Old Man himself sent for me one day and said "Pinwright, do you know what we are aiming at?" Like a fool I said "Quantity." The Old Man smiled and shook his head. "No, Pinwright," he said, "not Quantity. Nor Quality either. What we are aiming at is to try to bring the world more happiness through boilers. Always remember that." And I have always remembered it.

Naturally, then, the atmosphere in our works is a very happy one. We are encouraged to talk, sing, and even play musical instruments and non-gambling games at our work; and it is an understood thing that in the unlikely event of the works being totally submerged by flooding, water-polo will be laid on by Mr. Hargreaves, our popular works manager. Most of us keep pets of some kind, ranging from white mice and ferrets to the larger mammals. Dankshaw, whose aged mother combines taxidermy with taking in people's washing, has a large stuffed eagle by his work bench. Another operative, Josiah Heppenstall, at one time kept a fully-grown python of a particularly active variety, and many were the shouts of laughter as with flashing eyes it confronted some astonished visitor. As a rule it would merely chase its victim round the factory two or three times, and then, to show how fast it could really go, would race alongside the three-forty-five Huddersfield train for a few miles before returning home to its evening meal. However, in the end the factory inspector, on one of his annual visits, ruled that the python took up too much room, and Heppenstall, not without tearful scenes, had to hand over his pet to the professional care of old Mrs. Dankshaw. It is now one of the most admired exhibits in the Natural History Room at the Uggshaw Institute.

What an ideal factory! no doubt most people will say. Surely no work ever gets done there? Make no mistake. The Old Man's paternal rule can be stern and pitiless. For incompetence he has

336

no mercy. It will not be out of place, perhaps, if I give a short though horrifying example.

Some twenty years ago a certain Stanley Theakston was sent to us from Hilltop Labour Exchange as an apprentice boiler-maker. He was of course a friendless orphan. Even by the side of workers who suffered from such occupational diseases as phossy jaw, lantern-nose, Tubb's disease and double-ended syncope his appearance was not exactly prepossessing. A tow-coloured thatch of hair hung dankly over a thatch-coloured face, in which the greenish gleam of protruding teeth might have been glimpsed had not a huge black cloth cap, surmounted by a brass button of repulsive design, which he was never known to take off on any account, involved his whole person in murky though merciful obscurity. Thank you once again.

In spite of a certain prejudice we all did our best to help the new hand. But from the first his attitude was unco-operative. If he was given a boiler and told to get busy on it he would give it a few desultory taps with his hammer and then, evidently losing interest, would turn his back on it and go to sleep. Even when Mutcliffe, Heppenstall, or one of the other hands showed him the old boiler-maker's trick of reviving flagging interest by trundling the boiler smartly up and down the shed a few times he did not seem able to grasp the idea; he would trundle his boiler right out of the shed, down the road, and perhaps into some canal or waste dingle, where it would be found days afterwards in a rusted and unserviceable condition. Nor was this the worst. As most people are aware, it is dangerous to light a fire under a boiler *without first turning the water on*. Theakston was continually setting Nature at defiance in this way; it was his delight to start fires not merely under his own boilers but under other people's as well. Nature's rejoinder often took a violent form, and it was no fault of Theakston's if there was not heavy loss of life and damage to property.

No one was surprised when in the end the Old Man sent for him. As it happened, I had been taken off boiler-making that morning to do a few repairs in the Old Man's office, in which he had disinherited two of his sons the previous evening. So as I moved

337

about the room, patching up a torn curtain here and there, sweeping up the plaster from the floor, and removing traces of blood from the ceiling with Sugden's No. 2 Fluid, I was able to hear every word of the interview.

"What's your name, my lad?" began the Old Man, kindly enough.

"Theakston."

"Well, Theakston, so you don't take to boiler-making? The foreman in your shed tells me that you have no interest in your work. It seems that you have not completed a single boiler during the fifteen years you have been in the works. How is this?"

Theakston seemed to be struggling for breath.

"Come, lad," went on the undeviating voice. "Tell me. I am here to help you."

In a horrible gulping tone Theakston spoke. "Boilers? I thought they said bolsters. At the Labour Exchange."

There was a terrible silence. I laid down the shattered halma-board I was mending. The Old Man had gone white with anger. If looks could kill, old Mrs. Dankshaw might well have found an unusual object for her skill on her work-table that very night. Then the crisis passed. The Old Man pointed to the door.

"Go! And never again set foot in Clekersyke Clough."

Theakston staggered out of the door.

The end of the story is characteristic. Years later I heard that the Old Man had forgiven the friendless orphan sufficiently to set him up in a rather meagre way as a literary and dramatic agent in Tristan da Cunha. All things considered, I think it was remarkably generous of him.

F. MAYNE

Murder in the Making

"I NEARLY became a murderer myself," said Cox, while we were discussing a recent murder trial.

338

"Ha, ha," I said. "I remember once when I—"

"I was at school at the time," continued Cox. "It was during a clay-modelling lesson. I hated clay-modelling. I hated all lessons in which I was expected to do anything or make things. I liked sitting in my desk and watching my teachers wear themselves out. Clay-modelling I hated in particular."

"But how did you nearly murder somebody during a clay-modelling lesson?"

"The mere feel of the clay made my nerve-endings vibrate, and my more remote neurons used to jangle in sympathy."

"Who was the victim?"

"I remember each pupil was forcibly supplied with a grey tray, a large slab of grey clay, and a small puddle of grey water."

"Was it one of the boys or the master?"

"It makes me feel bilious to talk about it."

"About the murder?"

"I had up to then managed to fob the art master off by fashioning various objects like tennis-balls and pancakes. He was not keen on my tennis-balls and pancakes; but he soon grasped the idea that I was not good at clay-modelling, and he was not usually an unkind man."

"Then why did you try to kill him?"

"Once, after my father had explained some modern sculpture to me, I made an irregular shape and bored a large hole through it. The art master asked me what it was, but I could see that he was incredulous even before I had told him. I explained that it was an idea rather than an object. He said would I please stick to objects rather than ideas for the time being."

"Was that when you tried to—"

"One day I was seized with a wild ambition; I wanted to create a vase or urn. But I found it difficult to secure any graceful lines. After about ten minutes it was more or less the same width all the way up, so I seized it in the middle and squeezed it until it squirted out at both ends, producing a vase that looked like an hour-glass. But it was not symmetrical and all my efforts could not make it so. I kept on scraping little shavings off the bulges until it was again

339

practically the same width all the way up. Soon all the little pieces that I had whittled off had dried out and were quite intractable. Suddenly the vase itself collapsed into fragments. The puddle of grey water was now used up, and I was faced with a tray full of friable and frangible clay crumbs. I abandoned by Utopian vase. If only I could make a solid lump, all I wanted to do was to squash it flat into a pancake or roll it round and round into a tennis-ball. I scrabbled, kneaded, and massaged. Every now and then there was a catch in my voice even though I wasn't talking. I now saw that even a rudimentary pancake was out of the question."

"You tried to steal a model from the boy in the next desk," I exclaimed.

"I was leaning forward to retrieve a small piece of clay which had jumped over the edge of the tray when my attention was diverted from my crumbs to my teacher. There was a little table which the open door of the big cupboard hid from the rest of the classroom. I, however, was at the end of the front row, and in leaning forward I had a fairly good view. His extraordinary behaviour held me spellbound. After cutting up new pencils issued by the education authority into small lengths, he put these pieces into his mouth and began gnawing at them in a curious, tentative way."

"You acted in self-defence," I cried. "They took him away struggling violently."

"At first I was puzzled by his behaviour, but the true explanation quickly occurred to me. Earlier in the week he had been considerably worried about our losing a large number of pencils. For every used pencil, he said, he had to produce a stump. Now he was busy creating stumps that looked as if they had been used; and by the way he exposed his eye-teeth as he munched, I could see that they were poor quality pencils.

"Something caused him to turn his head, and for a few awful moments we gazed at each other—he with three or four pencil stumps hanging out of his mouth, and I mechanically rolling a clay crumb between my forefinger and thumb. I sank back, but he knew that I had seen all. A minute later, he emerged from behind the cupboard door, trying to look nonchalant."

Satisfied that I had located the victim and that the climax was at hand, I remained silent.

"He pretended that I was not his real objective and glanced at the work of other boys in a desultory way, pausing to praise a boy who was just putting the finishing touches to a model of the Taj Mahal. As he approached my desk I watched him carefully.

"For a few seconds he stood gazing at me like a recently converted cannibal. When he spoke, he spoke far too quietly, asking me what my tray of crumbs represented. I thought of trying to avert the storm by saying that it was a snowfall or a collection of very small tennis-balls, but I felt that my words would carry little weight. Suddenly he began screeching at me. He asked me if I had spent the whole afternoon putting my clay through a sieve. He told me that if I was tired of making tennis-balls that looked like lemons, I should make a lemon that looked like a tennis-ball. By now he had wound himself up so far that I thought he was going to fly to pieces. Becoming inarticulate, he rushed to the cupboard, produced a cane, and told me to bend over."

"Yes, yes!" I cried in excitement.

"I bent over, and he gave me four terrible cuts. I tottered back to my seat with rage in my heart, for I knew that I had been caned, not because I had failed to produce a clay model, but because he had been eating pencils."

"What about the murder?" I said coldly.

"Oh, I never tried to commit an actual murder," said Cox.

"Then why did you say that you nearly became a murderer?"

"Well, if I had been a weaker character, the injustice of it all would have warped my mind and slowly turned me into a particularly vicious type of murderer."

If Cox has a fault—and he has many—it is that he is too fond of talking about himself.

Charivaria

"Moscow Stirring the Kurds"
Manchester Guardian

But whey?

When a goldfish found abandoned in its bowl in Piccadilly was taken to the R.S.P.C.A. their comment was "We have no idea how a goldfish came to be in Piccadilly at such a time." At any other time, of course, the streets are paved with them.

"The chairman, however, said he could not alter his ruling, and Mr. Keesey, in protest, picked up his papers and walked out of the Council chamber, saying: 'It is contrary to Standing Orders and I shall not sit down and stand it.'" *Clevedon Mercury*

Thus clarifying his attitude.

The Church Speaks Out

"Do You Know What Hell Is?
Come and Hear Our
New Organist."

Notice outside a Toronto church

"Why does one see," asks a correspondent in a weekly journal, "a brimstone butterfly flapping its wings, in a main thoroughfare, on a cold and wet day in February?" Well, it has to do that or walk.

"Special note to ALL: if you'd like a brief, but to the point, criticism of a *short* MS., then send it along with a s.a.e. We pull no punches; you are not likely to do us credit if we pull blinkers over your eyes nor if you wear cotton-wool over the aforesaid peepers. If you are likely to figure on this page (to our advantage as well as yours), then we want you. If you would be wasting your time and ours, we'll tell you so—ever so gently!
    Yours, waiting joyfully, but calmly, for the first cuckoo of the spring
—————(Director of Studies)." *Advt. in The Writer*

That's candid, anyway.

"He is an unusual mixture of hard-headed business man and creative artist. Age, just turned 40, clean-shaven, with dark-brown hair and light-brown eyes and six feet. And a bachelor."—*Weekly News*

Well, think of darning all those socks.

Truth in Advertising

"Asahi Beer
You try it once! You will never want another beer."—*Advt. in Bangkok Post*

"Renee is a grandmother of 47, and mother of four."—*Daily Express*

Hats off to the second generation!

Two Tottenham children were given a severe warning by the magistrate for stealing toffee apples from a barrow. They were reminded that this sort of thing is apt to lead to a sticky end.

The Polish Communist regime have invented the word Spychalszczyzna to describe nationalist deviation in the Polish Army. Judges must take extra care when they pronounce sentence in such cases.

"Czechs Accuse Embassy
Prague Radio has accused two Britain of Sping."

Cyrenaica Observer

It's a lie, whatever it is.

Old American Custom

"Wrightsville was snoozing in the August sun. A few people drifted along under the elms on State Street. Two policemen were wiping their necks on the steps of the County Court House."

From a detective novel

Safety First

"Pierce with a pin to release vacuum. Then push off."

Instructions on the lid of a jam-jar

"Be Thou with Me (Bach), with Organ accomp.; My heart ever Faithful (from Cantata No. 68—Bach); Art Thou Troubled with the City of Birmingham Orchestra (from 'Rondelinda'—Handel)."

China Mail

Not much, but thanks for asking.

"The individual dosimeter looks like a fountain pen and can be carried like one. The wearer looks like a fountain pen and can be carried like one."—*Daily Graphic*

What a curious coincidence.

National Health opticians are complaining that their margins of profit are too low. All the same, for them prosperity is just around the cornea.

Sporting Losers

"I saw him land at least five big dace and roach. They expressed their admiration of the water, and of the Farnham Angling Society."—*Aldershot paper*

Among the articles which Germany would like to export to this country, we read, are collar-studs. This looks like another plot to bring Britain to its knees.

There were no psychiatrists in mediæval England, remarks a writer. But it must be remembered that in those days the country was sparsely inhibited.

A thief has been stealing wine by cutting round holes in vinters' windows—and then working his fingers to the Beaune.

"MACARTHUR
FLIES BACK
TO FRONT."

Bangkok paper

To keep the sand out of his eyes?

347

"Mrs. Brandon took the heavy piece of silk from the table, unfolded it and displayed to the Millers an altar cloth of her own exquisite embroidery sewn with pre-war silks from her hoard, upon which, everyone began to blow their nose or cough and Mrs. Brandon was quite dissolved in delightful tears. 'Let me offer you my handkerchief,' said a deep, pleasant, voice by her side . . ."—*From a novel.*

There was one gentleman there anyway.

Squish!

"BRITAIN STANDS FIRM ON
PALESTINE DATES."

The Scotsman

An American dietician is exciting comment by experimenting with various types of music during meals as an aid to digestion. Jealous rivals accuse him of playing to the calory.

New Look for Men

"W. ——, Trousers Maker. Entrance round back.
Notice in the window of a Leeds tailoring establishment

Handyman

"They had to pass through an iron grille and a wooden door. The officer opened the iron grille, and while he was opening the wooden door Jackson made a bolt for it."—*Star.*

"REMEDY FOR EXHAUSTION.—Beat up fresh egg in a little warm water and sweeten to taste. Heave for a ¼-hour then drink."

Recipe book

Not, as you might have thought, vice versa.

"Pedigree Scotch Terriers For Sale. Dog and Bitch Puppies, by son of Ch. Malgen Juggernaut; dam well bred."

Advt. in Cumberland Herald

Oh, jolly good show!

348

Fishermen report seeing blue-nosed sharks off the south coast. This bears out the general opinion that it is too early yet for bathing.

Whoopee!

"THIS CONCERNS YOU!
.... and YOU TOO,
For your Wedding, Funeral & other
merry making CEREMONIES
Remember
The United Yoruba Brass Band."

Advt. in Nigerian paper

"HAIRDRESSING
Good Horse Manure, delivered in 4-ton or smaller loads; reasonable prices."
Advt. in Lancs. paper

Nevertheless . . .

"Those repulsive little creatures, the familiar but mis-named earwigs, seem to be making a concerted attack on Wallsend just now.
A local butcher opening a paper bag of silver even found one in his soap dish."
Newcastle Evening Chronicle

And the gunpowder ran out at the heels of their boots.

"Luckiest woman in Brighton, to-day, is Mrs. Elizabeth Kibblewhite, who last week threw a dice to determine her pools selection—and won £2,398."—*Brighton Argus*

Never say die, eh?

"Many women, this year, I find, are buying plum puddings. Very good they are, too, and quite inexpensive. Mice-meat, however, is another proposition."
Scottish paper

Though also inexpensive.

349

"His heart beat against his breast in great heavy strokes. He felt his legs give way under him, but just saved himself from falling. He pressed his fingers against his eyeballs, withdrew them."   *Woman's Own*

Did that help?

"Americans Think British-made Cycles Are Tops."
                                            Southern Daily Echo

Back to the drawing-board, chaps.

Fashion Note

"Thursday, August 21st. 3 days
HERE COMES THE GROOM (U)
With interesting shorts."
                            Midhurst cinema programme

Pimpernel Fox

"They dared invade forbidden zones . . . in search of the man of mystery . . . kidnapped by fanatic underground killers! Released by 20th Century-Fox."   *Advt. in South African paper*

"(331) SWANS. Do swans fly across country? If so, how far?—Ignorant.

Yes. The distance depends on where they are going.—Ed., *The S.F.*"
                                            The Scottish Farmer

For long journeys, of course, they start farther away.